A

THE CHRIST OF THE FOURTH GOSPEL

THE CHRIST OF THE
FOURTH GOSPEL

IN THE LIGHT OF FIRST-CENTURY THOUGHT

E. M. SIDEBOTTOM

"May he who by his Incarnation gathered
into one things earthly and things heavenly,
grant you the fullness of inward peace and
goodwill . . ."

LONDON

S·P·C·K

1961

First published in 1961
by S.P.C.K.
Holy Trinity Church
Marylebone Road
London N.W.1

Made and printed in Great Britain by
William Clowes and Sons, Limited, London and Beccles

© E. M. Sidebottom, 1961

CONTENTS

ABBREVIATIONS

BASOR   *Bulletin of the American Schools of Oriental Research*

CH   Corpus Hermeticum

DSC   Fragment of a Zadokite Work (Damascus Document)

DSD   Manual of Discipline

DSS   Dead Sea Scrolls

ET   *Expository Times*

FG   Fourth Gospel

HTR   *Harvard Theological Review*

JTS   *Journal of Theological Studies*

LG   Left Ginza

L & S   Liddell and Scott, *A Greek-English Lexicon*, rev. H. S. Jones

LXX   Septuagint

MM   Moulton and Milligan, *The Vocabulary of the Greek Testament*

NTS   *New Testament Studies*

RG   Right Ginza

S–B   Strack–Billerbeck, *Kommentar zum Neuen Testament aus Talmud und Midrasch*

TWzNT   *Theologische Wörterbuch zum Neuen Testament*

PREFACE

I wish to thank those who have so generously given me of their time and personal encouragement. Professor C. K. Barrett was responsible for originally suggesting publication. The late Professor T. W. Manson also read the work in embryonic form and gave encouragement and advice. Professor H. E. W. Turner has kindly read the whole in its later stages and helped me to remove many a phrase that marred the style; he also suggested the substance of the introductory chapter. To Dr E. L. Allen my thanks are especially due for his unfailing kindness and patience over many years. I have to thank also the editors of *The Expository Times* and *The Anglican Theological Review* for permission to use again in much revised form some material which first appeared in their pages. It now constitutes part of chapters 6 and 8. Finally, I tender grateful acknowledgement to the printers and to the editorial staff of the S.P.C.K. for their helpfulness and accuracy, and to my wife and father for their help with the indexes.

E.M.S.

ACKNOWLED'GEMENTS

Thanks are due to the following for permission to include copyright material: Basil Blackwell, S. Mowinckel: *He That Cometh*; Gerald Duckworth and Co. Ltd, S. Cave: *The Doctrine of the Person of Christ* and W. F. Howard: *Christianity according to St John*; the Cambridge University Press, F. C. Burkitt: *Early Christianity outside the Roman Empire* and C. H. Dodd: *The Interpretation of the Fourth Gospel*; the Clarendon Press, S. H. Hooke: *In the Beginning*; T. and T. Clarke, G. Dalman: *Words of Jesus*; the Lutterworth Press and the Beacon Press, Boston, Mass., R. Otto: *The Kingdom of God and the Son of Man*; A. and R. Mowbray and Co. Ltd, G. Quispel: *The Jung Codex*; the Oxford University Press and the author, W. A. Curtis: *Jesus Christ the Teacher*; the S. C. M. Press, James Robinson: *A New Quest of the Historical Jesus*. The quotation on the title page is taken, by permission, from the Service of Nine Lessons and Carols of King's College, Cambridge.

CHAPTER 1

INTRODUCTION: THE WORLD OF THE FOURTH GOSPEL

Before it is possible to assess the significance of an ancient writer for the present day it is necessary to find out as far as possible what his words meant when they were first written. This is a typically modern approach, and is the method of biblical criticism. No writer, not even a genius, creates his style and forms of thought *ex nihilo*; the beliefs and language of his circle are the material with which his thinking operates. The writer of the Fourth Gospel is generally supposed not to have written in isolation but to have belonged to a circle from which he derived his distinctive idiom. If the character of that circle can be determined, a clue is at hand to the meaning of some essentials of this gospel. If John is a Jew, for example, who thinks in what is regarded as a typically Jewish manner, he will be inclined to stress personality in God and man and think less in terms of substance, of "celestial chemistry" as it has been called; or, in academic language, less metaphysically. This immediately influences the way we regard the concept of the Logos and the value of the gospel as a record of actual events. Most of the controversy which has raged over the Fourth Gospel has indeed turned upon the question of the milieu of the writer. The indecisiveness of the discussion is probably due to the fact that the various cultures were far more inextricably intermingled than has sometimes been assumed. This remains true even though the idea can be taken too far until all the extant writings of the ancient world become a gigantic jigsaw puzzle to be fitted together with the ingenuity of, say, the later Reitzenstein, to mention a scholar whose name is honoured as that of a pioneer in this field. However we may criticize extremes of this sort, it has to be remembered that our historical sense and our procedure in borrowing ideas

I

and symbols were not shared by the ancient writers. The author of the Epistle to the Hebrews, for instance, begins his work with a series of quotations from the psalms, which he takes as addressed to Christ. The modern mind feels uncomfortable about such direct application, because it thinks first of the "setting in life", to borrow a phrase from form-criticism, of the psalm in question, and asks to whom it was originally addressed. Our insights of course have their value and are indeed indispensable to our way of thinking. In this particular respect we can use them to distinguish between the more or less valid speculations of early writers. Not indeed that the writers themselves were entirely devoid of such criteria. The character of the writer himself and the sort of religious development he has attained contributes to his understanding of the "real" relations between ideas and to his ability to construct a valid theology. The Gnostics in general shared with modern Hindus and theosophists an apparent inability to recognize the importance of distinguishing between various conceptions, not only in respect of their mythical character but also in respect of their moral quality. But it does not follow that whoever used such methods and drew on concepts divorced from their context was thus blind, and the fact that the original significance of an idea is lost in its final construction must not be considered necessarily to vitiate the construction itself. Where the confusion arises is where the modern writer fails to distinguish between various types of thought to the extent that discrimination becomes impossible between the writers themselves.

We have then to consider in relation to any study of the Fourth Gospel the various types of literature we possess which may throw light on the writer's beliefs. Much of what follows will be concerned with the attempt to distinguish between what really influenced him from what only appears to do so. Those who are familiar with C. H. Dodd's book on the Fourth Gospel will require little introduction to the subject, since in this readily-available work the author has provided a clear account of the various relevant types of literature. As this present essay is concerned only with the Christology of the gospel no detailed introduction will be expected. It is perhaps only fair, however, to offer some brief remarks on the literature referred to. Direct quotations will be avoided for the moment, since they appear later on.

In the first place, then, it is generally accepted that John was a Jew, and this immediately opens up the question whether his leaning was towards the Palestinian or Hellenistic type of Judaism. This distinction is illustrated in its extreme form by the difference between the work of the rabbis which was later incorporated into the Talmud and related literature on the one hand and the Wisdom literature on the other. The writings of the rabbis as we now have them are characterized by the exclusion of "Greek" ideas, prompted perhaps by opposition to the Christians, who had adopted the Septuagint or Greek version of the Bible made at Alexandria as their Bible and whose thought was eventually determined by these Gentile ways of thinking. As products of this school and reflective of its tendencies are to be classed the Targums, the Aramaic paraphrases of the Old Testament which probably began as commentaries on the lessons in the old synagogue after the decline of Hebrew as the spoken language. It is in the Targums that the famous "Memra" appears as a name for God or his interposition. In their extant form these rabbinic writings are later than the first century and must therefore be used with caution in the quest for first-century ideas.

Further Palestinian material has, however, unexpectedly appeared with the discovery at Qumran in the Judean desert of the Dead Sea Scrolls. These contain biblical texts, copies of apocryphal books, and original writings of a kind which has aroused much interest. The document of most importance perhaps for the study of the Fourth Gospel is called by scholars the Manual of Discipline. This contains the rules of the sect and bears striking resemblance to a fragmentary work found at the turn of the century in the now famous Cairo Geniza (or repository for rolls discarded by the synagogue) and called variously the Zadokite or Damascus Document. Of the other rolls the commentary on Habbakuk has perhaps aroused most controversy, but for our purpose only the Thanksgiving Psalms need be mentioned. Almost everyone has heard of the Dead Sea Scrolls by now, but some of the controversy has obscured their true value for biblical studies.

In a class by itself, distinct from both the rabbinical and Wisdom literatures, is Apocalyptic. This is a style of writing which has deeply influenced the New Testament, although it contains only one book called an apocalypse. It belongs to the soil of Palestine and more particularly to that period of disruption and recurrent anarchy which falls between 200 B.C. and the collapse of the Jewish state at the end of the first century A.D. The rabbis seem to have been averse to this whole style of thinking, and the Wisdom authors, although some lived at the same time as the apocalyptists, display an entirely different bent. The apocalyptists in the first instance are identified especially with the anti-Greek party in the days of Antiochus Epiphanes, who sought to impose Greek culture on the Jewish people. The Greek leanings of the Wisdom writers constitute one factor which sets them apart. The apocalyptists see history as the scene of a conflict between God and his enemies which will only be resolved by the direct act of God in putting an end to the present order and establishing a new one, whether in the present world or in an entirely remade universe. This the writers describe under the forms of visions which they offer in the names of certain ancient personages such as Abraham, Enoch, or Moses. In the Old Testament the apocalyptists are represented by Daniel in particular, though traces of the typical style can be found earlier. Nearer to New Testament times is the famous work called the Book of Enoch, which contains much that recalls the New Testament. It is the first of a loosely-connected series of Enochic writings and is therefore styled "1 Enoch". The section which has aroused most discussion is the so-called "Similitudes". Here the question is whether the pre-Christian date assigned to it by R. H. Charles is to be accepted, and, if so, whether the references to the figure called "that son of man" are significant for Jesus' own use for himself of the title "Son of Man".

In general the Wisdom literature belongs to an earlier period than the apocalyptic, and has affinities with a much wider genre of

literature which existed in the ancient world. It is represented in
the Bible by Job, Ecclesiastes, and Proverbs. But here too the
period is elastic; the Book of Wisdom in the Apocrypha belongs
perhaps to the beginning of the first century A.D., while the Ezra
apocalypse probably belongs to the end of the same century. Also,
in the Apocrypha is the book called Ecclesiasticus or the Wisdom
of ben Sirach: this is often distinguished from the Book of Wisdom as being more Palestinian in flavour. The Wisdom literature,
as the Book of Proverbs shows, has a timeless quality about it; it
is concerned with the perennial problems of mankind at large, and
is eventually given to generalized speculation. Apocalyptic, on the
other hand, is the child of a particular period of unrest, whatever
its relations to the fantastic in other religious thought, and is
dropped when that period in its special manifestations is over,
though again the rabbis were largely responsible for its demise
because of their dislike of that particular brand of speculation and
also perhaps because of its adoption by early Christianity. The
apocalyptic literature in fact owes its continuation and development to Christianity; the fantastic element reappears in Judaism
in a different form in the speculations of the Cabbalists and the
so-called Jewish mysticism with which writers such as Abelson,
Odeberg, and Scholem have made us familiar.

Philo the Jew of Alexandria is related to the Wisdom school
and deserves special place if only because of the voluminous
character of his writings. No rigid distinction is possible between
his writings and those of the rabbis, but he is essentially a man of
Alexandria, the home of Hellenistic Judaism. He represents the
acme of the process by which Jews attempted to reconcile their
religion with the thought of the outside world. Philo, while
remaining a staunch and courageous Jew, goes further than most
and incorporates more of the impersonal doctrines of Greek
philosophy than is really consistent with the Jewish idea of God.
For him God easily becomes the Absolute, and union with him
an intellectual absorption in the divine. Philo indeed represents an
advance upon Greek philosophy in some respects, and points for-
ward to neo-platonism. It is even arguable that the fashion in
which books on the Fourth Gospel have compared the Greek

"doctrine of the Logos" with the Johannine is inspired more by acquaintance with the writings of Philo than with those of the Greek philosophers themselves. By comparison the latter actually seldom use the term and then in a far less definite way.

Philo was a contemporary of Jesus. His thought, however, shows affinity with that of a series of later writers who are represented in the collection of writings called by modern editors the Corpus Hermeticum. The modern "hermetically-sealed" package perpetuates the name of the god under whose name these writings were produced. He is Thoth, the Egyptian Hermes. The Corpus Hermeticum exists in Greek manuscripts of the fourteenth century onwards, but the writings themselves go back to the Egypt of the second and third centuries A.D., or even, in some cases, earlier. They range over a variety of subjects, from alchemy to religion, but it is only the latter which concerns us. The religion of the Hermetic writers is of an exalted kind, consisting of an attempt, in theosophic fashion, to combine different elements of religion and popular philosophy in a single approach. The basic idea, as in gnosticism, is that of union with God by knowledge, but the writers display a religious zeal and have a *kerygma* to proclaim which sets them apart. The tractate which excites most interest in Christian scholars is the first, called Poimandres and containing a reinterpretation of the Genesis story as well as much Christian-sounding language.

The attention which Poimandres has attracted has much to do with the figure of a Man who appears as the equal of God and who has been likened to the New Testament Son of Man. This is the Anthropos whose presence has been detected in most of the nooks and crannies of ancient religion by such writers as Reitzenstein, Bultmann, Bousset, and Mowinckel. Mowinckel has recently incorporated a long section on the Son of Man from this standpoint in his book *He That Cometh*. Reitzenstein and Bultmann tend more especially to find the Anthropos in Zoroastrianism and Mandaism. Zoroaster or Zarathushtra was contemporary with the great prophets of the Bible and founded a lofty monotheistic religion with its supreme god called Ahura-Mazda and with a personification of evil called Ahriman. Later Zoroastrianism or

Mazdaism changed the name of the deity to Ormazd and is generally regarded as having established a strict dualism of light and darkness, truth and falsehood. Much has been made by the writers just mentioned of the idea that the Gnostics derived their distinctive tenets from this quarter. The Mandeans are a sect whose beliefs have been influenced by this Persian religion. But they also owe much to Christianity, and revere especially the person of John the Baptist. The chief books of the sect, which still exists in Iraq and Iran, are the Ginza or Treasure and the Book of John. The Ginza is divided into two parts, the Right and Left Ginza, concerned respectively with the living and the dead, and bound back to back and upside down to each other so that the book begins from both ends. Translations by Mark Lidzbarski which appeared in German in 1915 and 1925 of some of the more important Mandean writings are hard to come by. They have been added to in English by Lady Drower in several books. The contents of these writings constitute an extraordinary conglomeration of stories about angels and demons, theological speculation of a fantastic order, instruction, myth, and ritual. They are written in a dialect of Aramaic, and, according to some, go back to the Palestine of the first century. It is even said that they go back to John the Baptist himself and that Jesus held beliefs similar to those of the sect. In the field of Johannine studies these writings have been regarded by some as emanating from the fount from which sprang the Johannine Christology.

The Mandean doctrines have much in common with those of the Gnostics, who have been mainly known to us through the polemical writings of the Christian Fathers. Recently, however, finds have been made of original Gnostic writings, and here the name Nag Hammadi ranks with that of Qumran. Just before the discovery of the Dead Sea Scrolls an important collection of manuscripts was found at the spot in Upper Egypt where St Pachomius founded his earliest monasteries. The first of these documents to attain fame was the Gospel of Truth, from the Jung Codex, so called because it was acquired by the Institute of the famous psychologist and writer on mythological subjects. This work has been closely associated by some with the name of the

2

arch-heretic Valentinus, and appears to represent an early and more Christian version of his teachings. The other documents include the Apocryphon of John, a Gospel of Thomas (which has recently received much publicity), a Gospel of Philip, and a work entitled the Hypostasis of the Archons.[1] These writings may be expected to increase our knowledge of Gnosticism from the point of view of the Gnostics themselves as opposed to that of their opponents. Gnosticism was a serious threat to Christianity in the early days, and appears as such in an embryonic form in the New Testament itself. There is a strong current of belief in some quarters that the Fourth Gospel is indebted to it in important respects, particularly in regard to the "dualism" discernible in its pages. Gnosticism with a capital "G" usually means the definite systems of those heretics who were opposed by the early Church Fathers. With a small "g" it stands for the whole tendency which these writers exhibit to regard the world as a dualism of mind and matter and so to create a series of intermediaries between God and the world, and to seek redemption from the body by means of knowledge of certain esoteric doctrines. That the distinction is not always easy to maintain is illustrated by the case of Manicheism, which is systematic but late. Manicheism has features in common with Mandaism. Its name became (and has remained) a byword for dualistic heresy.

It must be accepted as at least possible that John was acquainted with some of the above types of thought where he was not influenced by the actual writings themselves. The extent of his indebtedness in either respect will be examined in succeeding chapters. An attempt will be made to give references, by means of the notes, to the relevant works in English wherever new types of literature are introduced. By this means and with the aid of this brief introduction it is hoped that the reader will not be hindered overmuch in his examination of the substance of the essay, which is after all not mainly concerned with anything but the Fourth

---

[1] Other works in the Nag Hammadi collection not included in the Jung Codex are listed in Doresse, *Secret Books of the Egyptian Gnostics*, pp. 142–5. A handy translation of the Gospel of Truth has recently been produced by Kendrick Grobel.

Gospel. The other writings constitute a fascinating field of study in themselves, but this work must be left to the expert. We are concerned with the relatively restricted subject of Johannine Christology and the light which the apparently related literature can cast upon it.

CHAPTER 2

THE APPROACH TO THE JOHANNINE CHRISTOLOGY

The theology of St John's Gospel, according to the dictum of C. A. Anderson Scott, is almost wholly a Christology. For this reason the study of the Johannine Christology involves, to a much greater extent than is the case with the other New Testament writers, the whole question of the nature and provenance of the work. It is true, of course, that Christianity in any case is mainly concerned with Christ and his significance, but St Paul, for example, who is the only other figure in the New Testament of like stature, chooses symbols and metaphors, snatches of credal formulae and hymns, for the purpose in hand at the moment of writing. Analysis of the Fourth Gospel is much more difficult, but the advantage is that, on the assumption of homogeneity, the various aspects under which Christ is presented may illuminate each other in a much more direct way, so that the same idea may recur in different forms throughout the same book. An obvious possible exception is the doctrine of the Logos, which has seemed to many so different from the other conceptions that they have separated the Prologue from the rest of the gospel. But even this is a matter for discussion. This and the whole question of interpretation depends almost entirely on the assumptions of the student, and these in turn on the background assigned to the Fourth Gospel itself.

This is in fact the significance of modern critical study of the Bible. For many years it has been no longer possible to regard the sacred books as reflecting the same timeless teaching in the same way, or as containing almost explicitly the doctrine of Chalcedon. With the rise of the new method the meaning was to be elucidated which occupied the writers at the time they wrote, and thus the background must be known. Each writer must be assigned his place and time. If in the Fourth Gospel more doctrine was to be discerned than in the first three, then so much the worse for its claim to record actual events and actual impressions of Christ as he was. John belonged to the second century and represented the beginning of that process of Hellenization of a Jewish religion which was so reprehensible to critics. Here perhaps E. F. Scott was as influential as any upon British thought. Westcott had found that "the didactic method and not only the language of St John is essentially Hebraic".[1] Scott assumed the other position. His *The Fourth Gospel, Its Purpose and Theology* (1906) came with the force of a revelation to many who were young at the time. Scott tacitly accepted, on the authority of continental scholars, a date early in the second century and interpreted the gospel in terms of polemic against Judaism, the followers of John the Baptist, and Gnosticism. Questions of authorship and historical value were relatively unimportant in comparison with the elucidation of the author's meaning. The Johannine Christ was little more than the projection upon the stage of history of the inward experience of the disciple who participated in the Church's heritage of the Spirit. The significance of the Johannine Christ was that he was the walking, talking expression of the Logos of Philo of Alexandria. "Jesus was the Light of the World and the Life-Giver, because he was himself the Logos, one in essence with God."[2] Nearly twenty years afterwards the characteristic remark of F. C. Burkitt was in the same vein: "I do not think the writer [of the Fourth Gospel] distinguished in his own consciousness between what he remembered (or had derived from the reminiscence of others) and what he felt must have been true, and I greatly doubt whether we can distinguish often in that gospel what is derived from tradition and what is derived from imagination."[3] At about the same time the work of Billerbeck and Moore

---

[1] *The Gospel of St. John*, p. xcvi.

[2] Sydney Cave comments, "Would it not be truer to say that the Evangelist called Jesus the Logos, because he had first found him to be the Light of the world and the Life-giver?" (*Doctrine of the Person of Christ*, p. 65, n 2.)

[3] *Christianity in the Light of Modern Knowledge*, p. 209.

on the Memra appeared to destroy at a blow the last remaining prop for a Jewish interpretation of the Logos. Yet, despite elements of truth in the Hellenistic approach, its general effect was that of distortion, which has not yet been fully lived down.

It cannot be denied that the language of Philo is close in many points to that of John. Here also alone outside the pages of the Fourth Gospel is a developed doctrine of the Logos.[1] But if Scott turned to Philo, others turned to the writings of Egyptian theosophists, represented in the so-called Corpus Hermeticum.[2] Loisy made the point that, while John did not draw directly upon these writings, the expressions and ideas he held in common with them, such as "truth", "light",[3] "life", and the Logos as organ of creation and mediator of divine revelation and regeneration for immortality, were too much of a coincidence to be accidental. C. H. Dodd has reached similar conclusions on the basis of a special study of Hermetism.[4] Here again there is plausibility. In this literature there is a striking parallel to the Trinity as well as much common language. There is a Father who is life and light, a Son who is the Word, and a Son who is the divine Man.

The tendency to find the key to the Johannine teaching in such quarters was of course not new. Augustine in a famous chapter of his Confessions[5] tells how in the (neo)Platonic writings he discovered "not indeed the express words, but the same thing in substance" as the doctrines of the Prologue. What he could not find was the doctrine of the humility of the Word, that "he came to his own, and his own received him not", and especially the teaching that "the Word became flesh and dwelt among us". In

---

[1] For a comparison of Philo and the Fourth Gospel, see Dodd, *Fourth Gospel*, pp. 54ff.

[2] The standard edition of the C.H. is Nock-Festugière. Walter Scott's is a mine of information but unreliable as to text. See Dodd, *F.G.*, pp. 10ff, for a comparison of Hermetism with the Fourth Gospel. There are useful lists of parallels on pp. 34f, 50f.

[3] W. Scott, following Griffith, derived the name Poimandres (which is the title of the first tractate of the C.H.), from the Coptic ⲡⲉⲓⲙⲉ ⲛ̄ⲣⲏ, "Knowledge of the Sun-God", rather than from "Shepherd of Men". The writer of the tract explains the name as "The Mind of the Sovereignty".

[4] See his work referred to above, and *The Bible and the Greeks*.

[5] Book VII, ch. 9.

recent times, however, the assumption that the Prologue cannot be paralleled in its doctrine of the humility of Christ has been challenged. The essential doctrine is claimed to have been derived by John from the same sources as those used by the (later) Gnostics. It is plain that this is an important deduction which, if true, calls in question the uniqueness of the Christian revelation at its essential point. British scholarship in general has tended to minimize the importance of this approach, which has found its chief exponent in Rudolf Bultmann. But it is perhaps safe to say that the notion of a divine Man who descends to enable his own to ascend with him to the heavenly places continues probably increasingly to attract expositors[1] in search of Johannine origins, and they are not slow to point out that the Fourth Gospel was popular among the Gnostics and circulated early amongst them. It is claimed that this Man appears in many guises, ranging from Adam to the philosophical meditation on Genesis 1 and 2 in Philo, and from the "one like a son of man" in Daniel to the fully-fledged Gnostic redeemer in Manicheism. Bultmann finds the figure most characteristically in Mandaism,[2] which if for no other reason thus remains a living issue. He deduces that John himself was a gnostic, oblivious to the historical religion which finds its expression in Judaism, presenting Jesus as the decisive timeless event as in the gnostic cult, in this sense "eschatological", the *locus* of divine confrontation and judgement.[3] Although few scholars perhaps go all the way with Bultmann, even C. H. Dodd,

[1] McLaren Wilson (*The Gnostic Problem*, ch. VII, "Judaism and Gnosticism", 5 : The Redeemer) claims that "The myth of the Urmensch-Redeemer has been adequately examined by others, and the view that such a myth, if it ever existed, exercised a formative influence on the early Church is now generally rejected", and instances W. Manson, *Jesus the Messiah*, pp. 174ff. But he goes on to list and examine views which are substantially the same or stem from this.

[2] For Mandaism see A. S. Pallis, *Mandean Studies*; Burkitt, *Church and Gnosis*; and for its relation to St John, Odeberg, *The Fourth Gospel Interpreted in its Relation to Contemporaneous Religious Currents*, and Dodd, *F.G.*, pp. 115ff. The writings of E. S. Drower should also be consulted.

[3] Cf. Grant and Freedman, *The Secret Sayings of Jesus*, p. 101 : "There is no real movement in the Gospel of Thomas. There is no real history; there is no real eschatology; there is no sin. . . . Practically everything directly related to life in first-century Palestine is gone. To be sure, something like this has already happened in the Gospel of John. . . ."

who rejects the hypothesis of a pre-Christian gnostic redeemer, holds that "Son of Man" in John is the equivalent of the heavenly Man of Philo and the Anthropos of Poimandres, the first tractate of the Corpus Hermeticum. As such he is inclusive of humanity and his "ascent" is theirs also.

During this time the advocates of Jewish influence on the Fourth Gospel were not silent, while not necessarily tying themselves to the traditional position of Westcott that the author was a Jew, a Palestinian, an eye-witness, an apostle, the son of Zebedee. In 1917 J. Rendel Harris published a monograph in which he sought to show that the Prologue was Jewish in origin. Over a period of years Adolf Schlatter pointed out the semitic idioms and traces of the language of the rabbinic schools in the gospel. C. F. Burney, in his famous book *The Aramaic Origin of the Fourth Gospel*, took a similar line. C. C. Torrey, and, more recently, Matthew Black, have incidentally dealt with the Fourth Gospel from this angle. The Swedish scholar Hugo Odeberg produced a stimulating commentary upon the first twelve chapters in which he extended the field to cover not only Hermetism and Mandaism but also the esoteric works of Jewish mysticism. Sir Edwyn Hoskyns, while dispensing with minute specific allusion, appeared to proceed on the assumption that no "Greek" influence is to be looked for in the Fourth Gospel at all. He also stressed the "historicity" of the "flesh" in the work, and this attitude has been paralleled by an increasing willingness to find historical elements in John. Both P-F. Menoud and A. M. Hunter in recent reviews of Johannine studies[1] have reached the conclusion that the atmosphere is now more congenial to the belief that the Fourth Gospel has its historical tradition. Even Bultmann, for whom it often seems that the historicity of the gospels is of little moment, has seen a "signs-source" of some historical value in the Fourth Gospel, which the author combined with a "revelation-source" from his own gnostic background, and has suggested that the gnosticism he finds in St John is nearer to the teaching of Jesus himself than that given in the synoptics. It may seem somewhat

---

[1] Menoud, *L'évangile de Jean d'après les recherches récentes*, Deuxième edition, 1947; Hunter, *Interpreting the New Testament*, pp. 78ff.

whimsical to turn to such a quarter for support of John's historicity, but that such views can be advanced at all goes to show that the wind is no longer blowing all one way. And alongside all this has gone a revision of the attitude adopted towards the synoptics which is related to the revival in "biblical theology" of the attempt to see the books of the Bible not as isolated units but as a whole. It is no longer possible to regard the Fourth Gospel as the culmination of a process of Hellenization whereby the historical Jesus of the synoptics is transformed, by way of St Paul, into the cosmic Revealer of St John. This construction was the result of an evolutionary interpretation which was forced upon the documents without due regard for their contents. It is clear now that the first three gospels are more "theological" than was formerly recognized, and this in itself narrows the gulf between them and the fourth.

The latest change of opinion, however, is towards a realization that the distinction between Jew and Greek was drawn too rigidly. In the words of David Daube, "it is becoming ever clearer that Palestinian Judaism of the first century was far more varied and flexible than preoccupation with the particular line which ultimately prevailed would lead one to assume ... the sharp distinction between a Hellenistic and a Rabbinic Judaism in the New Testament period is being abandoned as it is found that many Hellenistic ideas had crept into, or been consciously taken over by, Rabbinism long before, and that the process, though slowed down, was not halted".[1] Previous Jewish scholars had not failed to anticipate such a conclusion. Thus A. Cohen wrote, "The theories of Aristotle and Plato about the constitution of the Universe were probably not unknown to some of the Rabbis and were not without influence upon them"; and he connects the

[1] *The New Testament and Rabbinic Judaism*, p. ix. Hort wrote in 1871, "The thoughts and ways of other nations had for a considerable while been creeping in among the beliefs and customs of the Jewish past, and it was vain to exclude them" (*The Way, the Truth and the Life*, p. 23). That Daube's words are of more than formal significance may be clearer if we add the part left out: "A notion like that of virgin birth, however incompatible with orthodox tenets, may not at the time have been universally so considered. The effect on one another of the numerous sects, major and minor, is not to be underrated."

Platonic idea of "creation" taken over by Philo with the rabbinic teaching that God used the Torah as a "blueprint" for the world.[1] Similarly, if Philo derived man's intelligence from God and his body from the earth, so did the rabbis. "Man's soul is from heaven and his body from earth."[2] The body is "the scabbard of the soul",[3] and the soul has the same relationship to the body as God to the universe.[4] J. Abelson had also pointed to similarities between Philo and the rabbis, particularly in regard to the doctrine of angels. It has long been held by some that, in the words of Westcott, "Philo is naturally regarded as the creator of teaching of which he is in part only the representative".[5] Lebreton wrote: "Even though the writings of his predecessors have disappeared to the last fragment, one has only to go through his works to see how numerous were these predecessors who loved to discover in the Bible the whole philosophical teaching of Greece; her physics, her psychology, and her ethics."[6] Now it seems that among these were some who trod the soil of Palestine. The result is to make it much harder to tie John to any particular milieu and interpret his views accordingly. We are thrown back on internal evidence.

But if Judaism was influenced by Hellenism, the opposite process also took place. Dodd makes the namelessness of God in the Septuagint a factor contributing to the definition of monotheism in the Hellenistic world.[7] Of particular interest from our point of view is the Jewish influence upon systems which show some verbal affinity with the Fourth Gospel. Philo and the Wisdom writers were themselves Jews. Certain tractates of the Corpus Hermeticum show plain traces of Jewish influence, not only from the Septuagint (which provides the creation story upon which the vision in Poimandres is based) but also perhaps, as Walter Scott

---

[1] *Everyman's Talmud*, pp. 27, 29; Philo, *De Opif.* 4.

[2] Sifre Deut. § 306; 132a.

[3] b Sanh. 108a.

[4] Cohen, p. 76; cf. 6 and 68.

[5] Op. cit., p. xvi.

[6] *The History of the Dogma of the Trinity*, p. 135.

[7] *Bible and Greeks*, p. 4. See p. 137 for the tendency to admit demiurges into Judaism. Norden held that the LXX influenced the idea of the "knowledge" of God: *Agnostos Theos*, p. 63.

suggested, through the teaching of Jewish schools on the fringe of what later came to be accepted as "orthodoxy".[1] The Gnostics properly so-called, typically Hellenistic as to their fundamental ideas (whatever their origins their pessimism is the outcome of the Hellenistic situation) may be taken as characteristic.[2] Though often violently anti-Judaic, they made great use of Hebrew-sounding names in their systems. The pagan Naasene document, which has been isolated from its Christian context, has inseparable Old Testament elements. The Book of Baruch, attributed to the Gnostic Justin, from which Dodd thinks the Christian episode involving Jesus as the first initiate into the true gnosis "could be removed without seriously affecting the system",[3] consists then mainly of allegorizations of the Old Testament. The appearance alone of the names Seth and Adam in the system of the Barbelo-gnostics shows acquaintance with the Old Testament; Seth also appears not only in the Sethite doctrines but also in the Nag Hammadi documents. The Apocryphon of John consists largely of a reinterpretation of the Genesis story, as does Poimandres. Mandaism also at a further remove shows plain signs of esoteric Jewish speculation; here too the Adamites appear: Hibil, Sitil, and Anush are Abel, Seth, and Enosh. These instances are more calculated to show what the Gnostics did not know about Judaism than what they did. But we are concerned with the fact that the language is the same and that it derived from Judaism. The Nag Hammadi Gospel of Truth shows less Old Testament influence than some of the others, though perhaps more acquaintance with Jewish ideas. Van Unnik is disposed to believe that pre-New Testament influences are not to be looked for.[4] But much is made of the Name theology which is of Jewish origin; there is more of this than use of the New Testament can explain. The passage quoted on page 41 below shows, as well as probable acquaintance with the Fourth Gospel, also traces of such ideas as the Beginning

[1] On the doctrinal relation of Judaism to Gnosticism see McLaren Wilson, op. cit., ch. VII.

[2] Neither Greek nor Near Eastern thought alone is sufficient to account for this pessimism, nor a combination of the two.

[3] *F.G.*, p. 99.

[4] *The Jung Codex*, p. 125.

and the Glory, which connect it with the Wisdom and Shekinah speculation. These few examples are sufficient to show the marks of Judaism upon the Gnostics. If John shows resemblances to these, it may well be because they used common themes and single conceptions, though not necessarily in the same way. The question of these common themes will now occupy us briefly.

The rabbinic turns of phrase in John extend to some of his most characteristic terms. Thus, for example, Light, Life, Holy Spirit, Paraclete, are all technical terms in rabbinic Judaism. So also, to take a different instance, is the word "abide"[1] for the dwelling of the Shekinah, and the latter has left traces on the Johannine language and thought. The concept of the Image, too, although not mentioned by name in the Fourth Gospel, was, as we shall see, evidently familiar to the writer. It is significant that some of these common terms were actually borrowed from the Greek and used in transliteration by the rabbis. Examples are: παράκλητος in the form פרקליט or פרקלטא, used in the Fourth Gospel of the Holy Spirit;[2] κατήγωρ in the form קטיגור used in the Fourth Gospel of Moses;[3] εἰκών in the form איקונין or איקונין. The fact that some of these terms and others were used by Philo[4] and such diverse writers as those of the Corpus Hermeticum, the Wisdom literature, Mandaism, and the newly-discovered Gospel of Truth, points to a common pool of these technical terms. Space forbids a lengthy examination, and in any case we are only illustrating the approach adopted in succeeding chapters, so a few examples will suffice. These are all words reminiscent of the Johannine vocabulary. The words Paraclete and Image are

---

[1] Aboth 3:7, "When ten people sit together and occupy themselves with the Torah, the Shekinah abides (שְׁרוּיָה) among them. The word is from the root שרה, שרי.

[2] But not in the rabbis; the Spirit is once named סניגור, which is the Greek συνήγορος. Billerbeck, ii, pp. 560-2 indicates two passages which show that the notion of the Holy Spirit as Israel's intercessor was not unknown: cf. Rom. 8.26 where the Holy Spirit is described as an intercessor, but the word Paraclete is not used.

[3] John 5.45.

[4] We are not concerned here with other than Gk words: Philo of course shares other words with the rabbis in translation, thus τόπος for מקום; τόπος appeared in the rabbis as טופס, but only in a non-technical sense.

common to Philo and the rabbis;[1] Beginning is used in the rabbis, the Wisdom literature, the Gospel of Truth, and Philo for Wisdom or the Logos;[2] Image appears not only in Philo and the rabbis[3] but also in Wisdom, the Corpus Hermeticum, and Mandaism: in some of these places (Philo, the Corpus Hermeticum) it stands for the Logos, and in others (Philo, the Corpus Hermeticum, Mandaism, the rabbis, the Wisdom literature) for the ideal Man. Philo used the word "first-born" of the Logos,[4] whereas the rabbis used it of the Torah as used in creation;[5] μονογενής appears in the Book of Wisdom.[6] The words light and life occur in all these sources with varying frequency, and in others such as the fully-developed Gnostic writers, the Dead Sea Scrolls, and the Testaments of the Twelve Patriarchs. The Odes of Solomon ought also to be mentioned as sharing some of the common language, but, given their Christian provenance, this is not so striking as with some of the others; and enough has perhaps been said to show the significance of this line. It must be emphasized, however, that it is unlikely that John was acquainted with any of the writings mentioned as we know them with the solitary exception of the Wisdom literature, and here even those who have acknowledged his dependence have not always realized its extent.[7] John undoubtedly belonged to some branch of the Wisdom school, and the "Johannine" flavour of the Odes of Solomon which also show strong Wisdom influence, bears this out; but the point we are making here is that this school was not

[1] The use of ἀρχή as a metaphysical principle occurs in early Christian thought. It is also one of the Names of Jesus. Theophilus of Antioch, *Ad Autolycum*, ii, 10, P G, vi, 1064, C, gives Spirit, Beginning, Sophia, and Dynamis. See Burch, *Jesus Christ and his Revelation*, p. 96, n 77. On ἀρχή see also J. Daniélou, *Théologie du Judaeo-Christianisme*, pp. 219–22.

[2] Cf. John 1.1 and 8.25.

[3] Gen. Rab. 68.18.

[4] Cf. Heb. 1.6; Rev. 1.5; and Rom. 8.29; Col. 1.15, where it is used in conjunction with Image. Philo uses πρωτόγονος υἱός of the Logos (Dodd, *F.G.*, p. 67).

[5] "Through the first-born (רֵאשִׁית) God created the heaven and the earth, and the first-born is no other than the Torah" (S-B ii, p. 357). The word translated First-born (firstling) also of course means Beginning.

[6] And in Plato with εἰκών of the universe.

[7] See Appendix B.

so divorced from the Palestinian Judaism of the first century as used to be thought. That there was a difference, however, is clear enough if only in the difference between the synoptics and John. The former seem to be nearer to the Palestine of Jesus' day than the latter, whose style obviously belongs to a special circle.

A word must be inserted here about the attitude adopted towards the Dead Sea Scrolls. Since their discovery the onset of "Scroll fever" has been at least as sharp as that of "Mandean fever" in the Germany of the twenties, and John has been freely compared with them. Here, it has been said, is John's true background at last, his *Mutterboden*, to use Kuhn's term. Though some have found in the Scrolls evidence of the contamination of Palestinian Judaism by gnosticism, others have declared that they provide an alternative explanation of those elements in John once attributed to gnosticism—namely, dualism and the light theology. Confusion has often been caused, however, by a failure to see or to make plain that these writings are not entirely *sui generis*. In Gaster's words, "In order to get this whole question into the right perspective, it should be observed that just as many things in the Dead Sea Scrolls as can be paralleled from the New Testament can be paralleled equally well from the Apocrypha and Pseudepigrapha of the Old Testament—that is, from the non-canonical Jewish 'scriptures' that were circulating between 200 B.C. and 100 A.D.— and from the earlier strata of the Talmud."[1] This puts the matter exactly. The doctrine of the two spirits, for instance, is closer to that of the Testaments of the Twelve Patriarchs than to John.[2] The same is true of the dualism generally: the Testament of Levi 5.20 says, "Choose either the light or the darkness, either the Law of the Lord or the work of Beliar", while the Testament of Naphthali has, "Neither while you are in darkness can you do the works of light." The doctrine of the two ways was of course commonplace in later Judaism. In the Scrolls "truth" and "light"

---

[1] *Scriptures of the Dead Sea Sect*, p. 30.
[2] Cf. T. Ben. 6.1; T. Jud. 20 has two spirits, one the "spirit of truth". T. Naph. 10.9 reads, "Blessed is the man who does not defile the holy Spirit of God which has been put and breathed into him." Possible Christian influence has to be taken into account in the Testaments, but this doctrine of the two spirits is obviously a development of the Yetzer Ha-ra'.

figure often; but so they do in the rabbis, where the Torah is truth[1] and light.[2] The refrain in certain Qumran hymns,

> By his knowledge everything came to be
> Everything that is he established by his purpose
> And apart from him nothing is done,

which has recalled for some the Johannine Prologue, is not so near as the passage from Sir. 42.15 (Heb.), "By his word were his works" or that from Wisd. 9.1, "who madest all things by thy word". We may refer also to the Odes of Solomon 16.19,

> And the worlds were made by his Word
> And by the thought of his heart.

The use of "Amen, Amen" after oaths is compared with the "Verily, Verily" of the gospel, but it is the standard response to oaths.[3] "Peace be upon me" is likewise scarcely an outstanding example of "Johannine" usage, being simply an obvious variant on the common *salaam* of the East. "Sons of light" occurs in the Scrolls as in John 12.36, but it appears often elsewhere. In the New Testament instances are Luke 16.8; 1 Thess. 5.5. The doctrine of "works" also appears which we shall have cause to consider in some detail later on: a spirit of truth enlightens a man to "an understanding and insight and mighty wisdom which believes in all the works of God".[4] But this is from Wisd. 9.9 (cf. 13.1) upon which John also depends.[5] In fact the parallels to John are only of the most general kind. Three further examples will suffice to show that when the matter comes down to specific comparison there is little resemblance. The use of Belial is not a true parallel to the Johannine "Prince of this world"; it is rather a variant of the Beliar of the Testaments of the Twelve Patriarchs. Gaster says that John 16.13 "who shall guide you into all truth" is an almost

---

[1] Midrash on Ps.25.

[2] 4 Ezra 14.20f; Talmud Ber 17a; see also S-B ii, pp. 357, 521f.

[3] Num. 5.22; Deut. 27 *passim*; Mishnah Shebu 5.2. I am indebted to Gaster for some of these references.

[4] D.S.D. 4.2.

[5] See below p. 158. Note the verbal affinities between the D.S.D. and Wisdom passages.

perfect translation of the term rendered "right teacher" or
"teacher of righteousness".[1] But the Holy Spirit is not the
teacher of righteousness in the Dead Sea Scrolls. Allegro in a
popular work refers "he gives not the Spirit by measure" (John
3.34) to the inheritance of good and evil spirits according to the
numerical reckoning of stars at a man's birth. But the verse is a
quotation from Sir. 1.10.[2] In any case the likeness between John
and the Scrolls is not nearly so obvious as that between John and
Philo or the Corpus Hermeticum or Mandaism or the Wisdom
literature, where identical language appears. Nor is there any
doctrine of the manlike one to compare with the New Testament
Son of Man, and it has been doubted whether the sect looked for a
supernatural messiah. Nevertheless their writings do provide
additional evidence for similarity between the Judaism of Palestine
and those outside movements which used to seem so different, and
will of course be drawn upon if comparison seems illuminating.

This, then, is the sort of approach which informs the present
study. While certain inferences for doctrine have been tentatively
offered, the main intention has been to see what John himself
thought, so far as this is possible in view of the complicated nature
of the background. For this the approach through language has
seemed inevitable. The only way open to us is to examine his
language in the light of contemporary (or near contemporary)
usage and to see in what respects his thought follows that of those
who share a common vocabulary. This last point is of course
vital: mere similarity of vocabulary, while it cannot be accidental,
does not of itself prove dependence of ideas. The very fact that
John was a Christian must be allowed to count for something.
But it must not be allowed to determine the issue in advance. Like
both the orthodox and the heretics after him, John chose what
seemed to him the most appropriate vehicles for his understanding of Christianity. Lest, however, too artificial an impression be

---

[1] Op. cit., p. 23.

[2] See J. M. Allegro, *The Dead Sea Scrolls*, pp. 124–33. The same writer goes on
to quote the Johannine teaching about the "prince of this world" who was "a
murderer from the beginning" and points out how often demon-possession is
mentioned in the gospel stories. Yet it so happens that it is never mentioned in
John.

given of a writer choosing this and that from different cultures to get his message across, it must be added that John himself seems to have belonged to a circle where Greek and Jewish ideas were inextricably blended, and both vocabulary and ideas were part and parcel of his mental background. Moreover, genius as he was, he was less concerned with putting across a message in intelligible terms than with setting on paper his own meditations, often allusive, sometimes tantalizingly ambiguous. The allusions crop up in a manner which often makes it impossible to point to one single origin for an idea or even to say whether one idea alone is intended. The Johannine *double entendre* has often been noted before: here it appears in his use of images. The Prologue offers several examples of this, one of which is the way the Logos itself appears now against the background of Wisdom, now of the Shekinah, now of the related concept of the Name, and all along it is an evocative symbol for what is to be found in a certain human being and his relations to God, the world, and to mankind in general.

In the course of the discussion stress will be laid on the names of Jesus in the Fourth Gospel. We are so used to taking expressions like Son of God and Son of Man for granted as traditional titles that it takes an effort to realize that they may be meaningful phrases for the author, if not coined anew by him yet understood by him and even charged with new meaning by him. It is obvious of course that Jesus had been called Son of God and Son of Man before the Fourth Gospel was written; but it does not follow that John did not have his own doctrine of sonship; and indeed that he did have it will be the purpose of many subsequent pages to show. Since, then, he applies these titles to the same person they are to be taken as different aspects of his being and function and none is to be taken by itself without distortion of the whole picture. Yet some significance is to be attached to the differences in the association of each title. What then is the significance, for example, of the fact that Jesus is never spoken of as descending (or as ascending either, except possibly at 20.17) in his character of Son of God, but only as Son of Man? Is this a relic of the Gnostic Anthropos, or is it original to John's theological presentation? This investigation of names has its justification in the fact that early Christian theology proceeded on such lines. The nature and functions of Christ were expressed in the names used for him.[1] These included Son, First-born, God, Lord, Man, Son of Man, Apostle, High Priest, Faithful One, Righteous One, Wisdom, Power, Shepherd, and later Beginning, Pearl, Lamp.[2] Even the word hand seems to have been used.[3] That John was acquainted with some of these is obvious, and they derive largely from Old Testament and apocryphal sources. This usage is connected also with the idea that Jesus was the Bearer of the Name of God, and it will be suggested later that this is a primary meaning of Logos in the Fourth Gospel. But it should be possible also to penetrate beneath the surface of this type of theology and see what the names were intended to express about the one to whom they were applied and what associations they would have for the user. This is the initial procedure for New Testament Christology. Hence the emphasis on discovering the background. There is thus entire acceptance of the interpretative element in John. But the problem of the relation between these high themes and the down-to-earth question whether Jesus actually did and was what is depicted in the Fourth Gospel must not be neglected. This is a full-scale subject in itself, but it is part of the Christology and must receive comment. As has been indicated, the historical value

[1] Recent books to devote particular attention to the names used are Cullmann's *Die Christologie des Neuen Testaments* and Vincent Taylor's *Names of Jesus*. V. Burch in his various books gave lists of references where names were used of Jesus in the early writers, though he did not himself develop the idea to any extent. (See *Jesus Christ and his Revelation*, p. 83 and n 58; p. 85 and n 63; p. 88 and n 65; p. 96 and nn 77,78; *The Epistle to the Hebrews*, pp. 39, 41ff.) These writers include also Philo, the Wisdom writers, the author of the Odes of Solomon, etc. In the New Testament the first two chapters of Hebrews are significantly prominent. Burch wrote of the latter author, "What his Old Testament material yields is not support for argumentative doctrine but a series of names" (*Ep. to the Hebrews*, p. 39). See also J. Daniélou, op. cit., pp. 190–226.

[2] See the references from Burch above, and for some other names the quotation from Aphraates below p. 195.

[3] Cf. Isa. 66.2; Irenaeus, *Adv. Haer.* IV. 20, 1; V. 28, 4 where God has two hands. The possible influence at an earlier stage of the Aramaic expression "by the hand of" must not be lost sight of: cf. John 1.2,3 in Syriac: "Everything came to be by his hand."

of the work is not now at such a discount as formerly, and even if we can only leave the two aspects of interpretation and history in uneasy juxtaposition it will make for a more balanced presentation of the subject.

In what follows the First Epistle of John will be used as additional evidence for the views of the Johannine circle if we are not indeed to allow that the authorship of both is the same. The study is grouped around the titles Logos, Son of Man, and Son of God, because it seems easiest to subsume the other titles and concepts under these. If later theology and formulae cannot be taken as definitive for these terms neither can they be regarded as mere names abstracted from Christian or extra-Christian tradition. John takes the meaning of the words and distils the full significance of the metaphors involved, and, to change ours, surrounds them with allusions which produce an impressionist portrait that only appears distinct at a distance.

CHAPTER 3

THE LOGOS AND GOD

The religious use of the term "word" has affinities Greek and Hebrew, and in the course of Johannine studies both sources have had their advocates. The only way to decide one way or the other (or both ways at once) is to inquire into the available possibilities and narrow them down by reference to the way the incarnate Word, Jesus, is treated in the body of the gospel. Caution is of course required with the last part of this in view of the widespread feeling that the Prologue is not an integral part of the work.

It was the custom not so very long ago to derive the Johannine "word" almost exclusively from Greek sources. The Greek word λόγος had such a wide variety of meanings that this fact lent itself to speculation. The primary meaning was "speech" or "expressed thought", and from this could be extended to cover thought itself, relation, principle, hypothesis, pattern, and reason or ground of things. The earliest thought does not distinguish religion and philosophy, so that when a single unifying element in the constitution of the universe is sought—water, air, fire—this element is regarded as divine. That is to say, "the divine" is sought for in a first principle: in short, religion and philosophy are one. Heraclitus of Ephesus,[1] called the Obscure, found in his "perpetual flux" one fixed factor on which the mind of man could rest, the Logos. He seems to have thought of it as the pattern or rhythm discernible in the continuous change, and as such as the voice of the divine without and within.[2] It must be said, however, that some suspect that the meaning throughout is simply

[1] See Weber, *Hist. Philos.*, pp. 18ff; James, *Concept of Deity*, p. 97; Webb, *Hist. Philos.*, pp. 14ff.

[2] Stoic thought tends to pantheism; the Logos is the world order regarded as God in place of a transcendent deity. (See James, *Deity*, pp. 96f; Adam, *Religious Teachers of Greece*, p. 222.)

"speech", i.e., Heraclitus' own oracle, which initiates men into the universal secret. Not for nothing was he called "the Obscure", and the elasticity of the term λόγος is to a large extent responsible for the obscurity. Anaxagoras[1] is the first thinker to move towards a spiritual interpretation of the universe and away from the pre-philosophy which has not reached the point of distinguishing between the material and the non-material. In dispensing with the search for a single element to represent the whole Anaxagoras fastened upon Logos as the unifying principle in everything. It was Reason which sorted out the different elements of the universe and assigned its proper place to each. Hence for him Mind or Intelligence (Νοῦς) is supreme, and although it is never referred to directly as divine, "divinity is attributed to its epithets".[2]

It remained for the Stoics to popularize the concept of Logos as immanent in the cosmic process, half hidden, half revealed, in the visible world, but discoverable in the self.[3] The Stoics were impressed by the order observable in the natural world, in the regular movement of the stars and seasons and of natural functions. Man should live in accord with this Reason or Principle; in all men perhaps, in some men at least, dwelt a spark of this divine Reason (the λόγος σπερματικός). It was each man's guide, like Socrates' δαίμων. By virtue of it man was a rational (λογικός) animal. The popular philosophy of John's day was a mixture, in different parts, of Stoicism and Platonism, both of which influenced the Wisdom literature, and, to a greater extent, the Hermetic writers. Philo also combined Stoic and Platonic thought, and for him the Logos is the world of Ideas, of which this world is a copy, as well as the Reason innate in the universe and man.

The Greek Logos influenced subsequent Christian thought more than it did that of the New Testament writers. Justin Martyr was, as Eusebius[4] puts it, an ambassador of the divine Logos in the guise of a philosopher, and claimed Heraclitus and

---

[1] See Webb, *Hist. Philos.*, pp. 35ff; Weber, pp. 30ff.
[2] James, *Deity*, p. 98.
[3] Cicero, *De Nat. Deorum*, II, 20ff; 45ff.
[4] *H.E.*, IV, vi, 8.

Socrates as Christians before Christ.[1] He thus set the fashion for later Christian theology, and his Logos differs far more radically from that of John than from that of Origen, for instance.

We shall return later to the question of the distinction between the Greek Logos of speculation and the Jewish word of the Lord. At the moment attention must be drawn to the fact that the identification of John with the Greek view landed commentators in considerable difficulties. Thus Stanton, to take a comparatively representative example,[2] felt himself forced to say that the becoming flesh of such an entity as the Johannine Logos would reduce the cosmos to chaos. The difficulty as it stands is insuperable; but it was of the critics' own making. It does not lie in the gospel itself, nor did it occur to St Paul in a not dissimilar context, and it is from his language that the modern kenotic theories derive their terminology. Presumably it was the Jewishness of John and Paul, their dependence upon the Wisdom rather than the philosophical Logos conception, which explains the circumstance. St Paul had found the secret of life in Jesus, and therefore could declare that by him the world hung together.[3] This recalls the Stoic idea that the reason within is akin to the Reason which orders the universe but it does not *begin* from a metaphysical standpoint, and therefore the metaphysical difficulties remain below the horizon. John likewise found that "in him was life" and therefore "everything came to be through him".[4] At the back is the Wisdom idea, not a metaphysical theory but a moral conviction. The writers of the New Testament were religious men, not philosophers. To look for exact theological definitions in their work is to miss what they have to give. This is particularly true of John. In such a one we must expect to find something new which draws upon the language of various usages to express what he has seen without exhausting his meaning in any of them.

It nevertheless remains that the Johannine Prologue has a philosophical ring. This is increased by the punctuation "what came to be in him was life" or "was life in him", adopted by Westcott and Hort, though not without hesitation on the part of

---

[1] I *Apol.*, xlvi, 3. [2] *Gospels as Hist. Docs.*, iii, pp. 168f, 171, etc.
[3] Col. 1.17. [4] John 1.3.

the latter.[1] Since "what came to be" seems to refer back to the "all things" which "came to be through him", the κόσμος appears to be in question; and this is a favourite term with John.[2] We are reminded of the saying in the Corpus Hermeticum, "the cosmos is the fullness of life".[3] Is this the Greek notion of the world as a living being, like a cow in a field, as someone put it? Estlin Carpenter thought it was[4] and quoted Plato's *Timaeus*[5] to the effect that "we may say that the world became a living creature truly endowed with soul and intelligence by the providence of God". (The words in the dialogue are spoken by Timaeus.) Westcott, however,[6] found difficulty with the form of words "is life", not "has life", and, like others before him, found an edifying meaning in the style of Anselm that God not merely *has* life but *is* life. The difference is that between the "idea" and the temporal realization of the idea. But Carpenter had to make it part of his case that "what came to be in him was life" was a parallel to the Hebrew idiom "I was a reproach", "This man shall be peace", "You once were darkness." If this is the case it introduces a doubt as to whether John could have been thinking in such a "Greek" way at the same time. What follows, "and the life was the light of men", is difficult to construe with life = a living universe. In what sense could the κόσμος be the light of men? The suggestion of Stoic influence—the world soul, and the σπερματικὸς λόγος—is a superficial impression, and in any case Hort's suspicion that the later punctuation may convey the correct sense has also to be reckoned with. As he pointed out, the earlier has no textual authority, "being only an embodiment of ancient interpretations",[7] and the later "has high claims to acceptance on internal grounds".

The connections between John and the Greek philosophers in the use of the term Word are, in fact, slight. The same is true of other connections which have been drawn. Thus it has been

[1] *App. to Gk N.T.*, pp. 73f, 1896 ed.
[2] Cf. 1.10.   [3] C.H. 12.15.
[4] *The Johannine Writings*, p. 318.
[5] 30B.   [6] Op. cit., p. 30.
[7] The newly discovered P⁶⁶ (Pap. Bodmer) seems to have the "later" punctuation, if it can be said to have any consistent punctuation anywhere.

compared with the Eastern Tao, and even with the Brahman of the Upanishads.[1] More seriously perhaps, the comparison has been made with the Vohu Manah or Vahista Manah of Zoroastrianism —more seriously, because in the view of many John was dependent upon Iranian thought for many of his ideas and much of his terminology, particularly in respect of his indebtedness to what Reitzenstein called the "light theology". Vohu Manah, "Good Thought", is, however, not parallel to the Greek Logos. As J. H. Moulton put it: "The common comparison with the Greek Logos is therefore at best only partial. Plutarch, who rendered Εὔνοια, 'Goodwill', did not think of it."[2] Vohu Manah is close to the concept of "Wisdom" as "practical righteousness", i.e., thought in accord with "the Wise Lord", Ahura Mazda. There is, however, no evidence that John had such direct contact with Iran as this. If the contact can be traced through the Jewish Wisdom, well and good; but that lies outside the scope of this investigation.[3]

Bultmann is responsible for what is considered by many a more promising line by which John can be connected with Iran. This is through the concept of the Word as a source of revelation, an idea which will occupy us in much of the remainder of this chapter. Jesus in John, says Bultmann, is the divine Bearer of revelation, and he traces the origin of this idea to Mandean sources. Here Anush-Uthra is called "a word (*malala*), a son of words".[4] This is taken to mean that he was a deity of revelation, and, since Mandaism is influenced by Iranian religion, it implies that Persian mythology is the ultimate origin of the concept of the Word as a divinity of revelation. We shall be concerned elsewhere with the question of whether Anush-Uthra is to be identified with the "cosmic, heavenly Man", or, so far as can be told, whether the Johannine presentation is indebted to Iranian sources. Suffice it in the present connection to note that the application to him of the

---

[1] Bollou, *Pocket World Bible*, p. 219.

[2] *Early Religious Poetry of Persia*, p. 61.

[3] The same is not true of the Anthropos, which, it is claimed, was always a rival to the central idea of Christian theology.

[4] *Malala* is properly applied to Adakas.

term *malala* merely signifies that, in Kraeling's words, he "has something to do with the promulgation of truth".[1] The question of a more precise identification of Anush with the Word of the Johannine Prologue may be left over for the time being. That the Mandeans in their extant writings made so little of the Word goes to prove that their connection with the doctrine of the Word had not the intimate nature required by the theory we are considering.

It was, however, in Alexandria that the combination of Greek Logos and Jewish Wisdom was effected. Λόγος is the translation of the Hebrew דָּבָר, the Word of the Lord by which the heavens were made. The distinction between the Jewish and Greek contributions does not consist in the fact that Logos for the Greek could have an independent existence. For most primitive peoples, the Hebrews included, the word once spoken has autonomous power and substance,[2] and this idea is apparently not given up in later thought. A word was, as Moore declared, "a concrete reality, a veritable cause".[3] It was but a short step from the psalms, where the "God said" of Genesis had taken on substance as "the word of the Lord" by which the heavens were made, to the combination of this Word with the substantive Logos of Greek speculation. The step was made easier by the fact that in the Wisdom books, the Word is the enunciation of the divine Wisdom which originated and now sustains and directs the world. Thus in Sir. 24.3, Prov. 2.6, Wisdom comes from God's mouth and is presumably therefore regarded as his Word. The idea is never fully developed, but in Sirach, as in John, "by the Word of God are his works",[4] and in the Book of Wisdom the identification of Wisdom with Word is already clear enough from the parallelism of clauses in

> O God of the fathers . . .
> Who madest all things with thy word
> And with thy wisdom formedst man.[5]

It is certainly not sufficient argument for approaching the Johannine Logos from the Greek side that no explanation is possible of

---

[1] In *Anthropos and Son of Man.*
[2] Dodd, *F.G.*, p. 264.
[3] *Judaism*, i, p. 414.
[4] Sir. 42.15.
[5] Wisd. 9.1f.

how "Wisdom" became "Word".[1] The two ideas must have grown up together until they coalesced. The doctrine of the Word with which John was acquainted owed much to Wisdom, as is clear from his indebtedness to Wisdom language. To outline the characteristics of Wisdom is to show how they have left their impress on the Prologue. Thus Wisdom is the spirit which was with God in the beginning, in which the universe was created, which is more precious and brighter than light, unique (i.e., only-begotten), and loving, and which the ungodly reject. The Johannine Prologue could almost be regarded as an elaboration of these ideas alone.

Where John goes beyond Wisdom language is not only in his developed use of Logos but also in the terms he associates with the Logos—life and light in particular. Even Philo does not use the word "light" of God without some misgivings, and never says directly that the Logos is the source of light. On the other hand, Philo is deeply influenced by the popular Greek philosophy, with its mixture of Stoicism and Platonism, and seems to regard the Logos sometimes as the world of Ideas, the ideal universe of which ours is a copy, and sometimes as the Reason inherent in us and God. The former idea is expressed as follows: "If the whole creation . . . is a copy of the divine Image, it is manifest that the archetypal seal also, which we aver to be the intelligible world (κόσμος νοητός), would be the very Logos of God."[2] The Stoic idea is expressed in the contrast between the λόγος προφορικός and the λόγος ἐνδιάθετος, the uttered reason and the innate reason.[3] But, because he was a Jew, Philo strove to bring the Platonic-Stoic view into some sort of accord with the biblical idea of creation by the Word of the Lord and the notion of the creative Wisdom. Thus his Logos is the image of God "through whom the whole universe was formed"; it is the instrument (ὄργανον) by which everything was prepared.[4]

Close to the Johannine use of "life and light" is the Corpus Hermeticum. Here too Stoic and Platonic ideas coalesce, and here

[1] As Carpenter held, *Johannine Writings*, p. 314.
[2] *Opif. Mund.* 25.   [3] *Vit. Mos.* 2.129.
[4] *Spec. Leg.* 1.81; cf. *Cherub.* 35; *Quod Deus Immut.* 12.

too in certain tractates Jewish thought appears. Dodd has in fact shown that the creation vision in Poimandres is based on the Septuagint account.[1] In these passages Logos loses its predominantly psychological and philosophical character and assumes something of the Jewish connotation. The Word of God from the Light "comes upon" the chaos at the beginning and creates order.

The fourth evangelist is not really so much concerned with creation as with manifestation, as the climax of the Prologue proclaims: "he hath declared him". His emphasis upon "everything came to be through him" is part and parcel of the polemic against the view of the world which regards it as inherently evil, just as he is working up to the conclusion "the Word became flesh". Thus "in him was life"—and still more clearly if we read "what came to be in him was life"—recalls the Wisdom teaching that "God created not death". As Bultmann observes, for John sin is essentially murder. In the same way the Genesis creation story stresses that "everything was very good". John's language recalls this myth. "In the beginning was the Word; all things came to be through him; in him was light", writes John; and the author of Genesis says, "In the beginning God made heaven and earth; and God said, let there be light." The Genesis Rabba comments, "From the opening of thy mouth light came to us."[2] The same symbolism is used of the earthly ministry: as God "called the light day, and the darkness he called night" so "We must work the works of him that sent me while it is day; the night comes when no one can work."[3] Yet all this of course only deepens the darkness of the rejection: "He was in the world, and the world came into being through him . . . and his own received him not." There would be no tragedy if there were no goodness.

Philo's Logos is "the Beginning", amongst other things, and this recalls the rabbis who read "as the beginning" in Prov. 8.22 instead of "in the beginning" and understood the first word of

---

[1] See his *Bible and the Greeks.*   [2] Gen. Rab. 3.1.

[3] John 9.4; cf 11.9f, "Are there not twelve hours in a day?" Paul also uses the imagery of day—for the dawning of the new world, as does the writer of the 1st Ep. of John.

Genesis to mean "by Wisdom" which was "the Beginning". Wisdom for the rabbis was none other than the Torah,[1] and it was with the Torah in mind that God created. Once more we have a series of parallels to the Johannine Prologue. The Torah is pre-existent, first-born, is the means of creation, life, light, and truth. It is "light of the world" (אוֹרוֹ שֶׁל־עוֹלָם). It is the "word" of God (in the sense of "commandment").[2] In the Testaments of the Twelve Patriarchs the "light to lighten every man" is Torah.[3] For Jews the Torah is almost personal; in the words of Travers Herford: "It is near the truth to say that what Christ is to the Christian, Torah is to the Jew."[4] Or as Lev Gillett put it, the Torah "is the very communication of the mind and heart of God, of his essential truth and power, goodness and love".[5] Even if one suspects some romanticism in this (for what of St Paul and others like him?) there must have been some who thought this way. John may indeed be opposing some such idea when he writes, "For the Law was given through Moses; grace and truth came through Jesus Christ".[6] But if the Word, like the Torah, is the expression of God's heart, that is because all speech is the expression of the whole man,[7] and, as Odeberg wrote, in the Fourth Gospel Jesus "gives himself in his words, and so eternal life".[8]

Wisdom is the Torah, and Wisdom makes one of her appearances in the Prologue as the one who *tabernacled* with men,[9] i.e., as the Shekinah. The Transfiguration also recalls the Shekinah, the "cloud of glory";[10] and Lohmeyer, in an important exegesis

---

[1] The beginning of this identification is traced to ben Sirach, and Spicq tried to show that the clauses in the Johannine Prologue follow the sections of that work: 1.1–20; 16.24–18.14; 24.1–34; 32.14–33.19; 42.15–43.33. He noted that these are followed by the Prologue in the same order of succession.

[2] Ps. 119.89.　　　　[3] T. Levi 14.4.

[4] *Pharisaism*, p. 171.

[5] *Communion in the Messiah*, p. 61.

[6] John 1.17. חסד ואמת was used of the Law.

[7] Pedersen, *Israel*, i, p. 167.

[8] John 6.51; Odeberg, p. 269 on John 6.63.

[9] John 1.14; Sir. 24.8.

[10] Cf. 2 Pet. 1.17, according to which the voice at the Transfiguration proceeded ὑπὸ τῆς μεγαλοπρεποῦς δόξης. On the Shekinah see Cohen, op. cit., pp. 42ff.

of the Transfiguration story, has referred to the importance of words in the Fourth Gospel. He writes: "It shows the Son of Man, not in his function as Judge of the World, as the visions of Daniel describe him. . . . He is not saving, not sanctifying and glorifying the people. He is teaching three disciples who hearken to his word. If Mark elsewhere speaks of the healing and exorcising ministry, and places preaching in the background, here speaking and speech are the only instrument of this Son of Man, and his only efficacy. We have therefore a Johannine touch in this story."[1] In the Fourth Gospel the word of Jesus is the word of God and the truth; it will judge men at the last day.[2] It abides in them and they must remain in it, as they remain in God.[3] It makes them clean; it is given to them.[4] The possible significance of "The word which I speak is not mine but the Father's which sent me" must not be missed. If Jesus gives himself in his words, and his word is the Word of God, then this comes close to saying that Jesus' word is the Logos. And in fact in the First Epistle the message of Jesus is the Word of life,[5] here standing for the Gospel itself. Jesus is the Way, the Truth, and the Life; he *is* the Gospel. It is no great strain upon meaning to take this word, which is also the word spoken to the men of old and which constituted them "gods",[6] as identical with the Word which was at the beginning. Jesus not only gave this Word, he was it—the self-manifestation of God. Bultmann writes, Da das Wort Jesu die *aletheia* ist, das er selbst ist, so kann auch gesagt werden, dass Jesus das Wort ist. Or, as Loofs put it: "Jesus Christ not only brought the Word of God as the prophets did; he was the Word in everything he said and did, the Word was made flesh in him."[7] This is practically what the

---

[1] *Krit. Exeg. Kommentar über das NT, Das Ev. des Markus*, p. 173, quoted Howard, *Christianity according to St. John*, p. 28.

[2] John 14.24; 17.17; 12.48.

[3] John 5.38; cf. 8.37; 8.31; cf. 1 John 2.14 and 4.16.

[4] John 15.3; 17.14.   [5] 1 John 1.1.

[6] John 10.35f. Stanton thought the argument at 10.35 "would have taken a different turn" if the writer had had the Logos of the Prologue in mind (*Gospels as Hist. Docs.*, iii, p. 168. Hoskyns saw a "delicate reference" to it (p. 456). Cf. Strachan, *Fourth Gospel*, 3rd ed. rev., p. 229.

[7] Bultmann in *N.T.S.* i, 2, p. 86; Loofs quoted by Carpenter, *Johannine Writings*, p. 326.

exordium to the Epistle to the Hebrews says: "God, who at old time spoke to the fathers in the prophets by divers portions and in divers manners, has at the end of these days spoken to us in a son, whom he appointed heir of all things, through whom also he made the world. . . ." The wonder is that this writer did not use the term Logos. He was certainly thinking of Wisdom when he called the Son "the effulgence of his glory and the impress [character] of his substance, upholding all things by the word of his power", and the words recall Philo: "When the substance of the universe was without shape and figure God gave it these: when it had no definite character God moulded it into definiteness, and when he had perfected it, sealed the universe with an image and idea, even his own Logos."[1]

The Prologue, however, is concerned not only with manifestation but also with presence; not only "he has declared him" but also "he was in the world". So also the Torah is the symbol of the presence of God. As Wisdom was told to "tabernacle with Jacob",[2] so the Word "tabernacled with us, and we beheld his glory". As we have seen, the coincidence of "tabernacle" and "glory" (Heb. כבד, Ar. יקרא) inevitably recalls the Shekinah, the cloud of glory, the presence. The word comes from the root שכן, to dwell; and from originally signifying the abiding of God in a certain spot, came to mean God himself, "a new word for the Godhead apart from notions of place".[3] The Johannine Word is the light which lightens every man. The Shekinah is upon every man as the light of God.[4] The First Epistle of John speaks of "that which we have heard, that which we have seen with our eyes, that which we beheld, and our hands handled".[5] For the rabbis of the Talmud the Shekinah could be "heard, seen [feasted upon with the eyes], smelt, heard coming".[6] In John, the Presence

---

[1] Somn. 2.45.   [2] Sir. 24.8.

[3] Abelson, *The Immanence of God in Rabbinical Literature*, p. 78.

[4] Sifre on Numbers 41. "The earth shone with his glory" (Ezek. 43.2), provokes the comment, "This is the face of the Shekinah"; "The Lord make his face to shine upon thee" (Num. 6.25), is interpreted, "May he give thee the light of the Shekinah" (Cohen, op. cit., p. 42).

[5] 1 John 1.1.

[6] Abelson, *Jewish Mysticism*, p. 92.

is known in the bond of love. "If a man loves me, he will keep my word, and my Father will love him, and we shall come to him and make our home with him."[1] The word "abide" which occurs in this relation so often in John, is a technical term with the rabbis (שָׁרוּיָה p.p. of שָׁרָה, שְׁרִי). The following passage is typical of many in Pirqe Aboth: "When ten sit together and occupy themselves with the Torah, the Shekinah abides among them, as it is said, 'God standeth in the congregation of the godly.'"[2] The addition a little later makes the whole passage sound very like the Johannine sentence just quoted: "And whence can it be shown that the same applies even to me? Because it is said, 'In any place where I cause my Name to be remembered I will come to thee and I will bless thee.'"[3] Dalman points out[4] that while John writes of Isaiah "he saw his glory" (i.e., the glory of Christ), the Targum expands Isa. 6.5 to "mine eyes saw the glory of the Shekinah of the King of the ages . . .". So we may compare the *locus classicus* for the Shekinah, Ex. 33, with the Prologue.

Ex. 33	John 1
7 Now Moses used to take a tabernacle and pitch it outside the camp.	14 And the Word became flesh and tabernacled among us
9 And the pillar of cloud (the Shekinah) descended	
10 And all the people saw the pillar of cloud . . .	and we beheld his glory
18 And Moses said, Show me, I pray thee, thy glory.	17 For the Law was given by Moses; grace and truth came by Jesus Christ.
20 And the Lord said, Thou canst not see my face: for man shall not see me and live	18 No man has seen God at any time:
22 . . . when my glory passes by . . .	the only-begotten Son . . . has declared him.
23 . . . thou shalt see my back.	

---

[1] John 14.23.
[2] Ps. 82.1.
[3] Ex. 20.24; Aboth 3.7.
[4] *Words of Jesus*, p. 231.

But if John was thinking of the Shekinah, could he also have had the Memra in mind? Dalman wrote: "מֵימַר, as well as יְקָר and שְׁכִינָה, appears to be represented in John 1.14 καὶ ὁ λόγος σὰρξ ἐγένετο καὶ ἐσκήνωσεν ἐν ἡμῖν καὶ ἐθεασάμεθα τὴν δόξαν αὐτοῦ δόξαν ὡς μονογενοῦς παρὰ πατρός. ὁ λόγος is מֵימְרָא; ἐσκήνωσεν represents שְׁכִינְתָּא; δόξα stands for יְקָרָא."[1] He commented: "All the three entities became incarnate in Jesus; and in this, at least, a use is made of these ideas which is at variance with their primary application." In those days it was the fashion to derive the Johannine Logos from the Memra as proof of its "Jewish" origin. Billerbeck and Moore, however,[2] showed that it was not a "being of any kind". The Jewish scholar Abelson had already reached the conclusion "that it is not used as an intermediary between man and God; and this accords with the rabbinic anxiety to avoid all possible suspicion of teaching the existence of two beings having equal or nearly equal divine powers".[3] The literal meaning of the term appears to be simply "word" in a quite general sense. Thus we read in Deut. 21.20, "He will not receive our Memra"; in Gen. 45.21 mention is made of "the Memra of Pharaoh"; in Gen. 3.17 Adam hearkens to the Memra of his wife (למימר for לקול). In Onkelos Num. 15.31 it stands for the Jerusalem Targum's "the first commandment". Used in connection with God it has been variously described as a "buffer-word" or "smoke-screen" word, to keep him off; and indeed it often gives the impression of a tendency simply to heap up words: thus Ex. 14.31, "Israel believed in the Name of the Memra of the Lord."

The conclusion is that in this respect the expression serves as a direct verbal substitute for the divine Name, the sacred Tetragrammaton. But the Name of God in Jewish thought was more than a mere grammatical part of speech; it was the essence of deity itself.[4] Thus in the Old Testament, "the place in which the Lord

---

[1] Ibid., p. 231.

[2] S-B, ii, pp. 302ff; Moore, *Intermediaries in Jewish Theology*, p. 53.

[3] *Immanence*, p. 159.

[4] Name means "character" also, as in the Lord's Prayer.

will choose to cause his Name to dwell"[1] is "the place in which *the Lord* will choose to dwell". In a language poor in abstract nouns, words like "name" could stand for "person".[2] This would explain the otherwise curious uses to which Memra is put. In Isa. 63.14 "Memra of the Lord" occurs for "spirit of the Lord" (here, incidentally, there would also seem to be some "substance" about the conception). There is in fact little distinction between Memra, Shekinah, Yekara;[3] all are used in the same way to indicate God where a term like "angel" would be felt to be inappropriate and blasphemous.[4] But the latter two are both expressive of manifestation, which bears out what Abelson says, that the examples show Memra as pointing to a divine manifestation in the affairs of the world.[5] Bultmann concurs: "The 'word of God'—like the rabbinic equivalent מימרא דיי—does not mean a concrete figure (neither a person nor a cosmic power or 'hypostasis'), but the manifestation of God's power in a specific instance."[6] Memra then is not a mediating principle of any kind, and not the creative Word of the psalms, for which the Targums use *pitgama*, or, rarely, *milla*;[7] it is the Name of God himself, with perhaps the suggestion especially of God as self-revealing. Here then is a meaning of "word" which, along with Shekintha and Yekara, presence and glory,[8] suits best the whole bent of the Prologue.

It is tempting to pursue the matter further. Memra is never used outside the Targums. But we know that among the Samaritans God was called "the Name", and that the Jews, in *citing* from

---

[1] Deut. 16.2.   [2] Acts 1.15.

[3] The concept of the Holy Spirit is also practically identical: see Cohen, ibid., p. 45.

[4] Stenning, *Targum of Isaiah*, p. ix; see p. xii. For the angel in Hellenism, see Dodd, *Bible and Greeks*, pp. 21ff.

[5] *Immanence*, p. 164; cf. p. 151. The Memra may well have played a greater part in Jewish theology than appears from our sources, where it would be suppressed in reaction to Christianity. Even now, as we have suggested in the text, there is occasionally more "substance" in the Memra than it is now customary to allow. See Knox, *Some Hellenistic Elements in Primitive Christianity* (Schweich Lectures for 1942, pub. 1944); Lev Gillett, p. 79 on Nahmanides' remarks in this connection.

[6] *N.T. Theology*, ii, p. 64.   [7] Moore, *Judaism*, i, pp. 417ff.   [8] John 1.14.

Scripture, said, not אדני, "Lord", but השם, "the Name". And there are traces in non-rabbinic literature of much wider speculation about the Name than appears at first sight. Thus the Christian *Didache* contains this prayer: "We give thanks to thee, holy Father, for thy holy Name, which thou didst make to tabernacle in our hearts."[1] The same combination occurs in John 17.6 and 17.4, where the manifestation of the Name is the same as the glorification of the Father, that is, comments Odeberg, it is the bringing of the Shekinah to earth: the Logos "tabernacles" among men.[2] In the Odes of Solomon 39.8 occurs the expression, "Put on the Name of the Most High and know him." There seems to be reason for thinking that this is a Jewish expression,[3] and a comparison with the Pauline phrase "to put on Christ" and the like might support the belief that "the Name" was a title of our Lord, as it appears to have originally been in Mark 9.41. For Philo, not only is the Logos the Name,[4] but (referring to Ex. 23.20f) the Logos is the one with the Name of God upon him.[5] Later Jews, referring to the same text, could speak of the Name of God abiding in his representative. Thus it abides in Metatron, the angel with God's Name in him,[6] who was called "the Angel of the Face", "the divine Presence", and "the little Yahweh".[7] It is to be remembered that according to the rabbis the Shekinah had a Face, and the expression occurs again elsewhere in the Odes of Solomon, together with the word "Name":

> I have put on incorruption through his Name,
> I have put off corruption by his grace:
> Death hath been destroyed before my Face:
> Sheol hath been abolished by my Word.[8]

Harris and Mingana pointed out that the parallelism of Face and Word suggest that God is the speaker in the last two lines and that

---

[1] *Didache* 10.2.   [2] John 1.14.

[3] Scholem, *Major Trends in Jewish Mysticism*, p. 368, n 131, gives a late Hebrew equivalent for the Syriac phrase.

[4] *Conf. Ling.*, 28.   [5] *De Migr. Abr.*, 31.

[6] In accordance with Ex. 23.20f. He fulfils some of the functions of the Alexandrine Wisdom.

[7] For "the little Yahweh" see Odeberg, *3 Enoch*, p. 144; *F.G.*, p. 310.

[8] Odes Sol. 15.8f.

the Word is the Logos, and further that the Logos is also the Name.[1] Elsewhere in the Odes the Name "given to us" appears to stand for the Holy Spirit.[2] A similar phenomenon occurs in the gnostic works which were discovered at Nag Hammadi, and are supposed to emanate from Valentinian circles. Here, however, the speculation becomes confused and prolix. The following occurs in a long quotation given by G. Quispel.[3]

> And this is the Father, he from whom proceeded the Beginning and to whom all who have proceeded from him and who have been manifested for the Glory and for the joy of his Name will return. And the Name of the Father is the Son. He it is who at the first gave the Name to him who proceeded from him and who was himself. And he has begotten him a Son, he has given him his Name. . . . And the sons of the Name are those in whom the Name of the Father rests.[4] And they for their part rest in his Name.[5]

In John Jesus prays for his followers to be kept in the Name which was given to him[6] and in which he has kept them.[7] He has given them the Father's word,[8] and to be kept in the Name seems to be equivalent to abiding in the word of Jesus which is also the Father's word.[9] The Nag Hammadi work, may, of course, be directly indebted to Johannine language and idioms, but in any case it shows how these were understood in some circles. The other writers, Philo, the Jewish heretics, and the authors of the

---

[1] Harris-Mingana, p. 89.

[2] Ode 6.7; cf. the equivalence (noted above) of Shekinah and Holy Spirit and the use of Memra to translate "spirit" in Isa. 63.14.

[3] *The Jung Codex*, pp. 73ff; Gospel of Truth, 37.35—38.30.

[4] Cf. *Didache* 10.2 quoted above.

[5] Note in this passage the mention of the Beginning and Glory and the Wisdom reference by which the Beginning "proceeds" from the Father: Prov. 2.6; Sir. 24.3. Cf. the pronunciation of the Name in the system of Marcus (Irenaeus, *Adv. Haer.*, I. 14.1), where it is associated with the utterance of the Word. The "first word" of the Name is called ἀρχή, which is left untranslated by the old Latin.

[6] Cf. Phil. 2.9 where Jesus is given the Name that is above every name.

[7] John 17.11f. Note Burch's remark (*Ep. to Hebrews*, p. 39) that the writer of Hebrews 1 "is not moved . . . by any ideas of rank in divine agency. His concern is with the 'name'." He goes on to point out that the *Auctor* then produces from the O.T. not "support for argumentative doctrine but a series of names" (as John does). Cf. Lactantius, *Divine Institutes XIII* on Ps. 45.6,7, which is quoted in Heb. 1.8,9, "by which his name is shown forth".

[8] John 17.14.   [9] John 8.31f; 17.7.

Didache and the Odes of Solomon, are not apparently dependent upon the Fourth Gospel. In the gospel no attempt is made to draw any closer correspondence between the Name and the Word than that already indicated. So also Jesus is not identified with the Name—though he is not identified with the Word either in the body of the gospel. Similarly, though he has life in himself and bestows life,[1] he is never the life itself, except possibly at 11.25, where, however, Moffatt would render, "true and living way". John prefers to hint and not define.

It cannot be ignored, however, that in the Fourth Gospel the Logos is involved in creation. Is there any evidence that at some point the Name was similarly involved? The proof of the dwelling of the Name in Metatron was achieved by the curious method of adding up the numerical values of the letters in his name, which amount to 314 and thus are equivalent to "Shaddai". In the later Cabbalistic doctrines much was made of this line, according to which also "all things exist only by virtue of their degree of participation in the great Name of God, which manifests itself throughout the whole Creation".[2] Quispel traces this doctrine back to the beginning of the third century,[3] and adduces other instances of the connection with creation of the Name and the various names of God in the esoteric writings of those early days.[4] He quotes among other things the following from 1 Enoch: "The angel requested Michael to show him the hidden Name, that he might pronounce it in the Oath, so that they [the fallen angels] might quake before that Name and Oath [by which] . . . the heaven was made fast and suspended . . . the earth was founded upon the water . . . the sea was created . . . and by which the stars complete their course."[5] Here apparently creation is effected and sustained by the pronunciation of the Name. The notion of pronouncing the Name occurs in the passage from the Gospel of Truth quoted already: "Who then is there who could pronounce a Name for him, the great Name, except he alone, to whom this Name belongs?" Quispel refers in a footnote to the interesting

---

[1] John 5.26.
[2] Scholem, *Mysticism*, p. 133.
[3] *The Jung Codex*, p. 69.
[4] Id., p. 67–76.
[5] 1 Enoch 69.14ff.

form of words in the *Didache* (from the passage already drawn upon): "Thou didst create all things on account of thy Name." On the surface this simply means (in Old Testament fashion) that God made the world for his glory, and we are back at the idea of creation as manifestation. J. B. Lightfoot long ago saw in the Alexandrine Logos "a philosophical term to express the *manifestation* of the Unseen God, the Absolute Being, in the creation and government of the world".[1] Whether Quispel is justified in finding that the Name in pre-Christian times "was considered as a cosmological principle, and thus in a certain sense as a distinct hypostasis"[2] is open to doubt, and is certainly not necessary for our argument. It is more than enough that the Name of God, the sacred Tetragrammaton, has something to do with the creation of all things. This idea too probably underlies the Prologue among the other implicit ones.

We may now proceed further. It is impossible not to connect the "Name" in John with the "I am" sayings. Jesus is given the Name, so that he in turn can give it to others, manifest it. He says, "I am." Foreshadowings of this appear in the synoptics, where Jesus warns against false Christs who will say, "I am",[3] and himself says, "I am", before the high Priest.[4] The risen Christ of Revelation says, "I am the first and the last."[5] With predicate the phrase occurs in pagan inscriptions, "I am Isis", "I am Osiris". The Mithras Liturgy has "I am the son . . . .". The expression is an inevitable one. Yet Norden[6] showed that the use of ἐγώ εἰμι in Hellenistic religions owes much to Jewish influence, and Oriental usage in general. From the Old Testament comes "I am thy God"[7] (LXX ἐγώ εἰμι ὁ θεός σου) and "I am thy salvation".[8] In John also a predicate can always be assumed: "I am the light of the world"; "I am (he)." At John 9.9 it is the blind beggar who says, "I am (he)." Where "I am" by itself occurs in the Septuagint it is generally a translation of the Hebrew אני הוא,

---

[1] *The Epistle to the Colossians*, p. 141.
[2] *The Jung Codex*, p. 70.
[3] Mark 13.18; Luke 21.8.
[4] Mark 14.62.   [5] Rev. 1.17.
[6] *Agnostos Theos*, pp. 177–223.
[7] Gen. 17.1.   [8] Ps. 35.3.

43

as in Isa. 43.1, "That you may know that I am (he)"; and this refers exclusively to God. It may be that we need go no further for the background of the Johannine usage; certainly Odeberg's objection that this would make Jesus say, "I am God, I am the Father"[1] is not decisive.

However, the use of ἐγώ εἰμι in John recalls also the Name of God revealed to Moses in the burning bush. This is given as אהוה אשר אהוה and is translated in the Septuagint ἐγώ εἰμι ὁ ὤν. In the Book of Wisdom and in Philo also God is ὁ ὤν. Dodd comments that Hellenistic Judaism was thus provided with a designation for the Deity of profoundly philosophical import.[2] The original motive of the translators was, however, reverential; the Name of God could not be pronounced. Where the philosophical element is introduced this fact is obscured; thus ὁ ὤν in Philo sometimes becomes τὸ ὄν, the neuter. Something analagous happens to Wisdom and Word where they achieve a metaphysical status; from being originally reverential circumlocutions for God they become independent hypostases. This is particularly true of Philo. In the Wisdom literature even Wisdom is only a quasi-personification; so Burch could write that in the New Testament itself the use of "the Sophia as a name for the Lord Jesus Christ did not convey that he was the Creator of the world, but that the God revealed in him was the Creator".[3] In the Wisdom literature the Word is only personified once in a highly poetical figure as a warrior leaping down from heaven.[4] But Philo's Logos stands over against God: "The primal existence is God, and next to him is the Logos of God."[5] The Logos is a second God, the bridge between the begotten and the unbegotten, "the oldest and most generic of things which have come into being". Philo is in advance even of Greek philosophy in this respect; Bevan wrote: "It is sometimes said that the Stoic σπερματικὸς λόγος was paral-

---

[1] *F.G.*, p. 310. On אני הוא cf. E. Stauffer, *Jesus, Gestalt u. Geschichte*, pp. 130ff; Dodd, *F.G.*, pp. 94ff.

[2] *Bible and Greeks*, p. 4.

[3] *Jesus Christ and His Revelation*, p. 96.

[4] Wisd. 18.15; cf. Rev. 19.12,13, where the rider of the white horse has a Name which only he knows, the Word of God.

[5] *Leg. All.* 2.86.

lel to the cosmic Logos of Philo or the Fourth Gospel, but in the
fragments of the old Stoic books the word is habitually used in the
plural, σπερματικοὶ λόγοι, for the multitude of specific types
reproduced by propagation. *Stoicism knew of no cosmic Logos distinct from God or the Divine Fire.*[1] This fact is very relevant to
the question whether the Johannine conception of the Logos is
Greek or Jewish in character.

But Philo himself is not consistent. Thus he can write that the
Logos is God's instrument in creation; and yet, "He used no
assistant (παράκλητος)—for who was there but himself alone?"[2]
This is close to the attitude of the Wisdom writers. In Wisd. 13.1
God is ὁ ὤν and the τεχνίτης,[3] craftsman, of the universe. Wisdom
is τεχνῖτις in 7.22, and therefore presumably one with ὁ ὤν. The
Stoic colouring of the surrounding language does not require us to
see here an independent hypostasis; rather we should take the
apparent identity at its face value. We are reminded of the rabbinic use of circumlocutions for the sacred Tetragrammaton, and
Dodd has recently recalled that Philo's use of Logos has some
affinity with the (probably later) use of Memra as denoting the
divine Name.[4] Philo actually says that the Logos is called "the
Name of God".[5] The whole point of such terms as Wisdom,
Memra, Logos, and Name, is lost when they become independent
mediators with substantive existence of their own. Their original
raison d'être is the sense of the numinous which surrounds the
person of God himself, the Name.

In the place where Wisdom is the τεχνῖτις and therefore presumably identical with ὁ ὤν, she has in her a spirit which is
μονογενές, or, to adopt a different reading more in accord with
9.17 where she is identified with the Holy Spirit, she is herself this
spirit. And Wisdom is in fact used in the same sense as Shekinah
and Glory, both of which leave their marks on the Johannine Prologue at its climax. Here μονογενής is used of the incarnate Logos:

---

[1] *Later Greek Religion*, p. xv (my italics).
[2] *De Opif. Mund.*, 6.
[3] This verse shows connections with the Johannine doctrine of "works": see
below, p. 158.
[4] *F.G.*, p. 68.   [5] *Conf. Ling.*, 28.

"the Word became flesh and dwelt among us, and we beheld his glory, the glory of the only begotten from the Father", and then with an even stronger expression, "God only-begotten, who is in the bosom of the Father, he has declared him."[1] The word μονογενής means "unique": Plato applies it to the world, Parmenides to the Existent, Clement of Rome to the Phoenix.[2] That it is common for an only child is shown by Luke 7.12; 8.42; 9.38; Heb. 11.17.[3] In its Stoic context in Wisd. 7.22 μονογενές would seem to be simply "unique" in the sense of being in a class on its own. If, however, Wisdom is to be in some sense identified with God, and the divine Logos is the Name, then it may be that there are religious overtones in the use of μονογενής which this bald translation misses. Abelson, in support of his idea that the Johannine Logos from one point of view is not so much a separate entity as an attempt to preserve the divine unity, found a parallel to the gospel μονογενής in the expression שם המיוחד. "The term שם המיוחד applied to God means 'the distinguished Name', i.e., the Tetragrammaton which is marked off by a special sanctity from the other divine names."[4] And again, "the gospel translation 'only-begotten Son' corresponds to the Hebrew יחיד used in this specialised sense".[5] Μονογενής is in fact the translation of יחיד in Ps. 22.20f; 35.17. Isaac in Gen. 22.2 is called יחיד, "only" son, and the יחיד is translated in the Septuagint ἀγαπητός, a word which is interchangeable with μονογενής.[6] Now Daube has pointed out that in the Genesis Rabba on this passage the place is called Moriah because the Law, "horaya",

---

[1] Hort's arguments in *Two Dissertations* (1877) still seem to hold good. They are supported by B ℵ pesh boh and several Fathers. P⁶⁶ now confirms that this was the Alexandrine reading c. 200. Burney's theory that the phrase was a mistranslation of the construct state has to face the criticism that so incompetent a translator would scarcely be able to begin (Black, *An Aramaic Approach*, p. 10).

[2] Plato, *Timaeus*, sub fin.; Parmenides, *On Nature*; Clement, *Ad Cor.* (A), 25.

[3] Πολυμερῶς occurs in Heb. 1.1; Wisdom in Wisd. 7.22 is a spirit μονογενές and πολυμερές.

[4] *Immanence*, p. 171, n 27.   [5] Op. cit., pp. 164f.

[6] Cf. L & S *sub voc.* ἀγαπητός; Bernard *in loc.* John 1.14, C. H. Turner in *J.T.S.*, xxvii, pp. 113ff, 362, on the Marcan Baptism account; N. Turner in *E.T.* Jan. 1960, p. 107, on the definitions of the lexicographers Julius Pollux and Hesychius.

came from there.[1] It is noteworthy then, that μονογενής appears for the second time in John immediately after "The Law came through Moses".[2] If the Logos is the Name, the connection of μονογενής with שם המיוחד suggests that μονογενὴς θεός in John 1.18 may be another way of indicating the equivalence.

The Septuagint translation of ἀγαπητός for יחיד in the Isaac story recalls the synoptic Baptism account, where Jesus is called ὁ υἱός μου ὁ ἀγαπητός.[3] The ἀγαπητός stands for the *chosen* in Isa. 42.1, "my *chosen* in whom my soul delights". Abelson points out that the rabbinic equivalent of בחיר[4] (chosen) is once more יחיד. But, according to some authorities, Jesus is called "chosen" at John 1.34, the Johannine version of the Baptism, where the usual text has ὁ υἱός.[5] There are thus three usages in John which have connections with יחד, only-begotten, chosen, and Name. The cumulative evidence supports Abelson's suggestion. Μονογενὴς θεός is after all a curious expression, and Stauffer has pointed out that the omission of the article is striking, and reminds one of Philo's (anarthrous) δεύτερος θεός as applied to the Logos.[6] If John was aware of the term used by Philo this is further evidence for his desire to safeguard the unity of the Godhead.

Starting as he does then with two persons, Jesus and God, John must needs insist upon the divine unity by drawing upon conceptions which maintain it while suggesting separateness. He nowhere makes Jesus claim directly to be divine, and nowhere calls him

---

[1] *N.T. and Rab. Jud.*, p. 213. "Morah"="Torah"; like Torah, "Horaya" means "instruction".

[2] John 1.17f.   [3] Mark 1.11.

[4] The similar word בחור, ὁ πρωτότοκος (cf. Col. 1.15) "used absolutely, became a recognized title of Messiah" (Lightfoot, *Col.* p. 144). Lightfoot quotes R. Nathan, *Shemoth Rabba*, 19 fol, 118.4, "God said, As I made Jacob first-born (Ex. 4.22), so also will I make King Messiah a first-born (Ps. 89.28(27))."

[5] ὁ ἐκλεκτός in John 1.34 is supported by P⁵ א* and the old Syr among others (see Souter's apparatus). As might perhaps be expected, the reading is not supported by P⁶⁶. The late T. W. Manson wrote in a private communication, "I have little doubt myself that in John 1:34 'Chosen' is the true text" and listed in support Burkitt, Zahn, Blass, Merx, Harnack, Lagrange, Joüon, Cullmann, and, "with some hesitations", Barrett and R. H. Lightfoot. Still more doubtful was Schrenk in *TWₜNT*, IV, p. 194, n 18.

[6] *TWₜNT*, III, p. 106 quoted Moule, *Idiom Bk. of N.T. Gk.*, p. 116.

"God", though the word is placed on the lips of Thomas in a statement without parallel elsewhere in the New Testament.[1] By implication he makes Jesus say, "I am Son of God";[2] he puts the words "I am" into his mouth, and says that the Word who was God became flesh in him. Throughout the Prologue, although it is the career of the divine Wisdom which is in mind, the references to Jesus' earthly ministry are unmistakable: he came to his own . . . as many as received him . . . born not of the will of the flesh but of God (cf. the Nicodemus story). . . . So the pronouns can be taken as referring to Jesus as well as to the Word. He too is θεός. To give a *name* to anything, to find the *word* for it, is to make it known, to establish relations with it. Jesus is the word for God. To have seen him is to have entered into personal relations with the Father. "His earthly life made visible to men the life which existed with the Father. This life has now become an experience of men enjoying fellowship with the Father and the Son, who is none other than Jesus Christ."[3] Hence "the reiterated emphasis upon the reality of the Lord's human life".[4]

It will seem that our review has reinforced the contemporary inclination to see only Jewish influences in the Johannine use of λόγος. That there are dangers in this approach from the point of view of a developed theology Vincent Taylor has done well to point out.[5] But if John does not think as a metaphysician his position is the true starting-point for Christology. Jesus is in fact God. One cannot help feeling that the tendency to write "the Word was divine" for θεὸς ἦν ὁ λόγος[6] springs from a reticence to attribute the full Christian position to John. It will not do to say that the meaning is that the Word "belongs to the same sphere of being as God"; Philo could have accepted some such formula as that. We

---

[1] But see Heb. 1.8 and 9, where the psalms are apparently addressed to Christ as God: this is another connection between the Christology of Hebrews and the Fourth Gospel.

[2] John 10.36.

[3] Howard, *Christianity acc. to St John*, p. 55.

[4] Ibid.

[5] *E.T.*, Feb. 1959, p. 140, in review of Cullmann's *Die Christologie des N.Ts.*

[6] See Moule, *Idiom Book of N.T. Gk.*, p. 116, for the significance of the anarthous predicate.

may compare *De Somn.* I.229–30, where ὁ θεός is said to be properly used of the Self-existent, and θεός without the article of the Logos.[1] But Philo was a Jew. He could not have accepted what the Church taught about Christ. And he was a most inconsistent theologian: there cannot be a "second God" because God is in a class of one. That John had some idea of the problem which was later to occupy the best minds of the Church may seem difficult; but the constantly-recurring theme of discussions on the "equality" and the like of Jesus with his Father seems to point in that direction. Yet John was no metaphysician. It may require, in Taylor's words, that we launch out into Greek thought to put all this into our terms; he is at least right that we are Christologically unsound without the conviction itself.

[1] Dodd, *F.G.*, p. 72.

CHAPTER 4

THE LOGOS AND MAN

The Word of God is the expression of God's mind. Logos therefore stands first of all for the revelation of the divine. But this
revelation takes place in a man. It was inevitable, then, that writers
should cast about for a link between the Word and manhood. In
an oft-quoted article, J. M. Creed wrote: "At first sight it would
appear as if the belief in Jesus as heavenly Son of Man might easily
blend with a Logos Christology, and indeed it is possible that an
interpretation of the term Son of Man on these lines was not
absent from the mind of the fourth evangelist. . . . It would seem
that the fourth evangelist was prepared, like Philo, to identify the
heavenly Man with the Logos and perhaps to suggest that the
Logos was archetypal Man."[1] This is a fascinating avenue of
thought. For many it leads to the various heavenly men of
gnosticism and on to the figure of Gayomart the original man of
Iranian religion. But for the moment we are only concerned with
the relation between the Logos and Man.

The Prologue of St John's Gospel declares that the Word is the
"light which lightens every man", that "in him was life, and the
life was the light of men". That much it says; and if the translation is allowed, "the light which lightens every man coming into
the world", then that also means the same thing.[2] The language
belongs to that strain in the Prologue which resembles the Jewish
statements about the Torah. A passage in the Testaments of the
Twelve Patriarchs,[3] which may or may not betray signs of

[1] *J.T.S.*, xxvi, p. 134.

[2] Lev. R. 31.6 is usually quoted as a parallel: אתה מאיר . . . לכל באי עולם
exactly equals "thou lightest all who come into the world".

[3] T. Levi 14.4. Charles, *Test. of Twelve Patr.*, p. 58, takes this as referring to
Alexander Jannaeus. He recalls Josephus, *Antiq.*, XIII.xiv.2.

Christian influence,[1] reads thus: "But if ye be darkened through transgressions, what, therefore, will all the Gentiles do living in blindness? Yea, ye shall bring a curse upon our race, because the light of the Law which was given *to lighten every man*, this ye desire to destroy by teaching commandments contrary to the ordinances of God." Here the reference to the Gentiles shows that "every man" means what it says. The Shekinah, which again is hinted at in the Prologue, is likewise upon every man as the light of God.[2]

Another element in the Johannine Prologue which is connected with Torah and Shekinah is Wisdom. Prov. 8.31 represents her as at the beginning

> Rejoicing in this habitable earth
> And my delight was with the sons of men.

At Wisd. 9.1f once more God is addressed as

> Who madest all things with thy Word
> And by thy Wisdom thou formedst man.

So Wisdom is especially associated with men. Not only so, but the shadowy original man of Job 15.7f is even spoken of in language appropriate to Wisdom:

> Art thou the first man that was born?
> Or wast thou brought forth before the hills?
> Hast thou heard the secret counsel of God?
> And dost thou restrain Wisdom to thyself?

And in practically identical fashion Wisdom says:

> The Lord formed me in the beginning of his way . . .
> Before the hills was I brought forth.[3]

Moreover, it was Wisdom who "guarded to the end the first-formed (protoplast) father of the world".[4] Thus there was precedent in John's background for his emphasis on "man" in the

---

[1] De Jonge, in a recent book on the Testaments, regards them as post-Christian in date.
[2] Sifre on Num. 41.
[3] Prov. 8.22.
[4] Wisd. 10.1.

Prologue, his insertion of the (apparently unnecessary) ἄνθρωπον in John 1.9.[1]

When we turn to Philo we find a correspondence drawn between his Logos itself and man. Dodd uses some carefully-chosen words here: "In Philo the ἄνθρωπος ἀληθινός is identified with the λόγος, or, to speak more accurately, that aspect of the cosmical Logos which is specially related to mankind is the ἀληθινὸς ἄνθρωπος."[2] The reason for this caution is that the real identification of ἄνθρωπος with λόγος is through the fact that the latter is the world of Ideas in the platonic style.[3] Doubtless the Stoic notion of a σπερματικὸς λόγος in every man, a seed of the divine Reason, would help towards the final result. "Every man in respect of his intellect is connected with the divine Reason, being an impression or a fragment or a ray of that blessed Nature."[4] The Stoics were able to preserve the paradoxical position that there is a divine element in all men and yet that it is possible only by choice, a trait which has reminded some of the Fourth Gospel.[5] It was, of course, this philosophical idea which finally won its way in Christian theology. We find Westcott quoting Theophylact from Thomas Aquinas: "He says not the Light of the Jews only but of all men; for all of us, in so far as we have received intellect and reason from that Word which created us, are said to be illuminated by him."[6]

The notion that man is akin to God is not a merely philosophical idea, however. Stoicism was a religion, and as a religious idea the conception is probably basic. Its denial, from humanist or

---

[1] But, as we shall see, John has a habit of using an apparently redundant ἄνθρωπος, a fact which, if it is relevant here, upsets two contrary arguments upon this issue. For the ἄνθρωπον of v. 9 is relied upon both by those who see in it a reason for taking φῶς with ἐρχόμενον and translating "the true *light coming* into the world" (Bernard, p. 10(1) (a)) and by those who see the insertion of ἄνθρωπον as an intentional indication that πάντα is not a neuter plural so that the translation is to be "the light which lightens *every man coming*", etc.

[2] *F.G.*, p. 279.

[3] *Alleg. Int.*, 1.12; *De Opif. Mund.*, 46; *De Plant.* 5.

[4] *De Opif. Mund.*, 51.

[5] Knox, *St Paul and the Church of the Gentiles*, p. 224; cf. the "essential man" of the Stoic-Platonic Corpus Hermeticum, Dodd, *F.G.*, p. 42.

[6] Westcott, *Gosp. of St. John*, p. 4.

from theological motives, has disastrous results, as was emphasized by the Russian exiles, notably Berdyaev.[1] It is common both
to the philosophically-tinged doctrines emphasizing the intellect
and to the mystical doctrines of all kinds. As Odeberg pointed
out, most of the systems of the ancient world reflect it, among
them rabbinic Judaism, Mandaism, Hermetism, gnosticism.[2] It
occurs in two special modes, which might be designated ethical
and ontological. In the New Testament both find place. "Love
your enemies . . . and you will be sons of the most High, for he
is kind to the ungrateful and evil"[3] is an example of the former.
The parable of the Prodigal Son is an example of the latter. "The
'Father'", wrote S. L. Frank in this connection, "is not merely a
loving being upon whose protection we may rely but is truly a
Father—a being from whom we have originated, to whom we are
akin, to whose 'house' we belong and whose 'kingdom' is prepared for us from all eternity."[4] Perhaps some temperaments need
the sense of "belonging" more than others, but it is clear that the
metaphor of adoption, if pressed too far, undermines not only the
doctrine that we are "partakers of the divine nature",[5] but also the
validity of the notion of the Spirit in our hearts crying "Abba,
Father".[6] More than the legal metaphor is needed to explain "The
Spirit himself bears witness with our spirit that we are children of
God: and if children, then heirs, heirs of God and joint heirs with
Christ".[7] The point of Jesus' use of the metaphor of family
relationships is that only these are indissoluble. For him we are
sons while we stray and not merely after we come back. Presumably the doctrine of the Fall was intended to preserve the primordial nature of our sonship.

In the Johannine writings our kinship with God is apparently
solely ethical. As the writer of the First Epistle puts it: "In this
the children of God are manifest, and the children of the devil:
whoever does not do righteousness is not of God, neither he that
loves not his brother."[8] John does not believe that all men in fact

[1] See S. L. Frank, *God With Us*, pp. 150ff; Berdyaev *passim*.
[2] *F.G.*, p. 172.   [3] Luke 6.35.
[4] *God With Us*, pp. 156f.   [5] 2 Pet. 1.4.
[6] Gal. 4.6.   [7] Rom. 8.16,17.   [8] 1 John 3.10.

share the divine nature, and this for two reasons at least. First of all, under the influence of Plato, through the Wisdom literature, he inclines to connect God only with the good. J. L. Stocks wrote: "God is the cause not of all things but only of the good, said Plato, but wrongly: his God was not a God of love."[1] Like all epigrams this is an over-simplification, but it serves to throw into relief the idealist bias against personalism. However, the writer of the Book of Wisdom combines the notion of God's "innocence" with that of his creatorhood by insisting that God made all things good; "the generative powers of the world are healthful, and there is no poison of destruction in them. . . . But ungodly men by their hands and their words called death unto them . . . and they made a covenant with him."[2] This is not far from the story of the beginnings in Genesis: "and behold it was very good". The Book of Wisdom, whether or not by a different author,[3] expresses what is not really a different view when it says: "For thou lovest all things that are, and abhorrest none of the things which thou didst make; for never wouldst thou have formed anything if thou didst hate it." (11.24.) Nevertheless, the tendency in this type of thought is to stress moral values and their significance in relationship. Thus the Shepherd in John is almost startlingly different from that in the synoptics. He is in fact concerned solely with the ninety-nine in the fold. The question is one to which we must return when we come to the divine sonship in John.

The other reason for John's elective tendency is his doctrine of love. This is of course connected with the previous reason, but owes much to the particularity of the biblical idea. Thus John hints at the concept of the Shekinah, which originally signified the

---

[1] Quoted Raven, *Natural Religion and Christian Theology*, ii, p. 32. This trait shows itself in such various writers as Marcion, the authors of the Gospel of Truth from Nag Hammadi, the Epistle to Diognetus, and the Odes of Solomon, to say nothing of the gospels and epistles of the N.T. in certain aspects. It appears later esp. in German mysticism, e.g., the *Theologia Germanica*; and is a *problem* for Boehme and his English follower Law.

[2] Wisd. 1.14ff.

[3] John would in any case regard the book as a unity. This is an instance of the different approach of a first-century writer.

presence of God in a particular spot, and still abides with this one
and that one as they are occupied in the Torah. In this idea of love
the initiative is with God: "We love because he first loved us."[1]
So John will call no one "son" save Jesus alone. We are τέκνα
θεοῦ. Dodd claims that in 10.34, after the fashion of the rabbinic
quotations, the conclusion of the words from Ps. 82.6 is assumed:
"I said, You are gods, *and all of you sons of the most High*."[2] Yet
the fact that we are never "sons" to John suggests that he deliberately omitted the underlined words.

It may be possible, however, to make too much of this. The
difficulty is that in this very saying the words occur, "You are
gods"; it was not, then, doctrines of deification which troubled
John at this point. There is in fact another strain in the Fourth
Gospel, on the subject of humanity's relation to God, underlying
the ethical one. The specifically Hebrew version of the notion of
man's kinship with God was conveyed in the words "man was
made in the Image of God".[3] Hooke wrote: "The original meaning of this phrase is uncertain, but it is at least certain that the
Hebrew words rendered 'Image' and 'likeness' invariably have a
concrete meaning in the Old Testament, and will not bear the
interpretation of a spiritual or moral likeness to God imparted to
man at the Creation. It is clear from passages even in the later
books of the Old Testament, that God is conceived of as in human
form."[4] He went on to say that the prohibition of graven images
is to be understood as implying "that no other image of God was
necessary than the image which he had himself created", and "the
Priestly writer implies in this phrase that man is the only divinely
sanctioned 'image of God'".[5] With the rabbis there is a characteristic oscillation between the two notions of an "ethical" and an
"ontological" kinship between man and God. In the first place:

[1] I John 4.19.
[2] *F.G.*, p. 271, n 3; *According to the Scriptures*, p. 47, n 1.
[3] Gen. 1.27.
[4] Cf. Ezek. 1.26; Hooke, *In the Beginning*, p. 37.
[5] Some of the Christian Fathers established a distinction between "image" and
"likeness" (εἰκών and ὁμοίωσις) in Genesis, corresponding to the "ontological"
and "ethical" relationships of man with God (*Studia Patristica* 1.420ff; cf. E.
Lampert, *Divine Realm*, pp. 68f).

5

"All creatures which are formed from heaven, both their soul and
body are from heaven; and all creatures which are formed from
earth, both their soul and body are from earth, with the exception
of man whose soul is from heaven and his body from earth.
Therefore, if a man obeys the Torah and does the will of his
Father in heaven, he is like the creatures above; as it is written, 'I
said, You are gods, and all of you sons of the most High'. But if
he obeys not the Torah and performs not the will of his Father in
heaven, he is like the creatures below; as it is said, 'Nevertheless
you shall die like men.'"[1] This is John's use of the same psalm:
it is the sanctified and sent one who does the Father's will who
appeals to the saying, "You are gods." But we find that the rabbis
had another line. Rabbi Akiba deduced from the text "Thou shalt
love thy neighbour as thyself" the doctrine "You should not say
that inasmuch as I am despised let my fellow-man be despised with
me; inasmuch as I am cursed, let my fellow-man be cursed with
me." R. Tanchuma said, "If you act in this manner, know who it
is you despise, for 'in the image of God made he man'."[2] Here
evidently those who do not do the will of God—the despisers and
cursers—are also "made in the Image". And it is not impossible
that the writer whose Prologue is modelled on the Genesis creation story and who insisted that the men of old were called "gods"
because the "word" of God came to them should have seen the
same significance in "And God *said*, Let us make man in our
Image". The ambivalence of the rabbis is typical also of John.
Thus, with him as with them, the world is now antagonistic to
God, now loved by him.[3] We may compare and contrast in this
respect Augustine. John has his doctrine of predestination: "You
did not choose me, I chose you", says the Christ of the Fourth
Gospel; or, as the writer of the First Epistle puts it, "We love
because he first loved us."[4] So says Augustine: "We cannot love
God unless he already loves us."[5] But Augustine passes over

---

[1] Sifre Deut. 306; 132a; Cohen, p. 68; Ps. 82.6f.   [2] Gen. R. 24.7.

[3] Odeberg, *F.G.*, pp. 116ff; e.g., John 15.19; 3.16; 1 John 2.2.

[4] 1 John 4.19; cf. 4.10, "Herein is love, not that we loved God, but that he
loved us."

[5] *De gratia et libero arbitrio*, xviii, 38.

John 3.16 in his commentary. There is the difference. In Genesis the word of God brings light and man in God's Image; John writes that in the Word is the light of every man.[1]

It is possible to trace the Image in the other writings which show affinity with the Fourth Gospel. J. B. Lightfoot wrote that "Image" was part of "the Alexandrian vocabulary of the Logos".[2] In Poimandres the Father of all, who is life and light, brings forth Man, having his Father's image, and hands over all his works to him[3] as the Father in John has given all things into the hands of Christ.[4] In another tractate[5] the Word is also the Image of God in the sense of being God's intellect. This idea recalls Philo. The latter draws a distinction between the two accounts of the creation of man in Genesis for the purpose of making one the creation of the earthly being and the other the creation of the Platonic Idea of Man. "There are two kinds of man. The one is the heavenly man, the other the earthly. The heavenly, being made in the image of God, has no part in corruptible or earthly substance; the earthly was made of seminal matter, which he has called clay."[6] Philo finds his heavenly man in the oracle of Zech. 6.12, "Behold a man whose name is the rising." "Strangest of titles", he writes, "if you suppose that a being composed of soul and body is here referred to. But if you think that it is that Incorporeal one, who is none other than the divine Image, you will agree that the name 'rising' is given to him very appropriately. For that man is the eldest son, whom the Father of all raised up, whom he calls elsewhere First-born, and Begotten, who imitates his Father's ways."[7] This is the sort of language Philo employs of his Logos, and once again we note the similarity to the Johannine language about the incarnate Logos.[8]

---

[1] John 1.4. The verse with "ye are gods" in Ps. 82 is preceded (v. 5) by the "Johannine" expression, "they walk about in darkness", and the recognition that "all the foundations of the earth are out of course", so that John would see the statement against his own realistic assessment of the condition of mankind.

[2] *Ep. to Colossians*, p. 144.

[3] C.H. 1.12.   [4] John 13.3.

[5] C.H. 12.14.   [6] *Leg. All.* 1.32.

[7] *Conf. Ling.* 14.62f; see the LXX at Zech. 6.12.

[8] John 1.14; 5.19.

Yet again in Philo, in the passage in *Conf. Ling.* 28 which we shall have occasion to quote again shortly, the Word is both Ideal Man and Image. In the Wisdom literature too, still in Alexandria, we find the Image. Wisdom is the "Image of his [God's] goodness".[1] And in Wisd. 2.12ff the suffering righteous one is intended to represent man as God made him—"to be an Image of his own proper being (or, eternity)".[2] The righteous one closely resembles the Johannine Christ. He vaunts that God is his Father, professes to have knowledge of God, and is son of God.[3] Moreover, his ways are "different".[4] And even the rabbis were not immune to the influence of the Greek εἰκών, as is shown by the fact that with them "the ascription of a 'Face' to the Shekinah is sometimes expressed by the word *iqonin* (Greek, eikon, eikonion) and in one place it is used for the image of God which is immanent in the world".[5]

The Image teaching had of course already been baptized into Christianity. For St Paul a man—any man— is "the image and glory of God",[6] and we are to bear the Image of Christ the Second Man from heaven.[7] In the language of the Wisdom school and Philo he calls Christ "the Image of the invisible God, the firstborn of all creation".[8] And elsewhere too his language about the Image recalls the idiom of the Johannine Prologue: "In whom the god of this world has blinded the minds of the unbelieving, that they should not see the light of the gospel of the glory of Christ, who is the Image of God. . . . Seeing it is God who said, Light shall shine out of darkness, who shone in our hearts to give the light of the knowledge of the glory of God in the face of Jesus Christ."[9] Once more Christ the light of men is compared with the first light of creation. In two other places however where one might have expected the word εἰκών it does not appear. One is

---

[1] Wisd. 7.26.   [2] Wisd. 2.23.
[3] Wisd. 2.16; cf. John 5.18; Wisd. 2.13; cf. John 8.55; Wisd. 2.18; cf. John 10.36; 19.7; cf. also Wisd. 2.13 with John 13.1ff.
[4] Wisd. 2.15; cf. John 7.7.
[5] Abelson, *Immanence*, p. 103, n 6.
[6] 1 Cor. 11.7.   [7] 1 Cor. 15.47ff.
[8] Col. 1.15; cf. John 1.18.
[9] 2 Cor. 4.4,6; cf. John 1.9,14, etc.

Phil. 2.6, where μορφή is used of the one who "emptied himself, taking the form of a slave, being made in the likeness of men". The other is the proem to the Epistle to the Hebrews. Here the writer seems, in the words of W. F. Howard, "to challenge his readers to hail their Lord as ὁ λόγος τοῦ θεοῦ ".[1] "God having of old time spoken unto the fathers in the prophets by divers portions and in divers manners, hath at the end of these days spoken unto us in a Son, whom he appointed heir of all things, through whom also he made the worlds; who, being the effulgence of his glory, and the very impress of his substance, and upholding all things by the word of his power, when he had made purification of sins, sat down at the right hand of the Majesty on high."[2] Yet this writer, steeped as he was in Alexandrine idiom, not only omits the Logos but also the image, and strangely substitutes the word "character" or "impress".[3]

Image then belongs to John's thought-world. Two of his episodes also recall it. The first is the discussion with Nathanael, where the latter is promised that he will see the angels ascending and descending upon the Son of Man. Burney and Odeberg, followed by Dodd, quote a passage from Genesis Rabba on Jacob's ladder to explain this. In this passage the angels ascend and find Jacob's image, and descend to find the sleeping empirical man. One of the Servant Songs of Second Isaiah[4] is quoted to the effect that the Servant is the image of Jacob "which is engraved on high". Here a host of associations crowd in. Jesus has just referred to Nathanael as an ideal Israelite: in the Genesis Rabba passage the Image is the ideal man, that is, Israel and not Jacob.[5] As we shall see, the portrait of the suffering Righteous One of Wisd. 2, who is the ideal man created to be an image of God's proper being, is drawn from the Servant. And Wisdom, who was told to "tabernacle with Jacob" as the Word "tabernacled" with

---

[1] *Christianity acc. to St. John*, p. 42.   [2] Heb. 1.1–3.

[3] Heb. 1.3; cf. Philo, *De Plant.*, 5, σφραγῖδι θεοῦ ἧς ὁ χαρακτήρ ἐστιν ἀΐδιος λόγος.

[4] Isa. 49.3.

[5] For the notion of an "ideal" figure as including moral qualities ("without guile") see below, p. 145. This notion however includes more than moral qualities.

men, is the Image of God's goodness. But in Philo the Image is actually identified with the Word, and with the ideal Israel also, in a phrase that recalls Jesus' promise to Nathanael who is also the type of the ideal Israelite, "You shall see": "God's First-born, the Logos . . . is called ἀρχή and the Name of God, and the Word, and Man after his Image, and 'he that sees', that is, Israel."[1] Here we have practically all the associations of the Johannine Word in one sentence. This writer also deals directly with the Jacob's ladder story, making the angels logoi and the place where Jacob slept the Logos, as well as the vision which he saw.[2] The other episode is the conversation with Nicodemus. Here the Son of Man is to be lifted up "as Moses lifted up the serpent in the wilderness".[3] Some have seen in this the "exaltation" of the Servant;[4] but in any case not only Num. 21 but also Wisd. 16.7 is involved, where it is not the brazen serpent which cures the Israelites but "thy word, O Lord, which heals all things".[5] The idea which is being preserved appears also in the Jerusalem Targum on Num. 21.9: "If he direct his heart to the *Name* of the *Word* of Yahweh." But the same idiom occurs along with the Image in the tractate of the Hermetic Corpus called the Font: "This then is the Image of God which I have traced for you; if you gaze intently at it and think on it with the eyes of your heart, believe me, child, you will find the upward path. Or rather the Image itself will guide you. For the vision has some power of its own; it possesses those who have once looked at it and *draws them upward*, as they say the lodestone draws the metal."[6] The word for "to draw upward", ἀνέλκειν, recalls the Johannine ἕλκειν used where the Son of Man,

---

[1] *Conf. Ling.* 28.   [2] *De Somn.* 1.11; cf. *De Migr. Abr.* 31.   [3] John 3.14.

[4] Recently C. H. Dodd; see his *F.G.*, p. 247.

[5] Philo also introduces his Word into the serpent episode—through one of the cardinal virtues which comprise it (*Leg All.* 2.20f).

[6] C.H. 4.11. The lodestone is a common mystical symbol; see Clem. Alex., *Strom.*, VII, ii, 9, where he has been picturing the universe as a hierarchy of circles: "Thus, just as even the smallest piece of iron is moved by the influence of a magnet, which extends through a series of iron rings, so virtuous beings are drawn by the Holy Spirit and are closely united to the first 'mansion'." The image was a favourite of William Law, and was used by Jeremy Taylor (*Doctor Dubitantium*, 1660, II, p. 440). See Hobhouse, *Selected Mystical Writings of William Law*, p. 239. The word "draw" was part of the rabbinic religious vocabulary.

when he has been "lifted up" like the serpent, will "draw" all men to him.[1] The foregoing examples then show that John moved in circles where the Image was a common idea; wherever he turned it met him. Some of his language comes from spheres where the Image is man in the likeness of God, some from spheres where the Image is ideal Man. His episodes are sometimes derived from traditions where the Image and Logos appear, often as identical ideas. He makes certain points which are made elsewhere by means of the Image language and the identification of Image with Logos. All this makes it likely that John thought in terms of the Image, though he avoids the actual word as he avoids Wisdom, Faith, Knowledge, and Servant. If this is so it strengthens the view that the Logos of John was *in some sense* ideal Man.

The use of the word Image was very widespread. It appears in the Gnostic systems which are related to Christianity, for instance the Barbelo-gnostics, for whom the Ennoia, Barbelo, was the Image of the invisible. It occurs in Mandaism, where Hibil-Ziwa is the Image. Manda d'Hayye addresses the Evil One, Ur, thus: "There comes *one beloved Son* who was formed from the *bosom* of the splendour and whose *image* is preserved in its place; he comes with *enlightening* of *life* and with the *command* that his *father* commanded him; he comes in the garment of living fire and *descends* to thy world."[2] All the words in italics are Johannine, with the exception of Image, which, as we have just seen, underlies John's thought. The question of whether the "Gnostic redeemer" shows himself in the Mandean writings or has influenced John must wait; but here we need to notice the possibility that the identification of the Johannine Word with "Ideal Man" in some sense is a reflection from this quarter. The Man in Poimandres is the offspring of Nous and therefore co-equal with Logos. In the Barbelo-gnostic system the "Perfect Man" was produced from Autogenes who in turn came from the union of Ennoia and Logos.[3] Where the Anthropos and the Son of Man appear together as the transcendental Monad and its objectification, the Son of Man is the indwelling Logos, the seed of things,

---

[1] John 12.32.   [2] *R.G.*, 91.11–18.
[3] Irenaeus, *Adv. Haer.*, 1.29.2.

to be found in man after the seventh year.[1] Some scholars have been specific. Burney, Bultmann, and others have isolated the main part of the Prologue as a hymn in Aramaic, and this has won widespread acceptance;[2] Cullmann, for instance, in his recent *Christology of the New Testament* conceded the possibility of its being a Wisdom or Mandaic hymn. The attempt has even been made to find a reference to one of the Mandean messengers in this hymn. Schaeder thought it was in fact a hymn which identified the messenger Anush with the Memra. The disciples of John the Baptist associated this Anush with John as in the Mandean Book of John. The fourth evangelist reflects their point of view when he says that the "man" sent from God was John. But he parts company with them in distinguishing between Memra and "man" and using the distinction to minimize the importance of the Baptist.[3] If this contention could be sustained, the dependence of John on a Mandean document would be established, and the argument strengthened that Johannine Christology owes something to an external doctrine of a heavenly Man. Not only so, but this heavenly Man would be the pre-Christian redeemer professedly discernible in gnostic writings.

Schaeder believed that in John 1.6,9, where the fourth evangelist uses ἄνθρωπος, he found in the original Aramaic אנוש, the name of the Mandean messenger. In support of his argument, and by omission of prose additions after the style of Burney and Bultmann, Schaeder reconstructed the relevant verses as follows:

'Εγένετο ἄνθρωπος ἀπεσταλμένος παρὰ θεοῦ
'Ην τὸ φῶς τὸ ἀληθινόν, ὃ φωτίζει πάντα
ἄνθρωπον ἐρχόμενον εἰς τὸν κόσμον.

This he translated into Aramaic poetry thus:

הוא אנוש משדר מן אלהא
הוא נהורא דכושטא דמנהר כל
אנוש אתי בעלמא

The basis of this translation rests on Schaeder's criticism of Burney's translation of the phrase ἐρχόμενον εἰς τὸν κόσμον. Like

---

[1] Hippolytus, *Refut.*, V. 8.14.
[2] Howard, *Christianity acc. to St. John*, pp. 45f.
[3] Reitzenstein-Schaeder, *Studien*, pp. 306–41.

Burney he connected this with the rabbinic בוא לעלמא,[1] but pointed out that to translate כל אנש אתי בעלמא is pleonastic[2] on the grounds that the rabbinic idiom can by itself signify "man". Why then did John insert the word ἄνθρωπον? Schaeder answered that he found the name אנוש in the original and took it for a form of אנש (man), either because of his Semitic background or because the form was actually current in his circle as it was in the Nabatean communities.[3] Kraeling, however, objected to Schaeder's translation and maintained that an original Aramaic couplet could equally well have read

הוא נהורא דכושטא
דמנהר כל אתי בעלמא

His contention was that John used ἄνθρωπον to avoid the ambiguity which would have allowed πάντα to be construed as a neuter plural, so that ἐρχόμενον could have been connected with φῶς. This Kraeling held to be a modern misreading of the text. But, as we have seen, this argument is unnecessary. John uses the word ἄνθρωπος in a redundant manner all the way through his work.[4] Black suggested it might be his way of translating an Aramaic indefinite pronoun.[5] Πάντα ἄνθρωπον would therefore seem to be merely an example of his style. ἄνθρωπος cannot of course be excised from verse 6, whatever is true of verse 9. But here there is no need to explain its presence and no reason for preferring אנוש to אנש.

Kraeling, however, went on to point out that the whole objection to the theory is that the Prologue of St John is not essentially Mandaic. The Logos, he said, plays no important part in Mandean theology. As we have seen, *malala*, word, as applied to Anush has a quite general reference to his rôle as a propagator of truth. Moreover, if Anush were actually introduced in verse 6, he would necessarily remain the subject of all that was said in the original hymn up to verse 14. That would make Anush creator of the world and one who was rejected by his own. But there is nothing

---

[1] See above, p. 50.   [2] *Studien*, p. 328.   [3] Ibid., p. 326.

[4] John 2.10; 3.1; 3.27; 4.29,50; 5.5,7,12, etc. Many of these expressions are of course current: cf. 5.5 with the opening of the Lucan parables of the Prodigal Son, Dives and Lazarus, and the Good Samaritan.

[5] *Aramaic Approach*, 1954 ed., p. 236.

in the Mandean description of Anush or the Baptist to support these suggestions.

The Mandean Anush, nevertheless, seems at some stage of his history to be connected with the heavenly Man, whether or not the latter was ever a redeemer in the Christian sense. Anush is of course the biblical Enosh, and, as Dodd points out,[1] in Philo "Enosh in fact is ὁ κατ' ἐξοχὴν ἄνθρωπος, and his record is βίβλος γενέσεως τοῦ πρὸς ἀλήθειαν ἀνθρώπου". He goes on to connect Enosh with the heavenly Man whom Philo identifies in some sense with the Logos. The gnostics and people of similar temperament liked playing with names and deducing truths from them. Thus in the Gospel of Truth, *The Paraphrase of Seth* to which Hippolytus alludes is called *The Paraphrase of Shem* and Seth is the name of God.[2] But Shem is Hebrew for Name, and in Gen. 4.26 Enosh (= Man) is Seth's son, from which time men called upon the *Name* of the Lord. Dodd notes that Philo often comments on this very passage: καὶ τῷ Σὴθ ἐγένετο υἱός.[3] The measure of a true theology is to a large extent the absence of the fantastic in this sort of exegesis. But the attempt to connect John with the gnostic type of thought is confronted by various difficulties. In the first place John is consciously anti-gnostic. "The Word became flesh" is directed against the gnostic horror of matter. The writer of the First Epistle declares, "Whoever denies that Jesus Christ has come in the flesh is not of God." In the Fourth Gospel the words "Knowledge" (Γνῶσις), "Wisdom" (Σοφία), and "Faith" (Πίστις) are deliberately avoided. W. F. Howard in a few impressive pages[4] draws attention to the fact that although the exordium to the Epistle to the Hebrews shows definite signs of literary dependence on the Book of Wisdom[5] and that although the first chapter of Colossians is replete with Wisdom language, the word "wisdom" itself appears in neither place.

---

[1] *F.G.*, p. 69.

[2] See the quotation in Puech, Quispel, and van Unnik, *The Jung Codex*, tr. F. L. Cross, pp. 2of.

[3] Op. cit., p. 69. The Paraphrase of Shem explicitly identifies Shem (i.e., Name) with Jesus, in a context which contains the words Son of Man, Wisdom, Bosom, Beginning, and Place; see Doresse, *Secret Books of the Egyptian Gnostics*, p. 149.

[4] Op. cit., pp. 41–4.   [5] Wisd. 7.25f.

Paul in fact only uses it once, in 1 Cor. 1.30. Nor does the word Logos appear in a personal sense anywhere in the New Testament outside the Johannine Prologue.[1] The obvious inference is that in John's circle, whatever was true of Γνῶσις, Σοφία, and Πίστις, the word λόγος did not have purely gnostic associations; and the extant gnostic works indeed do not make much significant use of the term.[2] There is therefore no reason at all to suppose that John's use of it points to a gnostic background.

When we return to the fourth evangelist's doctrine of the kinship of man with God, we find that the word λόγος with a small letter, as it were, plays a prominent part. It is not unlikely that this may help to determine the meaning of the term as a title for Christ. The connection of Logos in the latter sense with Name would bear this out. Thus, as we have seen, the Name could abide in God's representative, e.g., Metatron. In John, likewise, to be "kept in the Name" seems to be the same thing as "abiding in the word" of Jesus which is at the same time the Father's word. In the *Didache* we read, "thy holy Name which thou didst make to tabernacle in our hearts" and the divine Word "tabernacled" with men in John 1.14. In the Odes of Solomon the Name could be "put on" as in Ephesians the "New Man" is put on[3] and Name and Word appear to be equivalent in Ode 15.8,9.[4] And in John God does not merely have dealings with men; he abides in them.[5] This explains the difference between those who believe and those who do not. Those who have not the word in them are those who are begotten of the devil;[6] those who are begotten of God have the "seed" abiding in them, which is a different thing from being simply "Abraham's seed".[7] "Word" here plainly cannot be

---

[1] Howard, op. cit., p. 41.   [2] Dodd, *F.G.*, p. 109.

[3] Eph. 4.24.   [4] See above, p. 40.   [5] John 5.38; 1 John 2.14.

[6] John 8.44. There is no philosophical dualism here. Carpenter (p. 389) is misled into saying that 1 John 5.19 "does not fit in with a Logos-made universe". But the "darkness" which surrounds the Johannine story (13.30; 11.9) is the darkness of lovelessness (1 John 3.8f). The "Jews" are culpable, children of the devil by their own deeds: cf. 9.41.

[7] 1 John 3.9. John 8.37 suggests that the idea of seed in the same sense as "word" is present here. The idea of the *spermatikos logos* in Justin *1 Apol.*, 46 ("Christians before Christ") is different; the love of God is not intended.

interpreted rationalistically; it has something of the "mystical connotation" which Nock and Festugière find in the Corpus Hermeticum,[1] where the word "immortalizes" men. Similarly in the Johannine writings the word abiding means the overcoming of the Evil One,[2] and if a man "keeps" the word he will never see death.[3] Rufus Jones dwelt on this "mystical" strain in the Johannine writings.[4] He fastened upon the "seed" which is once used in the same sense as "word" as we have just traced it, and saw the essence of it as Life. Whether the metaphor is "water" or "bread",[5] "we are dealing with a process by which the believer takes into himself the Divine Life, and by an inward change of his own, so that he actually has 'God abiding in him'".[6] Odeberg discovered a similar meaning in the phrase "begotten of water and the spirit" and connected it with the heavenly seed.[7] This idea of the indwelling of one life in another is only possible where persons are concerned; and it is the personal which informs John's thought. It enriches his conception of God as life and light, which in Poimandres is little more than a formula of divine vitality and radiance. Thus those who have the word abiding in them according to John are those who have the love of God abiding in them.[8] "Thy word is truth", says the Johannine Christ.[9] "For", writes the author of the Odes of Solomon, "the dwelling-place of the Word is Man, and his truth is love."[10] This could pass for a commentary on the Johannine texts we have just considered. There is no trace in the Fourth Gospel of the intellectual divine spark; it is by coming to the incarnate Logos and receiving him that men become men. But this surely implies that the Word is essentially man in the sense that he embodies the love of God.

[1] *Hermès Trismégiste*, p. 187, n 31, on C.H. 12.13.

[2] Cf. 1 John 2.14.   [3] John 8.51.

[4] The word "mystical" is difficult to avoid in this connection, though out of favour in some quarters. It expresses that phase of religion which stresses communion as against formalism and rationalism. Cf. the *Theologia Germanica*'s "I would fain be to the Eternal Goodness what his own hand is to a man" (*T.G.*, X), and see J. Bernhardt's intro., pp. 97ff, for the medieval German development of the Hermetic Logos and Ur-mensch.

[5] John 4.14; 6.35,58.

[6] Quoted Howard, *Fourth Gospel in Recent Criticism and Research*, rev. C. K. Barrett, pp. 201f.   [7] *F.G.*, p. 48; cf. p. 67.

[8] John 5.38,42.   [9] John 17.17.   [10] Ode 12.12.

It would be typical of John if his declaration "the Word became flesh" had two meanings. In the first place it is obviously the attack upon the dualism of contemporary thought which we have noted. For instance, as Davies says, "for Philo the heavenly Man belonged to another realm of being, a realm that could never come to terms with matter".[1] John insists that Jesus Christ came in the flesh, that the Word became flesh.[2] His Christ is no abstraction, no docetic revealer. But the evidence also suggests that John wrote "the Word became flesh" and not, with Justin Martyr, "the Word became Man",[3] because the Word was eternally Man. Jesus *was* the Word which only abides in other men. That which was from the beginning, the THAT WHICH IS at which Augustine arrived at the climax of his mystical ecstasy, had been manifested to John in and as man.[4] He had glory with his Father before the world was,[5] and that glory was manifested in him. The one who became a historical person as Jesus of Nazareth did not then become personal; he was ever so: "Before Abraham was, I am."[6] The difference between John's Logos and that of Philo lies just here, that in John for the first time the Logos is really personal and not merely personified.[7] The reason is obviously because John did not begin with the Platonic Ideas or the Stoic Reason or the

---

[1] Davies, *Paul and Rab. Jud.*, p. 52. The reasons were (a) the abstract was superior; (b) matter and the body were somehow evil.

[2] 1 John 4.2f; cf. 2 John 7; John 1.14.

[3] 2 *Apol.* 10—as he might have become an angel or a flame of fire. The Old Syriac incidentally translates "became a *body*".

[4] That which was from the beginning: John uses the phrase both personally and impersonally, 1 John 2.13; 1.1. In the latter place not only the Gospel but the ineffable mystery of the divine is denoted.

[5] John 17.5.

[6] John 8.58; cf. Abbott's paraphrase: "The Wisdom of God, the spirit that is in me . . . is a Spirit like that of Abraham, who was pre-eminently the lover of men. But it is also the Spirit in which God created men in his own image, long before Abraham was born." As we shall see, this is only half of the story, but it is an important half.

[7] Cf. H. A. A. Kennedy: "The Logos-hypothesis itself, as it appears in Philo, is full of confusion. . . . In part it depends on the fluctuating boundary in ancient thought between personality and personification, and on Philo's own tendency to glide from what is conceived as truth to symbols of truth." Also E. F. Scott: "Philo thinks only of a divine principle. . . . John of a distinct Person over against and with God." It speaks much for John's ability that it is Philo who gives the impression of a "second god"!

Jewish Wisdom but with Jesus of Nazareth. Burch pointed out that "the Prologue to the Fourth Gospel can keep its literary structure even if each of the names for Jesus Christ takes in turn the place of the Logos. And, what is more important, the Prologue keeps its sense when these alterations are made."[1] The further step which identified this man with the Word of God was made simple by the idea of revelation: the God who revealed himself partially in the prophetic oracle[2] would reveal himself wholly in a full human life. This human life, itself identical with the divine self-expression which originated the universe, *is* that Word by which all things came to be.[3] Yet the manner of John's thought upon the divine indwelling and upon the relations of the Son of Man to men and to God suggest that he rejected altogether the abstract doctrine which attracted Philo. So we may believe that the "theory of ideas" which Bonsirven detected in Israel, whereby no creature could come into existence without being previously present to the thought and will of God, would best serve as a predisposing factor in John's mind for his doctrine of the "pre-existent" personality of the Word. We may indeed suspect (with certain Jewish writers) that this putting of "modes fort métaphysiques dans des cerveaux tout concrets"[4] could scarcely take place in isolation from Greek influence, but the Jewish leaning would fit the personal and historical, in short, biblical, bent of John's thought. It will indeed appear more clearly later on that the whole point of John's doctrine is that the revelation of God was personal and of a person.

[1] *Jesus Christ and His Revelation*, pp. 96f.

[2] Heb. 1.1.

[3] Victor Gollancz, in one of his anthologies (*From Darkness to Light*, p. 233), quotes a paraphrase of a Sufi saying, "The Perfect Man was the cause of the Universe, being the epiphany of God's desire to be known."

[4] Bonsirven, *Le Judaïsme Palestinien au temps de Jésus-Christ*, vol. i, p. 169.

CHAPTER 5

THE JOHANNINE SON OF MAN AND HIS ANTECEDENTS

We have argued in the previous chapter that, even if John did not actually identify his Logos explicitly with Man in some sense, he did live and move and think in an atmosphere where the identification had already been made. If so, we should expect that the term Son of Man in the Fourth Gospel would reflect such a view. The argument which would dispose of the possibility of this by pointing out that the author uses Son of Man with the same connotations and in the same connections as Son of God, Only-begotten, Logos, Christ, Son, is without force. If valid, it would prove too much, for the Logos would be in the same case. But in fact the title Son of Man in the Fourth Gospel is used in connection with quite special associations, and moreover associations peculiar to that work. The Son of Man is the point of union between heaven and earth;[1] he is the gate of heaven of Jacob's vision;[2] he alone has descended and ascended;[3] he must be lifted up[4] and glorified;[5] he gives the bread of life which is his flesh.[6] The assertion that some of these associations are fragments of "popular Son of Man theology"[7] is mere baseless assumption

---

[1] John 1.51. Bernard objects to Burney's exegesis on the ground that Nathanael and not Jesus is the type of Israel, "an Israelite in whom is no guile" (1.47; Bernard, p. 69f). But John has combined the idea of the angels going up and down between the ideal and the empirical man with that of the *place* being the gate of heaven. Philo makes the Logos the place, John the Son of Man.

[2] Cf. 10.7.   [3] John 3.13; cf. 6.62.   [4] John 3.14; 8.28; 12.34.
[5] John 12.23; 13.31.   [6] John 6.48,51 *et passim*.

[7] This phrase was used by Windisch in a different sense for the doctrine of angels in the discussion with Nathanael, which he took to contradict the usual Johannine teaching of unmediated contact between Jesus and his Father. But the reference to the Jacob's ladder story is too plain, and the Son of Man in the synoptics comes *with* a retinue of angels, they do not come to him.

unless backed up by actual examples of relevant date. To infer the existence of such a tradition from the pages of St John himself is to perform the unedifying feat of arguing in a circle. The next chapters will therefore be devoted to the questions raised by these peculiar associations of "Son of Man" in John.

Alongside these peculiar associations, there are others held in common with the synoptic tradition: the Son of Man as Judge, as Messiah, as Servant of the Lord.[1] The Righteous One of Wisdom is not entirely unrelated either. This chapter will be a convenient place to consider some of these, as well as the use of "son of man" in some of the psalms and the notion of the Prophet. To take the messiahship first, the emphasis on the importance of this issue chains the Fourth Gospel irrevocably to history. In this respect there is also a great deal more to be said for the view that John wrote for Jewish readers than is often allowed. He constantly uses the word "Jews" in a quite arbitrary sense to denote those in opposition to the Christian message, and sometimes actually as distinct from others who are also in fact of Jewish race. "Salvation", he declares, "is of the Jews."[2] His first chapter begins with Moses[3] and ends with the true Israelite.[4] Students of the rabbis have pointed to rabbinic turns of phrase and methods of argument in his work. He also brings out the political situation in which Jesus' ministry took its course more clearly than the other New Testament writers.[5] Dodd acknowledges that "the fourth evangelist, even more definitely than the synoptics, is developing his doctrine of the person and work of Jesus with conscious reference to Jewish messianic belief",[6] and "no other New Testa-

---

[1] In the synoptics more than in John "Son of Man" is a name rather than an interpretation: thus Mark 8.31 has "the Son of Man", for which Matthew substitutes "Jesus Christ"; Mark 10.45 has "Son of Man" where Luke has "I" (cf. Matt. 16.13 and 12.8); Matt. 5.11 has "For my sake" but Luke 6.22 has "for the sake of the Son of Man".

[2] John 4.22.   [3] John 1.17.   [4] John 1.47.

[5] John 6.15 gives the reason for Jesus' withdrawal from the five thousand, which in Mark is unexplained; 7.26 gives the people's speculation upon the rulers' attitude to his messianic claims; 10.24 reflects the messianic ferment; 11.49–53 reveals the machinations of the authorities; 18.36 declares Jesus' attitude to a show of force; 19.12 and 15 explain the political reasons for Pilate's capitulation to the mob.   [6] *F.G.*, p. 90.

ment writer shows himself so fully aware of the Jewish ideas
associated with [the title 'Messiah'] as does the fourth evangelist".[1] He alone in the New Testament uses the transliteration
Μεσσίας,[2] and he declares his very aim to be "that you may
believe that Jesus is the Christ, the Son of God".[3] Moses wrote of
him, Isaiah saw his glory, he is the "holy one of God". Believing
in his name, believing that he is the Christ, and receiving the light
or the Word are practically the same thing.[4] As elsewhere, Jesus
is the fulfilment of the prophecy of Zechariah.[5]

Yet he is more prophet than king. His question to Pilate may
be paraphrased, "Do you mean 'king' in the traditional sense, or
have you divined my secret? I came into the world to bear witness
to the truth. Every one who is of the truth hears my voice."[6] The
people recognize him as prophet, having dimly glimpsed the pur-
port of his "signs".[7] John the Baptist denies that he himself is
"the Prophet" and points instead to "the Lamb of God" who is
to take away the sins of the world, the whole world—for truth is
universal.[8] Jesus confesses himself Christ to the Samaritan
woman,[9] but the Samaritans themselves recognize him as the
Saviour of the world.[10] When the five thousand men seek to compel him to be king and leader of a nationalist movement he with-
draws into the hills by himself.[11] Westcott comments: "So he
drove many from him,[12] while he called out a completer confession
of faith from the twelve.[13] Words which had been used before (ch.
1), have now a wholly different meaning. To believe in Christ now
was to accept with utter faith the necessity of complete self-sur-
render to him who had finally rejected the homage of force."[14] So

---

[1] Ibid., p. 228.   [2] John 1.41; 4.25.   [3] John 20.31.
[4] Cf. John 1.12 with 1 John 5.1.
[5] Zech. 9.9f; John 12.13–15; cf. Matt. 21.5.
[6] John 18.34,37.   [7] John 6.14; 7.40.
[8] John 1.21,29, etc., cf. 1 John 2.2.   [9] John 4.26.
[10] John 4.42. P. Fiebig commented that Schlatter could not quote rabbinic
parallels to "the Saviour of the world". Bultmann, among others, sees it as a
specifically Hellenistic term. But then while Odeberg could find reference in the
rabbis to the Johannine "double sense" of the expression "the world", he could
find no reference to God loving the world.
[11] John 6.15.   [12] John 6.66.   [13] John 6.69.
[14] Gospel of John, p. lxx.

when Nathanael hails him as Son of God in the sense of King of Israel, Jesus exchanges the title for "Son of Man" which, here as in Mark, he prefers to the narrow Jewish messianic names.[1] It seems in John 12.34 that the crowd is represented as identifying the Christ with the Son of Man[2] of whom Jesus spoke, and are confused because their idea of the Messiah was of one who abides for ever, that is, an invincible conqueror.[3] Bernard quoted from Justin's *Dialogue with Trypho* the comment of the Jew on Daniel 7: "These scriptures indeed compel us to expect that great and glorious One who as a son of man receives the eternal kingdom from the Ancient of Days; but this your so-called Christ was dishonoured and inglorious so that he fell under the curse of the Law of God,[4] for he was crucified." So the Johannine Christ surpasses all popular expectations: he is not the apocalyptic figure any more than the military Messiah;[5] only a man who does signs no greater than those of Moses.[6] Nevertheless, the officers sent to arrest him declare that no man ever spoke like this man.[7] For it is in his full acceptance of manhood and community with all men in their manhood that the salvation of men and the universality of salvation consists: the inscription on the cross is in the three languages of

---

[1] Cf. Mark 8.29 with 31.

[2] Bernard, p. 443, held that "Son of Man" in John 12.34 is an unfamiliar title in the ears of the crowd. It may be so, and "Son of Man" in 9.35 would lend support to this (see v. 36). But the whole bent of 12.34 suggests that the crowd identified the Son of Man with the Christ who abides for ever. As usual in John, the bystanders are represented as understanding the Johannine idiom—in this case the messianic implications of "Son of Man".

[3] Lowther-Clarke wrote in 1936 that "the usual distinction, common in sermons even if it has disappeared from the books of scholars, between the Son of Man who came to serve and to suffer and the Conquering King of Jewish expectation, does not hold good" (*Divine Humanity*, p. 15). But, as T. W. Manson said, "it must be remembered that the bulk of the hearers of Jesus were simple people. It is extremely unlikely that they possessed all the texts in Charles' Apocrypha and Pseudepigrapha (or even all that were in existence at the time); and it is certain that they did *not* have Charles' commentaries. Consequently the views of the average man may well have been less refined than those of the twentieth century experts on the subject" (*Servant-Messiah*, p. 24 n). This would apply to John's crowd.

[4] Deut. 21.23.   [5] John 7.27.

[6] John 6.30f. For similar conclusions see R. A. Edwards, *F.G.*, pp. 61f, etc.

[7] John 7.46.

the world, Hebrew and Latin and Greek.[1] It is at the true Image that men look and are saved as they contemplate the uplifted Son of Man. John leads his readers to a new conception of Messiah as Son of Man, prophet, and witness to truth, and therefore universal in his significance as in his manhood.

The expectation of the people who ask John the Baptist in John 1.21, "Art thou the prophet?", and hail Jesus in John 6.14 as "the Prophet",[2] is not simply a matter of interpretation. The Dead Sea Sect looked for "the coming of a Prophet and the Anointed Ones of Aaron and Israel".[3] The Samaritans awaited a Messiah who was prophet and not king.[4] John's crowd appear then to reflect the confused ideas of the actual time: they combine the prophet and the king; that is, they expect a prophet who is also king.[5] One possible origin of the expectation of a prophet is the prophecy of "Elijah who is to come",[6] but Deut. 18.18[7] has more to be said for it: "I will raise them up a prophet from among their brothers, like unto thee; and I will put my words in his mouth, and he shall speak unto them all that I shall command them." In John Jesus is connected with Moses; he gives the commands of God; he calls his disciples "brothers". The expression "Son of Man" does not, however, appear in the Deuteronomy passage. It is in fact rare in the singular in the Old Testament outside the pages of the prophet Ezekiel,[8] and can here moreover be taken as a title: only here in pre-Christian literature would this be so easy even to the mind of a first-century writer. It is also the title of a prophet, and it is perhaps to Ezekiel pre-eminently that we must

---

[1] John 19.20. Edwards, op. cit., p. 153, denies the symbolism, but why then did John remark the circumstance? The gospels are not collections of camera snaps.

[2] Pap. Bod. (P⁶⁶) has the same title in 7.52, "*the* prophet does not arise out of Galilee".

[3] D.S.D. 9.11. See *BASOR Supp. Studies*, 10–12, App D. The expectation of a prophet goes back to Deut. 18.15 as opposed to Mal. 4.5, where it is Elijah who "must come". Cf. Mark 9.11 and 6.15; 8.28. The idea in the D.S.S. seems to be government by a prophet plus the anointed high priest and king.

[4] See, e.g., Stanton, *The Jewish and the Christian Messiah*, pp. 127f.

[5] John 6.14f. [6] See above, n 3.

[7] The passage is interpreted messianically in 1 Macc. 4.46; T. Ben. 9.2; Acts 3.22; 7.37.

[8] Dalman, *Words of Jesus*, p. 235.

73

turn if we wish to find the original of the Johannine Son of Man-Prophet. Most scholars seem inclined to doubt that Ezekiel exercises influence in this matter on the New Testament, yet the possibility cannot be ignored. W. A. Curtis made a point of summarizing the resemblances between the Son of Man in Ezekiel and the Son of Man in the gospels.[1]

> The Prophet's transportation in a vision to the holy City and to the Temple and to a very high mountain[2] is recalled in the Wilderness Temptation of Jesus. He also like Jesus made use of parables, with the vine among other themes: "Ah Lord God! they say of me, Is he not a (mere) speaker of parables?"[3] . . . He invokes proverbs in his preaching. He sees Israel as a flock scattered and shepherdless.[4] He sets Israel over against her "sisters" Sodom and Samaria as meriting still sterner judgement. He is bidden to say "He that heareth, let him hear",[5] and to pronounce woes. He demands repentance and offers forgiveness and mercy and new life or resurrection of her dead bones. The Spirit lifts him up and bears him whithersoever it wills. He looks back across the wayward history of Israel and sums it up in vivid, terse and poignant pictures. He denounces gross abuses in the Temple.

Curtis goes on to enumerate other similarities. "But thou, Son of Man, behold, they shall lay hands upon thee, and shall bind thee with them. . . . But when I speak with thee, I shall open thy mouth, and thou shalt say unto them, Thus saith the Lord God: he that heareth let him hear."[6] And again, "Son of Man, thou dwellest in the midst of a rebellious house, which have eyes to see and see not, and have ears to hear and hear not."[7] ". . . Son of Man, cause Jerusalem to know her abominations."[8] ". . . Son of Man, speak unto the elders of Israel. . . . Wilt thou judge them, Son of Man?"[9] ". . . Son of Man, prophesy, and say, A sword, a sword."[10] One of these resemblances recalls the Deuteronomy promise of a prophet, and the Johannine parallel: "Son of Man, thy brothers . . . the men of thy kindred and all the house of Israel." And part of the promise is, "I will give them one heart

---

[1] *Jesus Christ the Teacher*, pp. 138ff.
[2] Ezek. 8.3; 11.1; 40.2.   [3] Ezek. 20.49.   [4] Ezek. 34.5f.
[5] Ezek. 3.27.   [6] Ezek. 3.25,27.   [7] Ezek. 12.1,2.
[8] Ezek. 16.2.   [9] Ezek. 20.3,4.
[10] Ezek. 21.9; Matt. 10.34.

and I will put one spirit within you."[1] Others of Curtis' examples
we leave for consideration later.

Outside Ezekiel, Son of Man in the singular occurs in Ps.
80.17, where "the term is applied either to Israel or to a messianic
figure representative of Israel".[2] This "son of man" is "the man
of thy right hand" and may have suggested the connection
between Dan. 7.13 and Ps. 110.1 made in Christ's confession
before the high Priest.[3] There is some correspondence between
this psalm and passages of Ezekiel. The vine (Israel) occurs in
Ezek. 17.6 and Ps. 80.8,14. In Ezek. 15.2 the vine is in a forest; so
also in Ps. 80.13. Cedars are mentioned in Ezek. 17.3 after "son of
man" in the preceding verse; so also in Ps. 80.10. God "plants"
Israel in Ezek. 17.5 and Ps. 80.15; with Ezekiel the allegory clearly
refers to the political situation under Babylon. The vine of course
recurs in John; and though it recalls Jeremiah and Isaiah, the
relation with the "parable" in Ezekiel is closer: the branches and
the cutting of the vine are mentioned, and the teller is, as elsewhere, called "Son of Man".[4] The connection between John and
Ezekiel's shepherd is likewise probable: "The Son of Man came to
seek and to save that which is lost" in Luke is a direct quotation
from Ezekiel, except for the name "Son of Man" which can be
supplied from the context.[5] The reference in Ezekiel is to sheep,
and it is generally admitted that John's allegory of the Good
Shepherd bears some relation to the synoptic theme of the Lost
Sheep and the Shepherd. In Ezekiel the Son of Man is bidden to
prophesy to the shepherds of Israel (cf. the "hireling" of John's
allegory): "Woe unto the shepherds of Israel that do feed themselves! Should not the shepherds feed the sheep? . . . The dis-
eased have ye not strengthened, neither have ye healed that which

---

[1] Ezek. 11.15,19; John 20.17.
[2] Ps. 80.17f. "Who by divine help emerges from humiliation to triumph"
(Dodd in Manson's *Companion to the Bible*, p. 374; cf. *Scriptures*, p. 117, n 2).
Dodd points out that in the LXX the parallel between Israel as the Vine and the
Son of Man is clearer: "Visit this vine and restore it . . . and the Son of Man
whom thou hast made strong . . .": cf. the Vine in John 15.
[3] Mark 14.62.
[4] John 15.1ff; Jer. 2.21; Isa. 5.2; Ezek. 17.6,8,9,2.
[5] Luke 19.10; Ezek. 34.16; cf. 5.2. God is the speaker; he sends the Son of
Man.

was sick . . . neither have ye sought that which was lost. . . . And they were scattered, because there was no shepherd. . . ."[1]

Some of the incidental language of John also may well reflect Ezekiel's words. The promise to Nathanael about seeing heaven opened and the angels ascending and descending upon the Son of Man of course refers first of all to Jacob's vision of the ladder in Gen. 28. But here there is no mention of "heaven opened". But in the only place where the term "Son of Man" is used as a title outside the gospels, the dying Stephen sees "the heavens open and the Son of Man standing at the right hand of God".[2] The fact that here the Son of Man is "standing" at the right hand of God instead of "sitting" as elsewhere is usually explained as proving that here a genuine reminiscence of the actual vision is involved. But this does not explain why the vision took that form; and when we recall that Ezekiel's Son of Man is bidden to stand upon his feet at the beginning of chapter two, the reference to the heaven opened at the beginning of chapter one seems certain. And the Matthaean, Lucan, and Johannine versions of the Baptism of Jesus all reflect the language of Ezek. 1.1, "the heavens were opened and I saw". To draw a parallel between the angels ascending upon the Son of Man and the continual ascents and descents of Ezek. 1 is doubtless a more hazardous proceeding. Nevertheless the angels are lifted up from the earth in Ezek. 1.19 and the next time angels are mentioned in John (omitting with the the best texts the angel that disturbed the water in the pool with five porches), namely at John 12.29, the Son of Man says, "I, if I be lifted up".[3] We know that the first chapter of Ezekiel exercised a fascination upon the Jewish mind; as Abelson says, "commentaries were composed upon it wholesale". And we do need a precedent for the prominent theme of ascent-descent in the Fourth Gospel.

There are other similarities. In John the Son of Man is sancti-

---

[1] Ezek. 34.2ff. Curtis, pp. 138f (abridged). There are of course, other parallels, as, e.g., Matt. 7.21 = Luke 6.46 with Ezek. 33.31f. Stauffer, *Jesus and His Story*, compares 1 Enoch 89.59–90.38, but the similarity with the gospels goes no further than the mention of shepherds and sheep.
[2] Acts 7.56.   [3] John 12.32.

fied and sent; so is Ezekiel's Son of Man. "Son of Man, I send thee to the children of Israel. . . . I do send thee to them . . . thou art not sent. . . . etc."[1] In John the ascription of the term Son of God to the "sanctified and sent" one is justified on the ground that those to whom the word of God came of old were called "gods".[2] The "Jews" criticize this on the ground that it makes a man God.[3] But in Ezek. 2.1 the word of God comes to the prophet so that the spirit enters him and he stands upon his feet before God, i.e., on an equality. God has been described as "a likeness as the appearance of a man" and the prophet is now addressed for the first time as Son of Man. The language about "sanctified and sent" recalls the Christology of Hebrews which we have already compared with the Fourth Gospel:

> For the sanctifier and the sanctified are all of one
> For which cause he is not ashamed to call them brothers,
> Saying, I will declare thy Name to my brothers.[4]

The Name is prominent in Hebrews 1 as in John: the citations there are all meant to explain Jesus' title to a "more excellent name". So in John 17.6: "I have manifested thy Name to the men whom thou gavest me."[5] Although the Name in John is not sanctified as it is in Ezekiel but glorified, nevertheless the Son of Man who is connected with the Name as the Word is sanctified. It is interesting also that in Hebrews the Name is connected with the idea of the brotherhood of believers with Christ: "For which cause he is not ashamed to call them brothers, saying, I shall declare thy Name to my brothers."[6] Likewise with the Image in one place in Paul: "Whom he foreknew he also foreordained to

---

[1] Cf. Matt. 15.24, and the Johannine "Sent One", and Mark 12.6: "They will reverence my Son."

[2] John 10.35.   [3] v. 33.

[4] Heb. 2.11f, cf. D.S.D. 2.12f, "and through his Messiah he shall make them know his holy Spirit and he is true and in the true interpretation of his name are their names", i.e., they share his messiahship or anointing.

[5] The *locus classicus* for the notion of the sanctification of the Divine Name is several passages in Ezekiel (e.g. 36.23). "Father, glorify thy name" is in fact the Johannine equivalent of the "Hallowed be thy name" of the Lord's prayer, the parallel to which in the Hebrew morning service obviously goes back to Ezekiel.

[6] See D.S.D. above.

be conformed to the Image of his Son, that he might be the first-born of many brothers."[1] Ezekiel receives the command beginning "Son of Man, thy brothers . . ." and this seems to go back to the Deuteronomy passage, "a prophet from among their brothers". But in John 20.17 the risen Son of Man tells Mary Magdalen pointedly, "Tell my brothers." Dodd declared that John moulded his portrait of the Son of Man in part "upon the prophetic model".[2] It is hard to resist the conclusion that Ezekiel was one of the sitters for the composite portrait. The recurrence of the unusual term Son of Man in the singular as the heaven-bestowed designation of a human being, along with the associations of the title borrowed by New Testament writers from Ezekiel makes this as likely a source for the use of the term even by Jesus as Daniel or Ps. 8 or Ps. 80.

The vine in Ezekiel, as we saw, has affinities with that in Ps. 80. Here the Son of Man passes from oppression to triumph, at least proleptically. The boar from the wood has ravaged the vine Israel[3] but God is asked to visit and restore him. This is the progression in Dan. 7, to which the modern mind seems naturally to turn for the origin of the term "Son of Man".[4] Here the "one like a son of man" who has been persecuted (v. 21, the one like a son of man stands for the saints, i.e., Israel) receives dominion and glory.[5] Another important occurrence of the term Son of Man is in Ps. 8, where the characteristics of man, the son of man, are summed up likewise as humiliation and glory.

> What is man, that thou art mindful of him,
> And the son of man, that thou visitest him?
> For thou hast made him little lower than God,
> And crownest him with glory and honour.[6]

"Glory" and "honour" are terms which regularly appear in John, and, as we shall see, this psalm is not only used by the author of Hebrews and Paul, but also has something to say upon the Johannine doctrine of Christ's manhood. The point at the

---

[1] Rom. 8.29.   [2] John 12.32; 11.52. Dodd, *F.G.*, p. 255.
[3] v. 13.   [4] *Bar Enash* is to be taken as equal to *Ben Adam*.
[5] v. 14.   [6] Ps. 8.4,5.

moment is that this theme of glory and humiliation, which is also Johannine, points to the Servant of Isaiah, who establishes the relation between the two aspects of man's status by passing from the one to the other. The form of triumph in Ps. 80 moreover, as in the final Servant Song, is described as renewed life: "Quicken thou us, and we will call upon thy Name."[1] This is also the form in Mark, not just apocalyptic son of man plus suffering Messiah.

The references to the Servant in Mark are sought in the words at the Baptism, "Thou art my Son my beloved; in thee I am well pleased";[2] in the words "for many";[3] and in the apparent quotation, "It is written that he will be ignored."[4] On this Dodd writes, "Once again 'Son of Man' takes the place of 'Servant'."[5] The Servant appears in Paul at least in Phil. 2, where manhood itself is practically defined as slavery: "taking the form of a slave, being born in the likeness of men".[6] The word "slave" (δοῦλος) is interchangeable with "servant" (παῖς) in the Septuagint version of Isaiah,[7] and the word for "emptied" in the Philippians passage ("emptied himself . . . unto death") is used elsewhere in the same version for the Hebrew word rendered "poured out" in Isa. 53.12 ("poured out his soul unto death").[8] Isa. 52.13 (LXX) tells of the exaltation and glorification of the Servant; Phil. 2.9 tells of the exaltation of the slave: "Wherefore God also highly exalted him, and gave him the Name which is above every name." We shall see that here too "Son of Man" though not used is implied.

In the Fourth Gospel itself the name "Servant" is avoided,[9]

[1] Ps. 80.18. Note the parallel with Hos. 6.2.

[2] Mark 1.11; Isa. 42.1.

[3] Mark 10.45; 14.24, thought to be from Isa. 53.11.

[4] Mark 9.12, cf. Isa. 53.3, "despised and rejected" (Mark 15.28 is an assimilation to the text of Luke 22.37).

[5] Dodd, *Scriptures*, p. 92, n 2. But cf. M. D. Hooker, *Jesus and the Servant*; C. K. Barrett in Higgins (ed.), *New Testament Essays*.

[6] Phil. 2.7.

[7] Isa. 49.3,5; see Dodd, *Scriptures*, p. 91; cf. p. 118 n.

[8] See Dodd, ibid., p. 93; *J.T.S.*, xxxix, p. 292; H. W. Robinson, *The Cross and the Servant*, pp. 72ff (incorporated in *The Cross in the Old Testament*, pp. 103ff).

[9] See Zimmerli-Jeremias, *The Servant of God*, p. 50, for the silence of rabbinic Judaism on the title "servant of God" for the Messiah.

yet the Son of Man for John is nevertheless the Servant of the Lord. The first appearance of the title "Son of Man" bears this out. Here Nathanael is addressed in terms reminiscent of the Jacob's ladder story. The extract from the Genesis Rabba quoted by Burney, Odeberg, and Dodd, in explication of this has already been mentioned. In it the angels ascend to find the Image, the ideal Israel, which is referred to the Isaianic words, "Thou art my Servant, O Israel, in whom I shall be glorified."[1] The Image, that is to say Israel as opposed to Jacob ("without guile"),[2] is the Servant. And the Fourth Gospel shows many traces of Isaiah's language: "witness", "know", "believe", "I am he"(?), and, if we accept the variant in John 1.34, "chosen"—all are from Isaiah. Isaiah, says, John, saw Christ's glory and wrote of him.[3] Moreover, despite Bernard,[4] the expression "to lift up" used in John seems to go back to Isaiah: "Behold, my Servant shall understand, and be exalted, and be glorified exceedingly."[5] John writes, "The Son of Man must be exalted."[6] The word for "exalted" is used for the "lifting-up"[7] on the cross. The glory of the Incarnation is manifested fully in the passion; John's theme is "glory in humiliation". So John narrates the account of the Feet-washing. "Jesus, knowing that his hour had come . . . knowing that the Father had given all things into his hands and that he had come from God and was to go to God, rose from supper, laid aside his garment, and girded himself with a towel. Then he poured water into a basin and began to wash the disciples' feet and to wipe them with the towel. . . ."[8] The Master and Lord

---

[1] Isa. 49.3; Gen. Rab. 68.18.

[2] John 1.47.   [3] John 12.41.

[4] Bernard, pp. 112ff, rightly rejects the equation "lifting-up" = "ascension" in John (on this see further below, ch. 9: The Way, the Truth, and the Life). It is not impossible, however, that John thought of the exaltation as the glorification preceding the Ascension in point of time, and finally accomplished on the cross: cf. 13.31 and Bernard, in loc.

[5] Isa. 52.13 (LXX).   [6] John 3.14; 12.34.

[7] Burkitt held that "to be lifted up" meant to be crucified only in North Syriac; but it seems to be established that it could mean this in Aramaic also. Kittel pointed to Ezra 6.11 and Targums on 1 Chron. 10.10, Esther I.9.13; II.7.10 (Black, *Ar. App.*, p. 103).

[8] John 13.1-5. See Jeremias, *Servant*, p. 92.

takes the part of the slave, and those who will not accept him as such have no part with him,[1] "who, being in the form of God, counted it not a prize to be equal with God, but poured himself out, and took the form of a slave, being made in the likeness of men".[2] The Son of Man in John is the 'Ebed Yahweh, Servant and Slave. It is a picture of what is to come, for the Lord is to be crucified like any slave; he claims no privilege in the humanity he shares with the lowliest: here John is at one with Matt. 25.31–4, with Paul, and with the Epistle to the Hebrews—but of this later. Judas goes out, and it is night.[3] At once Jesus says, "Now is the Son of Man glorified, and in him God is glorified. If God is glorified in him, God will also glorify him in himself, and will glorify him at once":[4] "My Servant will understand; he will be lifted up and glorified exceedingly."[5]

It is an easy step from the Servant to the Suffering Righteous One of Wisd. 2.

> Let us lie in wait for the Righteous One. . . .
> He professes to have knowledge of God,
> And names himself Servant of the Lord,
> And vaunts that God is his Father. . . .
> For if the Righteous One is son of God, he will uphold him. . . .
> With outrage and torture let us put him to the test.[6]

For, despite a sidelong glance at Plato,[7] the portrait in the main is that of the Suffering Servant of Isaiah. Moreover, chapter five of the Book of Wisdom takes up again the theme of Isa. 53.

> We fools accounted his life madness,
> And his end without honour:

[1] John 13.4,8.   [2] Phil. 2.6f.
[3] John 13.30.   [4] John 13.31f.
[5] Isa. 52.13 (LXX). Dodd, *F.G.*, p. 235, seems to be decisive against the theory that "lamb" = טליא = עבד in John 1.29,36, i.e. that Lamb of God = Servant.

[6] Burch (*Revelation*, p. 81, n 55) claimed to be the first to have pointed out the significance of this passage for the N.T. If this is so it is itself remarkable.

[7] *Republic*, II, 361, E, quoted Clem. Alex., *Strom.*, V, 14: "The righteous man, then, will be scourged, tortured, imprisoned, his eyes will be put out, and after enduring every evil he will be crucified." Plato has earlier explained, "Beside our picture of the unrighteous man let us set that of the righteous. . . . We must strip him of everything except his righteousness. . . . So we shall be able to test his righteousness. . . ."

How was he numbered among the sons of God?
And how is his lot among saints?
Verily we went astray from the way of truth. . . .[1]

We may compare the following excerpts from Isa. 53.3ff: ". . . as one from whom men hide their face he was despised, and we esteemed him not . . . he made his grave with the wicked . . . he was numbered with the transgressors. Therefore will I divide him a portion with the great. . . . All we like sheep have gone astray. . . ."[2] Here too the resurrection is, on the face of it, implied: the righteous one, like the Suffering Servant, confronts his foes after his sufferings:

Then shall the righteous one stand in great boldness
Before the face of them that afflicted him. . . .
When they see they shall be troubled with terrible fear
And shall be amazed at the marvel of God's salvation.[3]

John is, of course, steeped in the Wisdom literature, and there is some evidence in the synoptics that the Son of Man was treated as an embodiment of the divine Wisdom:[4] his activities are justified as "Wisdom is justified by her works (or, children)."[5] The declaration of "the Wisdom of God" in Luke 11.49 concerns the suffering of the righteous. It is scarcely necessary to quote parallels to show how close the remarkable passage quoted above is to the New Testament portrait of Christ. What has been called the "bolt from the Johannine sky", "No one knows the Father but the Son, etc.",[6] is Jesus' profession of knowledge of God; he says he came to serve; he calls God his Father; his Temptation is that God will uphold him;[7] he is to be tortured and outraged. In the Fourth Gospel the Son of Man calls God his own Father;[8]

---

[1] A sentence appears in Wisd. 2.12 which is almost word for word the same as the LXX version of Isa. 5.10—Wisd.; ἐνεδρεύσωμεν τὸν δίκαιον, ὅτι δύσχρηστος ἡμῖν ἐστιν. Isa.: δήσωμεν τὸν δίκαιον, ὅτι δύσχρηστος ἡμῖν ἐστιν. Cf. Wisd. 2.13 with Isa. 42.1 (παῖς); Wisd. 2.15 with Isa. 53.3. This justifies the translation "servant". The writer of Wisdom of course knew of no division into Isaiah first and second, any more than John knew of two parts to the Book of Wisdom.

[2] The title "the Righteous One" occurs in the LXX at v. 11.

[3] Wisd. 5.1–2.

[4] See e.g. J. R. Harris, *Prol. to St. John's Gospel*, pp. 57ff.

[5] Luke 7.34f; 11.49; Matt. 11.19,27–30.

[6] Matt. 11.27=Luke 10.22.   [7] Matt. 4.5f=Luke 4.9f.   [8] John 5.18.

he claims to know God;[1] he says, "I am Son of God";[2] he is "the Righteous One" in the First Epistle;[3] he is Servant of the Lord; he is crucified.

It seems then that the fourth evangelist thought of his Son of Man first of all in terms of the Messiah, the prophet, the Suffering Servant, and the Righteous One, i.e., in Jewish terms. And these seem to fit into each other like a set of old Chinese boxes, the one inclusive of the other and enclosing more, even altering the aspect. Thus the prophet is distinguished from the Messiah in important respects, while remaining identical in others; the Servant, like the prophet, is not the traditional Messiah, yet more than the prophet. In each case the Son of Man is *a man*, not a god or even a rôle, and in each case John's Son of Man is Jesus, with the "extra" which that implies. But further, these are all in the broadest sense *ideal* figures: they are more than ordinary men. This paradoxical conclusion carries on what we found in the Prologue.

[1] John 8.55.   [2] John 10.36; cf. 19.7.   [3] 1 John 2.1.

CHAPTER 6

THE SON OF MAN AS MAN

That the writer of the Fourth Gospel had access to the Old Testament and Wisdom traditions behind the synoptics cannot conceal the fact that his primary source for the use of the title Son of Man of Jesus is the tradition he also shares with them, that the Lord used it of himself. It is usual to describe the synoptic Son of Man as "eschatological". By this it is generally meant that the title recalls the Enochic manlike one who is to appear on the clouds of heaven and exact retribution of the foes of God.

> And this Son of Man whom thou hast seen
> Shall raise up the kings and mighty from their seats,
> And the strong from their thrones,
> And shall loosen the reins of the strong,
> And break the teeth of the sinners.[1]

And again,

> For that Son of Man has appeared,
> And has seated himself on the throne of his glory,
> And all evil shall pass away before his face,
> And the word of that Son of Man shall go forth
> And be strong before the Lord of Spirits.[2]

This is presumably to happen at the "consummation of the age", in Matthew's phrase: "As he sat on the mount of Olives, the disciples came to him privately, saying, 'Tell us when will these things happen? And what is the sign of your advent and the consummation of the age?'"[3] This element is certainly represented in the synoptic tradition. Perhaps it is the overwhelming impression that is left upon the mind. The Son of Man will "come in the glory of his Father with the holy angels",[4] and then will

---

[1] 1 Enoch 46.4 (Charles).   [2] Ibid., 69.29.
[3] Matt. 24.3.   [4] Mark 8.38.

"pay everyone back according to his deeds".[1] He will "sit on his glorious throne" and judge "all the nations".[2] Or his Advent, Revealing, or Day, will be like lightning flashing simultaneously at one side of heaven and the other. The παρουσία will be unexpected like the Flood.[3] Or perhaps it is that the day Noah entered the Ark is like the Day of the Son of Man or the Day the Son of Man is revealed,[4] a day of destiny. Certainly the Son of Man is a man of destiny. Upon their acknowledgement of him hangs the eternal weal or woe of men, the judgement of God: "Whoever is ashamed of me and of mine (or, my words) in this unfaithful and sinful generation, the Son of Man will be ashamed of when he comes in the glory of his Father with the holy angels."[5] And, on a different tack, the Son of Man has authority to forgive sins and to abrogate the Sabbath laws.[6]

In 1 Enoch there is a hint of hiddenness in the description of the manlike one which seems to be borrowed from Isaiah. For instance Enoch 62.2 says, "And the word of his mouth slays all the sinners"; and 43.1–7, where "that Son of Man" is "chosen" and will be the light of the Gentiles, reads, "And in that place I saw the fountain of righteousness, which is inexhaustible; and around it were many fountains of Wisdom . . . and at that hour that Son of Man was named . . . and for this reason he has been chosen and hidden before him." So Isa. 49.2–6 has, "And he has made my mouth as a sharp sword; in the shadow of his hand has he hid me. . . . I shall also give thee for a light to the Gentiles", and Isa. 32.2(LXX) reads, "And a man shall hide his words, and be hidden, as from rushing water, and shall appear in Sion as a rushing river, glorious in a thirsty land." But the hiddenness in the gospels is stranger: *this* man is a homeless man, though a human person ready to join in festivities;[7] if men say a word against him, they will be forgiven.[8] The very confession of his name will destroy one's reputation;[9] he will be betrayed, mocked,

---

[1] Matt. 16.27; Prov. 24.12. [2] Matt. 19.28; 25.31,32.
[3] Matt. 24.39. [4] Luke 17.28ff. [5] Mark 8.38; Luke 9.26.
[6] Matt. 9.6; Mark 2.10; Luke 5.24; Matt. 12.8; Mark 2.28; Luke 6.5.
[7] Matt. 8.20; Luke 9.58; Matt. 11.19; Luke 7.34.
[8] Matt. 12.32; Luke 12.10. [9] Luke 6.22.

suffer, die.[1] Yet it is the acknowledgement of this strange, unrecognized, persecuted man on which hangs so much.

Then afterwards he will come back to life.[2] This element is connected with the suffering but never in any explicit way with the coming in glory. Indeed, if we only had the gospels to go on, we might regard the coming in glory and the rising as the same thing, spoken of from differing standpoints and with the use, on the one hand, of more or less direct description (so far as description is the right word for such a thing as resurrection), and, on the other, of less imagery of a fantastic kind. Be that as it may, the resurrection-strain is associated more obviously with the manhood of the Son of Man: he is to come back to life after death, and after a very real death involving shame and suffering. As such, also, he is representative of all humanity at the general resurrection. But the "humanity" of the apocalyptic figure also is more ubiquitous than appears on the surface, though it could always be inferred from the fact that in all cases a man, Jesus, is in question. It will also appear, as we proceed, that this underlying *humanity* of the Son of Man is by no means unconnected with his office of judge—two things which at first sight appear wholly unrelated, and indeed antithetical.

ὁ υἱὸς τοῦ ἀνθρώπου is a possible translation of בֶּן־אָדָם used as a title in Ezekiel, and has obvious connections with the term in Pss. 8 and 80. But, of course, the original term used by Jesus was probably Aramaic, i.e., בַּר־אֱנָשׁ (or בַּר־נָשָׁא as the definite form) though some have recently been attracted by the theory that Jesus spoke Hebrew as his vernacular.[3] Because of his dependence on the Onkelos Targum as standard, Dalman was inclined to believe that בר־אנש was the quivalent of בֶּן־אָדָם in the sense that it was only used in poetical or semi-poetical passages. Recent

---

[1] Mark 8.31; Luke 9.22; Matt. 17.12; Mark 9.12; Matt. 17.22; Mark 9.31; Luke 9.44; Matt. 20.18; Mark 10.33; Luke 18.31; Matt. 26.2; Matt. 26.24; Mark 14.21; Luke 22.22; Matt. 26.45; Mark 14.41; Luke 22.48.

[2] Matt. 17.9; Mark 9.9.

[3] Harris Birkeland, *The Language of Jesus* (Oslo 1954); cf. Segal, *Mishnaic Heb. Gram.*, p. 17, who admits that Aramaic was the vernacular of Galilean Jews in Jesus' day, but holds that "even in Galilee, M.H. was understood and spoken, at least by the educated classes".

discoveries have produced evidence, however, to the effect that it could be used in narrative passages as a simple equivalent for "man" or for "anyone" as the earlier scholars[1] divined. Throughout the gospel strata, the basic meaning of "son of man" as "man" is understood. The "Q" sayings about the homelessness and ordinary social habits of the Son of Man imply this: "The foxes have holes and the wild birds have nests, but the Son of Man has nowhere to lay his head";[2] "the Son of Man came eating and drinking, and you say, Behold a man gluttonous and drunken, a friend of traitors and riff-raff".[3] In the saying, "all sins and evil-speaking will be forgiven the sons of men",[4] the writer of Matthew[5] substituted "men" for Mark's "sons of men",[6] thus showing that he knew the meaning of the expression. He throws the saying into parallelism:

> All sins and evil-speaking will be forgiven to men. . . .
> And whoever speaks a word against the son of man, it
> will be forgiven him.[7]

In this form of the saying "man" (generic) equals "son of man".[8] In Luke the Son of Man is here obviously not a figure of destiny as he is two verses previously.[9] The same is perhaps true

---

[1] E.g., de Lagarde, Wellhausen, Lietzmann. On the dialect used by Jesus see Bowman, *E.T.*, lix, p. 286 referring to Kahle, *The Cairo Geniza*, pp. 229ff: "Onkelos is neither Palestinian nor early, but represents an artificial Babylonian dialect. That Bar-Nash could be used for 'anyone' or 'a man' in early Palestinian Aramaic is shown clearly in the early Geniza fragments of the Palestinian Pentateuch Targum, for in Gen. 4.14, Bar-Nash is used for 'anyone', while in Gen. 9.5–6, Bar-Nasha (thrice) and Bar-Nash (twice) alike translate Ha-Adam man."

[2] Luke 9.58 = Matt. 8.20.

[3] Luke 7.34 = Matt. 11.19.   [4] Mark 3.28.

[5] Matt. 16.13 Pesh reads "What do men say about me—that I am the son of man?" (ܐ̄ܢܫܐ ܕܒܪ). Syr sin has, "What do men say about me—Who indeed is this son of man (or, Son of Man, so-called)?"

[6] Matt. 12.31. The Aramaic expressions are often translated better in Matthew (at whatever stage of his tradition the translation took place) than in Luke.

[7] Matt. 12.31f.

[8] Matthew is fond of casting his material into parallel form; cf. Matt. 6.19–21 with Luke 12.33f, where one of his favourite contrasts, "heaven-earth" comes out clearly. Here, however, he may in fact be original—Luke 12.10 has the other half of the parallelism—or Matthew may have conflated Mark and "Q".

[9] Luke 12.10,8.

of the saying, "The Son of Man has power on earth to forgive sins"[1] in Mark, which may at some level of tradition have expressed the truth that divine forgiveness is made effective in human community.[2] This may be the point of "on the earth", and Matthew actually adds, "they glorified God who had given such power *to men*".[3] In

> the sabbath was made for man . . .
> the son of man is master of the sabbath,[4]

the parallelism suggests that here too "son of man" means "man". And the identification of "son of man" with manhood runs through to the most advanced apocalyptic in the gospels. The late sermon in Matt. 25[5] contains what seems to be a direct reminiscence of the Similitudes of Enoch, "the throne of his glory";[6] yet here the figure determining the fate of nations judges by his relation to humankind, his identification with humanity in its lowliest representatives:

> Inasmuch as you did it to one of the least of these my brothers,
> You did it to me . . .
> Inasmuch as you did it not to one of the least of these,
> You did it not to me.[7]

The expression "the Son of Man" is Christian; Daniel and the Similitudes of Enoch (if this work is pre-Christian) have "one

---

[1] Mark 2.10.

[2] Matthew and Luke show no variation. This is in fact one of the proof-passages for the existence of "Q".

[3] Matt. 9.8.

[4] Mark 2.27f, cf. Mechilta on Ex. 31.13, "The sabbath is handed over to you, not you to the sabbath." See T. W. Manson's contribution to the *Festschrift* for Anton Fridrichsen. Cullmann, *Die Christologie des NTs* recognizes that in Mark 2.27f and Matt. 12.31 (Luke 12.10) *barnasha* denotes man or mankind. He adds however, "In the rest of the words of Jesus this explanation is excluded" (p. 157).

[5] Kilpatrick, *Origins of the Gospel acc. to St. Matt.*, p. 32.

[6] Matt. 19.28; 25.31. Cf. 1 Enoch 62.5; 69.27ff, etc. But see Sir. 40.1–3; T. Abraham, longer recension, XII.

[7] Matt. 25.40,45. The judgement on the unrighteous is on the broadest grounds, "inasmuch as you did it not to one of the least"; the blessing on the righteous, including the words "these my brethren" might be taken to restrict the relationship to the elect; though B and two Old Latin MSS. with some support from the Fathers omit "my brethren". The mention of brethren once more of course recalls the Deut. promise of a prophet, Ezekiel, Hebrews, and John.

like a son of man"[1] and a "being whose countenance had the appearance of a man",[2] who is afterwards referred to as "that son of man". As opposed to the animals in the Danielic passage, which are like beasts but are not real beasts, the "one like a son of man" appears to be of the genus man, though more than an ordinary man.[3] The language of Enoch where the figure is introduced in a manner reminiscent of the Danielic introduction and is afterwards "that son of man" (i.e., the one already mentioned), as well as that of 4 Ezra 13.3, where the being also introduced as "the likeness of a man" is referred to thenceforth as "that man", suggests that the tradition stemming from Daniel followed the same line. There is again something to be said for the view that the passage in Daniel looks back to the human dominion over the beasts in Gen. 1. Westcott wrote: "The divine kingdom is being contrasted with the kingdoms of the world. These are presented under the images of beasts. The brute forces symbolized them, just as man, to whom originally dominion was given, symbolized the rightful sovereignty which was to be established."[4] That sovereignty (and therefore "judgement") is the characteristic of manhood is the theme right through to the Wisdom literature. "Wisdom guarded to the end the first-formed father of the world. . . . And gave him strength to get dominion over all things";[5] "O God . . . who madest all things by thy word, and by thy wisdom formedst man, that he should have dominion over the creatures made by thee, and rule the world in holiness and righteousness, and execute judgement in uprightness of soul."[6]

---

[1] Dan. 7.13. Mowinckel, *He That Cometh*, p. 353, suggests that Daniel avoided the title "Son of Man" and substituted "one like a son of man" because he had interpreted the conception as a symbol for the people of Israel. See the next chapter for Mowinckel's adherence in the matter of the Son of Man.

[2] 1 Enoch 46.1.

[3] See Kraeling, *Anthropos and Son of Man*, pp. 143f. An angel is not meant here. The angels in Dan. 10.16 and 8.15 are not referred to as "like a son of man" but "like the appearance of a man". This, incidentally, is like the usage in Enoch.

[4] *Gospel of John*, p. 34. The point holds even if it be urged that no abstract symbolism was intended or possible, "the ideas of type and correspondence to type being the product of Western abstract thought" (Kraeling, *Anthropos and Son of Man*, p. 133).

[5] Wisd. 10.1.   [6] Wisd. 9.1–3.

In Ezekiel "the appearance of a man" is also "the appearance of
the likeness of the glory of the Lord",[1] and the Son of Man is
commanded to judge, "Wilt thou judge them, Son of Man?"[2]
Man in his ideal aspect is the type of divine dominion. The author
of Ps. 8 sets the two aspects of man side by side:

> What is man, that thou art mindful of him?
> And the son of man, that thou visitest him?
> For thou hast made him but little lower than God,
> And crownest him with glory and honour.
> Thou madest him to have dominion over the works of thy hands;
> Thou has put all things under his feet.[3]

The author of Hebrews declares that Ps. 8 refers not to man as
he is, who has not everything subject to him, but to Jesus, whom
we see "for a little while made lower than the angels, crowned
with glory and honour for (or, because of) the suffering of death,
so that by the grace of God he might taste death for every man".[4]
The picture leaps to mind of the thorn-crowned Christ presented to John's crowd: "Behold the Man." Jesus alone, says the
author of Hebrews, fulfils the purpose and nature of man, and
"brings many sons to glory". The drift of the passage shows that
the "children" of verse 13 are children of God, not of Christ. The
sons of verse 20 are then sons of God, whom Christ is not
ashamed to call brothers (vv. 11–13), because they and he are of
one origin (v. 11), and share the same nature (v. 14). The argument goes on in terms which recall the Johannine theology. "For
it was fitting that he, for whom and by whom all things exist, in
bringing many sons to glory,[5] should make the pioneer of their
salvation perfect through suffering. For he who sanctifies and
those who are sanctified have all one origin. That is why he is not
ashamed to call them brothers, saying, 'I shall declare thy Name
to my brothers. . . .' Since therefore the children share in flesh and
blood, he himself likewise partook of the same nature. . . . He
had to become like his brothers in every respect."[6] Man is ideally
of divine origin, "the sanctifier and the sanctified" together. But

---

[1] Ezek. 1.26,28; cf. Ex. 24.17.
[2] Ezek. 20.4.   [3] Ps. 8.4–6.
[4] Heb. 2.6–9.
[5] Cf. Rom. 8.29 and above, p. 77f.   [6] Heb. 2.10–12,14,17.

it is noticeable that the Alexandrine author does not present a doctrine of the platonic Idea of man: Jesus is the true man, the true representative of man.

This use of the psalm did not apparently originate with the author of Hebrews. It is quoted by St Paul in 1 Cor. 15.27. He has just called Christ ἄνθρωπος: "for since by man came death, by man came also the rising from death."[1] So now the reference to Ps. 8 ("for all things are put in subjection under his feet"), where "son of man" and "man" are in parallelism, suggests that ἄνθρωπος was Paul's way of translating "son of man". Later the Apostle writes: "So also it is written, The first man Adam became a living soul. The last Adam became a life-giving spirit. ... The first man is of the earth, earthy: the second man is of heaven."[2] Some have thought that here, as also in Col. 1.18, where Christ is "the head of the Body", there is a reference to the rabbinic metaphor of Adam's body for the unity of mankind.[3] Both passages, however, come from the Wisdom literature: the latter draws heavily upon Prov. 8.25ff, the former recalls Sir. 24.28: "The first man did not know her (Wisdom) perfectly; even so the last man has not traced her out." There is thus in Paul, too, a doctrine of Man with Christ as the embodiment of all he stands for or should stand for; and it is connected with Wisdom.

Phil. 2 contains a hymn on the Incarnation which, whether by Paul or not, is used by him. Here Christ was "made in the likeness of men" and is "found in form as a man" (σχήματι εὑρεθεὶς ὡς ἄνθρωπος).[4] Lohmeyer[5] declared that nowhere else in the Greek Bible is εὑρεθεὶς followed by ὡς, and that this is, moreover, contrary to Greek idiom, which has the nominative simply after the passive of εὑρίσκω. Consequently ὡς goes closely with ἄνθρωπος and recalls Dan. 7.13, where the Septuagint reads ὡς

---

[1] 1 Cor. 15.21.

[2] 1 Cor. 15.45,47. The Syriac version is interesting: "The first man, Adam" becomes ܩܲܕܡܵܝܵܐ ܒܲܪ ܐ݂ܢܵܫ. Qadmaya is used of Adam in the Gen. Rab. and of Manda d'Hayye in Mandaism.

[3] See e.g. Davies, *Paul and Rab. Jud.*, p. 57; Col. 1.21f; 1 Cor. 12.12–27; Eph. 4.25; Rom. 12.4f.

[4] Phil. 2.7.

[5] *Ursprung und Anfänge des Christentums*, iii, 482.

υἱὸς ἀνθρώπου. The word ἄνθρωπος in Paul, then, used of Jesus, in linked with the Danielic "one like a son of man" as well as with the "son of man" of Ps. 8. The latter is cited in 1 Cor. 15, "He put all things in subjection under his feet", along with a reference to Ps. 110.1, "till he has put all his enemies under his feet". But it was precisely such a combination of Dan. 7.13 and Ps. 110.1 which our Lord made before the high Priest. It looks as if St Paul used the word with an eye on the title that Christ had made so peculiarly his own, "the Son of Man". The Son of Man is Man as God intended him.

These ideas find their echo in the Fourth Gospel. The writer draws upon the Wisdom literature, has affinities of vocabulary and idiom with the writer of Hebrews, and moreover he bases his Prologue on Gen. 1. He makes play with the same notions as Ps. 8, which is also based on Genesis. The words "little lower than God" are "an obvious reference to Gen. 1.27, where man is declared to have been created *in his own image*". They also recall the argument "You are gods" and the doctrine of equality in Poimandres, which also makes use of Genesis. "Thou hast made him to have dominion over the works of thy hands; Thou hast put all things under his feet; All sheep and oxen and the beasts of the field" (Ps. 8.7,8) is based on Gen. 1.28. In John, as with the Man in Poimandres, the Father has "given all things into his hands". "Glory and honour" (Ps. 8.5) are "attributes ascribed to God as the supreme King of the universe.[1] He has bestowed them upon man as the king of the terrestrial sphere."[2] They also recur as themes in John.

In every case we have reviewed, Wisdom literature, Ps. 8 and Genesis, Paul, Hebrews, and Dan. 7, stress is laid on dominion as characteristic of manhood; and the function of the king for the Hebrew is chiefly judgement. When, therefore, John writes "he gave him authority to execute judgement because he is son of man",[3] the presumption is that it is the manhood which is in question. The omission of the article in the Greek strongly

---

[1] Ps. 29.1; 104.1; 145.5.
[2] The quotations are from Cohen, *Soncino Psalms*, p. 19.
[3] John 5.27.

THE SON OF MAN AS MAN

suggests a reference to Dan. 7.13, where this "represents the
original exactly".[1] The manlike one "symbolizes the rightful
authority which was to be established" as against that symbolized
by the beasts because to Adam dominion was given originally.
Against this is to be set the judgement of E. C. Colwell that the
anarthrous John 5.27 is normal; but C. F. D. Moule points out,
"in the New Testament the anarthrous υἱὸς ἀνθρώπου occurs
only in John 5.27, *except in quotations from the Old Testament*".[2]
Moreover the writer of the Fourth Gospel seems deliberately to
omit the article in the parallel phrase "Son of God" in order to
indicate the meaning "divine",[3] which would then be the con-
verse of "human"—just as the Suffering Righteous One of Wisd.
2.18 is "son of God". It would seem then that, contrary to current opinion, the meaning of John 5.27 is that Jesus judges by
virtue of his manhood.[4]

The Wisdom passage we have already quoted may provide
further support for this view. After the statement that God "made
all things by his Word and man by his Wisdom", the writer goes
on,

That he should have dominion over the creatures that were made by thee,
And rule the world in *holiness* and *righteousness*,
And *execute judgement* in uprightness of soul.

St Paul uses the same Greek words for "righteousness" and
"holiness" in speaking of the "New Man": "Put on the New
Man who after God is created in *righteousness* and *holiness* of
truth."[5] Here Christ the "New Man" is the man made by Wisdom. But the same passage seems to be echoed in John 5.27,
where the words "execute judgement" (κρίσιν ποιεῖν) recall the
similar expression "execute judgement" (κρίσιν κρίνῃ) in the
Book of Wisdom. Whether this has any force will depend on the
cumulative argument hitherto adduced, but it is inherently likely

---

[1] Westcott, p. 34. The original is כבר־אנש.
[2] Heb. 2.6; Rev. 1.13; 14.14; Moule, *Idiom Book*, p. 177. My italics.
[3] John 10.36 and 19.7.
[4] Cf. the Mandean messenger who judges because he is head of his tribe (of
men).
[5] Eph. 4.24.

that the doctrine of the Man if it came to John at all came by way of, or in conjunction with, the Wisdom teaching. Yet the notion of judgement and its relation to Man crops up in another way also.

That Adam and the Adamites were associated with judgement in the final sense is shown by the curious judgement scene in the Testament of Abraham,[1] where Adam is called the "protoplast" as in Wisd. 10.1.[2] Abraham sees the Judge on his dread throne, surrounded by all the paraphernalia of judgement, and the *angelus interpres* says: "Seest thou, most holy Abraham, the dread Man that sits upon the throne? This Man is the Son of the protoplast Adam who is called Abel, whom Cain, the wicked one, slew; and he sits thus to judge all creation, trying both righteous and sinners. For God has said, I judge you not, but every man shall by man be judged. . . . For every man has sprung from the protoplast, and therefore here first by his Son all are judged."[3] So this "Son of Man" judges all creation. The language about judgement recalls one special feature of the Johannine judgement, for, as God in the Testament of Abraham judges not but leaves all judgement to man, so in the Fourth Gospel "The Father judges no one, but has given all judgement to the Son."[4] But the connection is closer still. When the "Jews" declare, "Abraham is our father", Jesus replies, "You are of your father the devil. . . . He was a murderer from the beginning."[5] They intend to murder the Son of Man; is it fanciful to see here a reference to Cain and his murder of Abel, that "dread Man" who is "son of Adam"? It would seem not. The association of sin with murder and the devil occurs also in the First Epistle of John, where Abel is actually mentioned (though not by name): "And be not like Cain, who was of the evil one and

---

[1] There appears to be no question of Christian interpolation. "In fact, apart from some late Christological additions made in a few MSS. by copyists, there is not a single Christian interpolation found in the whole book. . . ." (Ginzberg: quoted Box, *The Testament of Abraham*, p. xvi.)

[2] T. Abraham, longer recension, XII and XIII. Adam is mentioned first, "this all-marvellous Man" on a golden throne.

[3] Box's translation. The first judgement is by man as such, the second is by the Twelve Tribes of Israel.

[4] John 5.22.   [5] John 8.39,44.

murdered his brother. And why did he murder him? Because his own deeds were evil and his brother's righteous." So in one Johannine judgement scene a man shuns the light because his deeds are evil.[1] And verse 8 of the chapter quoted above from the First Epistle reads, "the devil sins from the beginning".[2] The transition from the mention of Abraham in the gospel otherwise seems inexplicably abrupt; but on the assumption that John knew the legend related in the Testament of Abraham everything falls into place.[3]

At this point the "Jews" claim to be children of God, and Jesus takes up the theme again in chapter 10. He has been charged with making himself "equal with God" because he claims to judge and dispense life[4]—both divine prerogatives according to rabbinic ideas[5]—and now because he declares he is "one thing" with the Father. "We stone you for no good work but for blasphemy, because you, being a man, make yourself God."[6] John's readers would be familiar with the idea expressed in John 5.18, "making himself equal with God". The Man of Poimandres, to whom all things are handed over, is equal with God his Father who is "life and light";[7] and St Paul lays it down as an axiom that Christ is equal with God.[8] The plain meaning of the argument which Jesus uses in John 10.34f is that Jesus, being human, claims

---

[1] John 3.19.

[2] 1 John 3.12,8.

[3] John 8.34f. M. R. James thought the T. Abraham was originally written in Greek in the second century by a Christian who used earlier material; Kohler and Ginzberg that it was Jewish with Christian interpolations and originally written in the first century in Hebrew. Some argue that the distinctive eschatology of the work is Palestinian, others that it points to Alexandria. Box wrote that the original story "probably grew up in the first half of the first century A.D. when Enoch had fallen into the background, and Abraham had become the hero of Jewish legendary lore (cf. Matt. 3.9), and the 'seal of circumcision had become the pledge of life'". (*Test. of Abraham*, 1927, pp. xxviiif.) This fits the Johannine picture remarkably well.

[4] John 5.26f.

[5] S-B on 5.17; Schlatter on 5.21.

[6] John 10.33.   [7] C.H., 1.12.

[8] Phil. 2.6f. His words recall Ezek. 1.26; the one "in the form of God", equal with God, is "in the likeness of man". P[46] and several early writers read ἀνθρώπου for ἀνθρώπων.

to be divine by analogy with the judges of old whom the word of God constituted "gods".[1] John, who can be shown to be familiar with Aramaic idiom, was quite capable of the linguistic subtlety involved in taking "son of man" as meaning "human", just as Paul seems to do. The fourth evangelist in fact constantly uses the word "man" of Jesus, and, in view of the evidence that he thought of Jesus as "the Man", even the fact that he was fond of using the expression where an elliptical one would serve does not diminish the force of this.[2] The habit is especially striking in a writer who is often supposed to stress the divinity at the expense of the humanity. Thus Jesus presents himself at Jerusalem as "*a man* who has told you the truth which I heard from God";[3] and Pilate sets him before the people as "*the Man*".[4] Other examples of this mannerism are perhaps less convincing: the woman of Samaria calls her acquaintance to see "*a man* who told me all I ever did";[5] the blind man calls him "*the man* called Jesus";[6] the leaders say, "*this man* does many signs";[7] the high Priest prophesies that "*one man* is to die for the people";[8] being *a man*, he makes himself God.[9] Such language may be significant; the ἐγώ εἰμι utterances are not less compelling because the blind man says ἐγώ εἰμι of himself.[10]

It is thus, and perhaps surprisingly, as *a man* that Jesus appears

---

[1] John 10.34. The meaning in the psalm is of course shown by Ex. 22.28, "Thou shalt not curse the *gods* or a *ruler* of thy people." Odeberg, *F.G.*, pp. 266f, says that the "Jews" could have accepted an Elijah from heaven or a saint who had ascended, but not a man who was *of celestial origin*, one born of a woman who was yet a heavenly being. Yet on p. 333 he himself stumbles at the same teaching and gets rid of John 10.34f by calling the passage "scarcely Johannine in character".

[2] Cf. Black, *Ar. App.*, for the use of ἄνθρωπος for an Aramaic indefinite pronoun. This does not however explain the emphasis, e.g. in "Behold the Man".

[3] John 8.40. Bernard, p. 311, declares this use of "man" to be unique in the N.T.

[4] John 19.5.   [5] John 4.29.   [6] John 9.11.

[7] John 11.47. The idiom is uniform throughout the F.G. Thus the "Jews" also speak of "signs".

[8] John 11.50; 18.14.

[9] John 10.33; cf. 18.17,29. John 7.46, "No man ever spoke like this man" could point either way: it could be taken as a rejection of the manhood.

[10] John 9.9.

in the Fourth Gospel; and it is this fact which must be squared with any theory that he is regarded as representative Man. His humanity in this sense is indeed emphasized more obviously and deliberately here than in the synoptics. His origin and name are stressed: "They said, Is not this Jesus, the son of Joseph, whose father and mother we know? How can he now say, I have come down from heaven?"[1] Philip tells Nathanael, "We have found him of whom Moses in the Law and the prophets wrote—Jesus of Nazareth, the son of Joseph."[2] Sydney Cave wrote:

It is a misrepresentation of the facts to describe this gospel's portrait of Jesus as a mere Christophany. Faithfully this gospel narrates his human weakness, his weariness at the well, his sorrow and vexation at Lazarus's death, and his thirst upon the Cross. Nor is it true to say that the evangelist depicts Jesus as immune from inner conflict, praying only for didactic purposes, himself immune from human needs. His deep emotion at the visit of the Greeks is an indication of the strain with which he accepted the burden of the Cross. His soul was troubled, and it was by prayer that he gained the calm courage needed to endure the Cross, and so consummate his work and do the Father's will.[3] Much as in this gospel his power is emphasised, it is not an independent power. The signs he works are in answer to his prayers to God.[4] Of himself, he can do nothing; his works are those which the Father gave him to do.[5]

Yet this man is also the Man, representative man, in the sense that he is what we should be and is the means of our manhood. That he is *a man* and the doctrine of love are the complementary safeguards against the idea that he is an abstraction. The source of our personality is the love of God deep down under our consciousness which is brought out by contact with the Son of Man, so that

[1] John 6.42.
[2] John 1.45.
[3] John 12.23–7.
[4] E.g. John 11.41.
[5] John 5.19,36. Cave, *Doctrine of the Person of Christ*, p. 61. Bernard, who rejects the equation "Son of Man"="Man", yet writes: "The strict Hebrew doctrine of God left no place for the Incarnation. God and man were set over each other, as wholly separate and distinct. But even in the Jewish scriptures there are hints and foreshadowings of potential divinity in man (cf. Ps. 82.6; Zech. 12.8); and it is to this feature of Hebrew theology that attention is drawn in 10.34" (I.C.C. *St John*, p. 368). For a recent example of one inclined to make Son of Man="truly human", see R. H. Lightfoot, *F.G.*, p. 144.

not the cross, nor the *kerygma*, nor any event, but the Lord himself is salvation. As Bunyan sang,

> Blest cross! Blest sepulchre! Blest rather be
> The Man that there was put to shame for me.

And so each episode in the Fourth Gospel is an epitome of the whole gospel because Jesus is present in it.

CHAPTER 7

THE ANTHROPOS

The subject of this chapter is so enormous that it requires, to do it justice, at least a book by itself. It arises, however, at this point as a real issue. Westcott wrote of the expression "Son of Man", "The title was a new one."[1] But this is commonly denied to-day. And many writers are attracted by the theory that the early Christians borrowed the title from a god who was widely known in the ancient Near East, who was actually called the Son of Man, and who was credited with most of the attributes and work which Christians ascribe to Jesus of Nazareth.[2] Some say that Jesus himself drew on this mythology to interpret his work; and it is held by Bultmann, for example, that John represents his teaching better in this respect than the synoptists, who brought it more into line with "orthodox" Judaism. The question is then whether, since we have argued that John was acquainted with various doctrines which made him regard Jesus as Man in a special sense, we must go on to adopt the theory that he borrowed his Christology from this developed doctrine. The position maintained here can be expressed at once in the words of C. H. Kraeling: "To connect the Christian Son of Man as saviour with the Anthropos directly seems foredoomed to failure because of the fact that in his soteriological manifestation the Anthropos is definitely a product of the second Christian century. . . . Whether there is any common ground between the eschatological Bar Nasha of the Jewish apocalypses and the primordial champion Anthropos is another question."[3] That is to say, it is not a question of whether there was widespread speculation about the first man or the primordial

[1] *Gospel of John*, p. 33.
[2] See, for a recent example, Mowinckel, *He That Cometh*, ch. X.
[3] *Anthropos and Son of Man*, p. 127.

Man, but whether he was regarded as a Saviour in the sense that Jesus is in circles which can be shown to have got the idea from non-Christian sources. The argument cannot be allowed that it is impossible to distinguish between the various manlike characters which have cropped up in mythology and that therefore we must simply assume that the traits which liken them to the Christian Son of Man are original. If in fact it is impossible now to trace sources the presumption must be that the Christian Saviour is prior. This was the point which Edwyn Bevan set himself to labour. Nevertheless, despite the difficulty of the subject, a further effort must be made to try to disentangle the threads of this web, and into this the other question raised in the passage from Kraeling quoted above enters, namely, the rôle played by the manlike one of the Jewish apocalypses.

That there was a widespread myth about an original man and his extraordinary nature is certain. Scholars find traces of this myth in the Gnostic writers mentioned by Hippolytus and Irenaeus, in the Coptic-Gnostic writers, including now the newly-discovered Nag Hammadi writings, in Valentinianism, in the Hermetic Corpus, in Manicheism, and in Mandaism. They also point to the heavenly Man in Philo,[1] to Gayomart the original Man of Zoroastrianism,[2] to the Jewish speculation about Adam, the Adamites, (Abel, Seth, Noah, and so on) and Metraton, and to the Wisdom literature. The Odes of Solomon, the Epistles of Ignatius, the Song of the Pearl in the Acts of Thomas, and other peripheral sources are occasionally pressed into service, as are also the Jewish apocalypses, parts of Ezekiel, and even the messianic prophecies in the book of Isaiah. The most developed Man is the Primal Man of Manicheism who closely resembles, in some respects, the Persian Gayomart. Like the latter he descends from being a champion of light to being a thrall of the powers of dark-

---

[1] It is worthy of note that the heavenly Man of Philo is a counterpart of the earthly in Platonic fashion, and this is what informs the system of Valentinus in which, e.g., the Man and the Church are archetypes within the Pleroma of the earthly realities. The Man of Poimandres is merely a personification of earthly man; when the myth has fulfilled its purpose, the tale is seen to be about "man, any man" (Dodd, p. 43). The philosophical idea seems here to be prior.

[2] Whose name is supposed to mean "mortal life".

ness and is rescued. The glorious Adam of rabbinic speculation also resembles Gayomart, if only because of the glory. The brightness of the sole of Adam's foot before the Fall darkened the sun;[1] likewise Gayomart shone like the sun.[2] It must be admitted that here the resemblance ceases; Adam was of enormous size, extending from one side of the earth to the other,[3] whereas Gayomart was a sphere of four cubits' diameter. He was also not bisexual as Adam was. Nearest of all in language to the Fourth Gospel is the Mandean literature, though here the traces of the original Man are few. Manda d'Hayye is indeed called "first man" (*gabra qadmaya*),[4] "(this) man", and "that man whose fire did not sin".[5] Hibil-Ziwa (Abel) is called "first-born son of Manda d'Hayye and the Great Life", who descends to the "worlds of darkness" by commission from his fathers [*sic*]. His mother is the Image of the highest Being, Mana.[6] One of his helpers is Anush, whose name is the biblical Enosh and means "man". "The youthful Child, the Great Righteous Unique One"[7] is a designation of Hibil, who besides being son of Manda d'Hayye is also Son of Adam, though "he was begotten of no earthly man's seed".[8] So, says Odeberg, "he is the Celestial Son of Man".[9] But there is no single Anthropos in Mandaism, as the same writer implies when he points out that the different messengers in the same tradition are all termed "Unique" or "Son" or "Firstborn"[10]—evidently, then, not in the Christian sense. Both Manicheism and Mandaism are of course post-Christian; Hibil-Ziwa in the latter is a conscious counterblast to the synoptic Christ, and the career of Anush-Uthra is actually described in language borrowed from the gospels. Thus he comes in the years of "Paltus king of the world" (Pilate), heals the sick, makes the blind see, cleanses lepers, restores the lame, makes the deaf and dumb speak, and raises the dead.[11] The Naasenes described by Hippolytus[12] also know of Christ; they equate the Anthropos,

[1] S-B, iv, p. 887.   [2] Zaehner, *The Teaching of the Magi*, p. 40.
[3] S-B, iii, p. 325.   [4] Cf. Gen. Rab. 38.9.   [5] Odeberg, *F.G.*, p. 78.
[6] Ibid., p. 79.   [7] R.G., IX, 236.30.   [8] R.G., IX, 243.25.
[9] Op. cit., p. 82.   [10] Ibid., p. 89.   [11] R.G., I, 200ff.
[12] *Refut.* V, 7,36.

Adam, with "the Christ the Son of Man". Here, however, most are convinced that a pagan document has been touched up by a Christian hand, and that the Anthropos is original. Christ also appears in the doctrine of the Sethians or Ophites and Barbelo-gnostics of Irenaeus,[1] though not in very close connection with the Anthropos whose Ennoia appears as "the Son of Man, the Second Man" (Ophites), or who is "the Perfect Man" produced by Autogenes, himself the fruit of the union of Ennoia and Logos (Barbelo-gnostics). In these various writings the name Adam constantly crops up, which proves Jewish influence of some sort has been at work, and this is true of the chief pagan source, namely Poimandres. Here Mind, the Father of all, being life and light, gives birth to Man, equal to himself, and delivers to him all things that have been made.

It is plain, then, that anthropology was a chief concern of many minds in the religious circles of John's day. Naturally the various myths have features in common. The idea which generally informs those of the gnostic systems is that of man as a captive in matter because of the existence of the sexual instinct; the heavenly Man is then a personification of intellect which falls to become the divine spark in man. The Man of Poimandres is the classic instance of this, and the idea recurs in Mandaism. Here it seems that Adakas, which, according to Lidzbarski, means "the hidden Adam" (*Adam kasya*) is the inner aspect of Mana, the highest being. His descent is the coming down of the spirit of man into this world from the world of light to be imprisoned in the body. This myth naturally has affinities with the Zoroastrian doctrine of man's spirit as a divine spark, as also with that of the Titans or the Watchers who unite with earthly women to beget demigods. The Greek tale of the Titans and their rebellion was sufficiently similar to be combined with that of the Watchers, the sons of God who married the daughters of men and begat οἱ ἄνθρωποι οἱ ὀνομαστοί. But Zoroastrian scholars have protested against the idea that the Manichean view of the body as composed of the substance of evil

---

[1] *Adv. Haer.* 1.28. The Gnostic Marcus apparently thought the "power of the Highest" which overshadowed Mary (Luke 1.35) was the Anthropos, and this was why Jesus called himself "Son of Man" (Iren. 1.15.3).

reflects Zoroastrian doctrine. Thus Zaehner writes that such an idea is for the Zoroastrian "unnatural, perverted, and blasphemous".[1] There is really little evidence that Persian dualism was of this nature. Man's freewill is emphasized and the goodness of at least certain aspects of this world. But wherever the Man appears in gnostic sources, it is against this background. The Man is redeemed rather than redeemer. It is significant that the earthly counterpart of the heavenly Man in Philo is also said to be created by God, while in Poimandres, at a further remove from classic Judaism, this is not the case.

When we speak of the "gnostic Redeemer" we in fact mean one who comes to bring knowledge to the intellect of man which is sunk in the pleasures and cares of the body. This function is not performed by the Man, but by a messenger or messengers, as for example in Poimandres. In Mandaism salvation is brought about by the descent of a series of messengers who make the voice of light heard by the spirits of men,[2] i.e., recall to them their heavenly origin, so that they too, armed with the correct passwords can also ascend past the evil planets (of which Jesus is one) to their true home. So in Manicheism the Primal Man is saved by the piety of the individuals of whom he is composed; he is the soul of man writ large,[3] and the liturgy comprises a "mystery" in which is rehearsed the story of the human soul captive in matter. Here the messengers who awake the soul to itself are Adam, Seth, Noah,

---

[1] *Teaching of the Magi*, p. 54. In his larger work, *Zurvan, a Zoroastrian Dilemma*, Zaehner finds evidence of connection between Iranian religion and Gnosticism, but doubts its extensive influence. Ahriman was not in fact creator of the world but only of the evil in it; and Ormazd was not "unknown" in the way the supreme God of the Gnostics was. McLaren Wilson suggests that the existence of the Demiurge in Poimandres as a secondary creator but not one hostile to the supreme God shows that the development took place within Gnosticism itself. Bousset, *Hauptprobleme*, p. 118, admits that Persian dualism has to be much transformed to bring it into line with the Gnostic.

[2] Thus the name Manda d'Hayye is traced to the words "Knowledge of Life". "Life" in the plural is the Syriac for "salvation"; thus Burkitt pointed to the Syriac version of Luke 1.77, γνῶσις σωτηρίας = ܪܟ̈ܝܐ ܕܚܝ̈ܐ. Others think Manda = Mede (Drower, *Haran Gawaita and Baptism of Hibil Ziwa*, p. ix).

[3] This is true in Poimandres, where the Man who ascends to his Father is really only mankind personified. Here too, in this sense, they ascend with him.

Buddha, Zarathushtra, Jesus, and Mani. Even so, the very idea of the messengers seems to have sprung from the teaching about the biblical patriarchs and Jesus as sent by God. But the essential factor is always γνῶσις, as the following passage which Dodd quotes goes to show. Jesus in the Naasene hymn is made to say: "Behold O Father! this quest of evils upon earth is all astray from thy spirit. But it seeks to escape bitter chaos, and knows not how it shall come through. Send me, therefore, Father. Having the seals I will descend. I will traverse all aeons, and I will open all mysteries and I will reveal the forms of gods. And having summoned Knowledge I will communicate the secrets of the holy way."[1] No redeemer is necessary beyond γνῶσις itself. Thus redemption comes in the Song of the Pearl through a letter.[2] But in John it is knowledge of a Person and not of doctrine that saves.

It is a real difficulty in the way of the view that John borrowed his Christology from gnosticism that the gnostic idea of the redeemer is unintelligible without the gnostic idea of redemption, namely that souls need to be delivered from matter. Thus for the Mandeans, as Menoud pointed out, Death is the real redeemer, who "delivers and removes the souls and spirits from the body".[3] This is in contrast to John with his doctrine of "life eternal here and now"—to borrow Nairne's phrase. Incarnation in John is by divine intention and not by a "fall"; the incarnate One knows his own origin, unlike the Inner Man who has to be enlightened. The Johannine Saviour does not take his own out of the world after the fashion of the gnostic messengers.[4] Moreover, the Fall of the Man takes place before the worlds; he is the pattern which empirical man is to follow. John's Christ is rooted in history, as we hope to show. All the seven descents and ascents of the Mandean messengers take place before the creation of Adam, and the notion of time is really without meaning. Bultmann, to get over this difficulty, has to excise all passages in the Fourth Gospel

---

[1] Hipp., *Refut.* V.10, quoted Dodd, *F.G.*, p. 113.

[2] A letter is involved in the Mandean creation story, but in an entirely different way: see Drower, *Mandeans of Iraq and Iran*, p. 257. For a recent statement of the common misconception that every Gnostic system has a redeemer, see R. M. Grant and D. N. Freedman, *The Secret Sayings of Jesus*, p. 62.

[3] L.G. 1.1.   [4] John 17.18,15.

which point to belief in linear time by stressing the redemptive vocation of the Jewish nation.

Bultmann holds that John was a gnostic. "Gnostic terminology", he writes, "places its stamp mainly on the words and discourses of Jesus, but it is by no means confined to the revelation-source which presumably underlies them; rather it runs through the whole gospel and the epistles."[1] For John everything earthly is mere seeming: "the world's nature is designated as *falsehood*".[2] Against this it must be argued in familiar fashion that John makes a frontal attack on the essential gnostic dogma of the evil of matter: "the Word was made flesh". The humanity of Jesus is obviously and deliberately emphasized. The absence not only of demonology but of any trace of the influence of the planets or of a mediate creator or of an antagonistic being beyond the "prince of this world" is striking.[3] The discourses in the Fourth Gospel show no trace of the mythologizing or the pseudophilosophy which delighted the Gnostics. Its allegories come from the Old Testament. Compare, for instance, the allegory of the Vine in the Fourth Gospel with its Mandean counterpart in which the branches are gods. It can, of course, be rejoined that John absorbs gnostic elements in the process of opposing them, that he takes them and turns them against their protagonists. This is plausible in places, as when he makes Jesus pray that his disciples should not be taken out of the world but only be kept from evil. But in other respects the argument falls curiously flat. Thus the words Σοφία, Γνῶσις, and Πίστις are apparently deliberately avoided. As we have seen, Howard[4] pointed out that the same is true of Σοφία and Λόγος in Paul and the author of Hebrews. Why then did John use Λόγος? The answer must be, either, as we have suggested, because the word was little used by gnostics, or else that John was directly attacking a major tenet of gnosticism, the belief that the flesh was evil, by use of the term. The whole Prologue

---

[1] *New Testament Theology*, ii, p. 13.

[2] Ibid., p. 16.

[3] See S-B, ii, p. 552, who quote similar phrases, though the precise phrase "prince of this world" does not denote Satan but an angel.

[4] *Christianity acc. to St. John*, pp. 43f.

works up to the pronouncement, the Logos became flesh. The same could be true of his use of Son of Man. Either the name had not yet become notorious as the name of a God in syncretistic circles and so was "safe" for John to use, or else it was not; in which case we should expect an explicit attack on the Anthropos doctrine. The fact that we do not get it suggests that it was not in fact an issue. The Anthropos as known to John was not the name of a rival Redeemer.

At this point the argument changes its character. The origin of the Johannine Son of Man is found in myths which underlie the Gnostic systems as they now stand. In Manicheism the lost self of the Primal Man is often called the "son of" the Primal Man. The Naasenes made the Son of Man the son of the Anthropos. In the philosophical sense the Christian term is used for the immanent phase of being of the transcendent Anthropos. But it is extremely difficult to find evidence for the belief that "Son of Man" was the name of a popular god. Mowinckel[1] seeks to prove that "Son of God" was a title of "the heavenly Son of Man" in Jesus' day by reference to the cry of the Gergesene demoniacs, "Son of the Most High God",[2] and to the question of the high Priest, "Are you the Messiah, the Son of the Blessed?" which Jesus answers with the words "Son of Man". This, however, simply assumes that when Jesus called himself "Son of Man" he was identifying himself with such a god, and begs the whole question of its existence. Dalman[3] rightly emphasized that Jesus in Matthew claims that God must have revealed to Peter that he was Son of God because the title Son of Man in itself did not convey this information. The fact is that the latter title never occurs (except in Ezekiel) *as a title* outside Christian or semi-Christian circles, and that even here it is used outside the New Testament simply in the sense of "a human being" (as opposed to a divine being). Thus traces of the Anthropos-theology have been dis-

---

[1] *He That Cometh*, pp. 368f, and note his reference to this page on p. 294.

[2] Mark 5.7; Luke 8.28; Matt. 8.29. Bousset, *Hauptprobleme*, p. 90, notes the occasional appearance of θεὸς ὕψιστος in Gnosticism, but acknowledges its frequency in later Jewish literature.

[3] *Words*, p. 245, ref. to Matt. 16.17.

covered in the Ignatian epistles and in the Odes of Solomon, yet Ignatius writes, "Jesus Christ was of David's line in his human nature, son of man and Son of God",[1] and in this he is accompanied by Justin, Irenaeus, Origen, Eusebius, Athanasius, Gregory of Nyssa, Gregory Nazianzus, Cyril of Alexandria, Chrysostom, as well as by Tertullian, Ambrose, Cyprian, and Augustine.[2] The sole exception is Irenaeus where he is quoting the views of the gnostics.[3] In the Odes of Solomon, Christ says,

> (The Spirit) brought me forth before the face of the Lord,
> And although a son of man
> I was named the Luminary, the Son of God.[4]

And here the term means again "human" as distinct from Son of God which means divine, even if, as Harris and Mingana sought to show, the reference is to Dan. 7.13. Even in the Jewish apocalypses, where we are often told that "Son of Man" appears as a title, the position is doubtful. The part of 1 Enoch called the Similitudes is only extant in an Ethiopic translation and here the phrase is "son of a man" and "son of the offspring of the mother of the living",[5] which is the regular translation of ὁ υἱὸς τοῦ ἀνθρώπου in the Ethiopic New Testament. Even if the title has not been interpolated by the Christian translator the fact remains that it only appears after the original introduction of "a being whose countenance had the appearance of a man" who is afterwards referred back to as "that son of man". In 4 Ezra 13.3 the apocalyptic figure is introduced for the first time by the words "as it were the likeness of a man", and is afterwards referred to as "that man". By this cumbrous method of introduction both writers indicate clearly that they intend to be understood as harking back to the figure in Dan. 7.13, "one like to a son of man", and it is thus to the Danielic vision that all the apocalyptic writers point. Even the Christian author of Revelation uses the phrase "son of man" in exactly the same sense as Daniel two centuries

---

[1] *Ad Eph.* 20.2.   [2] Dalman, *Words*, p. 253.
[3] *Adv. Haer.* V.21.1; cf. I.30.1.   [4] Ode 36.3.
[5] Ethiopic *walda b'esi* (*b'esi*= vir) and *walda 'eg"āla 'emaḥeyaw* (**ወልደ፡ብእሲ** and **ወልደ፡ እጓለ፡ እመሕያው**).

before.[1] Later on the Syriac translators of the Old and New Testaments show by their curious translations of בר־אנשׁ (for which they have ܒܪ ܐܢܫܐ) and ὁ υἱὸς τοῦ ἀνθρώπου (for which they have ܒܪܗ ܕܐܢܫܐ and even ܒܪܗ ܕܓܒܪܐ) that it did not suggest to them a well-known name. Nor do these translations suggest that they were consciously avoiding such a name.

There are thus no traces of a popular deity called the Son of Man in the extant writings. As to the possibility that the existent figure in the Jewish apocalypses reflects an ancient myth it can only be said that as he stands he is entirely different from the gnostic Man. Mowinckel writes, "In spite of his pre-existence, the Son of Man [sic] in Judaism is a purely eschatological being with a purely eschatological task", and adds that the manlike one does not fall into matter nor draw the souls of the redeemed after him into light.[2] He goes on to quote Sjöberg with approval to the effect that the differences between the manlike one and the primordial man are greater than their similarities.[3] That Daniel himself depended on a developed myth of a Saviour-Man is not less obscure. To quote Mowinckel again: "It is difficult to say with certainty whether this figure lay before him as an element in a larger, connected narrative (a 'myth'), in which the monsters from the sea also played a part, or whether the picture in Dan. 7 was composed by the seer or by his apocalyptic tradition from symbols and other individual features, partly borrowed and partly newly devised."[4] The argument that Enoch must have known of an independent version of the myth because he introduces new elements—the "pre-existence" of the manlike one, his concealment by God, and his offices of revealer and judge is not decisive; as Mowinckel points out, the notion of the judge, for example, is implied by the "dominion" of the Danielic figure.[5] The pre-

[1] Rev. 1.13; 14.14; cf. the beasts, the third with a face "as a man", 4.7.

[2] Op. cit., p. 436.   [3] Ibid.

[4] Ibid., p. 352. Mowinckel himself in the next paragraph treats the problem as solved, as far as the implications for the manlike one are concerned. He writes, "Thus we can conclude from Dan. 7. . . . He was thought of as . . . a divine being in human form."

[5] For the connection of 4 Ezra with Daniel see Dalman, *Words*, p. 241, n 1.

existence may go back to the primordial man, but, in view of the total absence of other "primordial" traits in the manlike one, it is safer to assume that it has to do with Jewish predestinarianism, for which what is purposed by God exists beforehand in his mind and will. The "pre-existence" of the manlike one is thus the obverse of his eschatological office. Hiddenness is also characteristic of the messianic king, but it also appears in the description of the Suffering Servant of Isaiah, which, as we have already seen,[1] influenced the Enochic figure. In any case, why should the writers of Enoch and 4 Ezra refer so explicitly to Daniel if they were drawing upon a well-known tale? But that the "symbols and other individual features" of Dan. 7 are derived from tradition is not hard to show.

In Genesis God created man as an image of himself, and it is this which enables the writer of Ezek. 1.26 to use the expression "the likeness of the appearance of a man" in his description of God; but in fact the apocalyptic writers do not follow him in this —they do not make the manlike one divine—though they use similar expressions for the manlike one, and give him, like Adam and the son of man of the psalms, divine prerogatives. In Dan. 7 man retrieves his rightful dominion over the beasts, originally given in Gen. 1, and the symbolic beasts of course appear in Ezekiel, though in Daniel they have degenerated, with the times, into symbols of evil. Some details of the Danielic vision of God appear in Ezek. 1.15ff. Gen. 1 also provides the sea and the winds which probably originally derive from the Babylonian story of Tiamat, the chaos monster who is disturbed by the winds (רוח and תהום). Tiamat may also be the horrible monster of Dan. 7.7. The "clouds of heaven" are regular in Old Testament theophanies, for example in Ezek. 1.4 and in Ex. 19.9, where God comes to Moses on the top of a mountain. But in Ezek. 28.12ff the garden of God is also up a high mountain; here the anointed Cherubim walk in the midst of stones of fire—probably the stars are meant, says Oesterley.[2] The mysterious mountain of the gods was placed by the Indians and Persians, and, as Isa. 14.12 shows,

[1] Above, p. 85.
[2] *Judaism and Christianity: The Age of Transition*, p. 94.

by the Babylonians also, in the extreme north.[1] This feature probably explains the difficulty that in Daniel the figure comes on the clouds to God who is apparently enthroned on earth. There is no descent: here too the scene is probably a mountain. And the paradaisical man who inhabits Ezekiel's mountain[2] is actually compared with the patriarch Daniel. It is not improbable even that the use of בן־אדם in Ezekiel is connected with Daniel's כבר־אנש; he first appears immediately after the vision of "the appearance of a man".[3] The new thing which Daniel added is the eschatological motif which derives from the *Weltschmerz* of the second pre-Christian century, perhaps with some stimulation from the supernatural Messiah, who is also connected with the first man, as in the Testament of Levi 18, where he does all that Adam did in reverse. But in all this there is no justification for the view that a God-Man persisted in Jewish circles.[4] The divinity of the manlike one cannot be proved even in Enoch, where "worship" is offered to him, and the glorious Adam of the rabbis, who was worthy of the worship of angels, always remained purely human[5] before as after his Fall. The same applies to the eschatological figures of Zoroastrianism, the *Saoshyanto*, "restorers", who are of the seed of Zarathushtra and in no sense gods.

The paradaisical man who appears in Ezekiel is by no means the same as the primordial man, but the two conceptions are linked by the notion of Wisdom, which seems to accompany all the manlike figures. It is through his Wisdom that Ezekiel's man is compared with Daniel; the Adam of the rabbis is wiser than the

---

[1] Skinner, *Isaiah*, p. 54. Cf. also Doresse, op. cit., p. 284f. In Isaiah as well as Ezekiel (28.2) the question of wishing to be a god (as Adam and Eve wished) arises, as it may do in Phil. 2.6.

[2] Ezek. 28.3.

[3] The Son of Man of Ezekiel has possible connections with the heavenly denizen in 1 Enoch through the title, and through the paradaisical man also in Ezekiel, though the two are kept apart in that work.

[4] Dalman points out that it is in the fact that he is "unarmed and inoffensive, incapable through any power of his own of making himself master of the world" that the characteristic of the manlike one of Daniel consists. He seeks to show that a subsequent writer has tried to minimize the divine element in the manlike one by substituting עַל עֲנָנֵי שְׁמַיָּא for עִם עֲנָנֵי שְׁמַיָּא (*Words*, p. 242).

[5] Cf. Davies, *Paul and Rab. Jud.*, p. 46 and refs. there.

angels in that he can name all the beasts. But the shadowy *Ur-mensch* of Job 15.7ff is referred to in words which are almost indentical with the description of Wisdom in Prov. 8.22[1]. Wisdom is characteristic of the manlike one in Enoch; far back, in Babylonian religion, the first man, Adapa, is the son of Ea, "the wise one of the gods who knows all";[2] and in Persian religion Wisdom is prominent also, as the "Mazda" part of the name Ahura-Mazda, the earlier name for Ormazd, shows. When we turn to Greek parallels we find that the first man, born before the moon, who counselled Zeus in his quarrel with Hera and was Athene's tutor,[3] resembles the first man of Job. It seems that it is here that the real connection lies between the various men, Semitic and Greek. But the Greek idea of Wisdom has an intellectual twist which is foreign to the Semitic; it thus appears in connection with the gnostic myth of mind imprisoned in matter. In view of the dubious connection of this type of dualism with Persian religion, Quispel is probably right that the oldest form of the gnostic myth, which transforms the Man into a prisoner of matter, goes back, not to Gayomart, but to the Greek Wisdom who brings forth the seven planets.[4] We are back at the essential factor in all gnosticism.

If John, then, was influenced in his use of the Christian term Son of Man by any speculation about Man it was most probably through that form of it which was entertained in the Wisdom circles of Judaism. The later Gnostic Saviour-Man is a product of various factors, one of which is the Johannine Christology itself.

[1] See above, p. 51.
[2] Cod.Ham. 26.R.101.
[3] Hipp., *Haer.* V, 6.5.
[4] *The Jung Codex*, p. 76. Although there is a speculative tendency and an acosmism in Persian thought which are foreign to the mind of Zoroaster himself as well as to Semitic ways. For a survey of work in the whole field see Duchesne–Guillemin, *The Western Response to Zoroaster*.

CHAPTER 8

THE DESCENT OF THE SON OF MAN

The special characteristics of the Johannine Son of Man, it will be remembered, are that he is the point of union between heaven and earth, the gate of heaven; he alone descended and ascended; he must be lifted up and glorified; he gives the bread of life which is his flesh. All of these ideas cluster round the conception of the descent of the Son of Man, a conception which is given great prominence in the Fourth Gospel.

The notion of "descent" which is involved makes one connection of the Johannine Son of Man *in this respect* most unlikely. Here is a decisive contrast to the manlike one of the Jewish apocalypses in connection with whom the idea of "descent" never occurs. In Dan. 7 he comes to the Ancient of Days to be given kingship—and this is the meaning of Christ's confession before the high Priest. "Coming on the clouds of heaven" would in any case be a curious way of describing a descent, and this would also not be suggestive of receiving divine power but rather its opposite. If the Ancient of Days is regarded as being enthroned *on earth*—though the vision says nothing which requires this— then it must be on the top of a high mountain, as with the paradaisical man in Ezekiel.[1] In the Similitudes of Enoch, where the

[1] Christ's confession is a combination of Dan. 7.13 with Ps. 110.1; Mark 14.62. G. R. Beasley-Murray, *Jesus and the Future*, p. 259, has asserted that in Dan. 7 the manlike one *descends* to earth to receive dominion from an Ancient of Days already enthroned there. Whatever his reasons for holding this view, it is not new (see Dalman, *Words*, p. 241). But it seems most hazardous to make the details of the vision cohere so well that the Ancient of Days is enthroned among the beasts. In other respects they do not: what, for instance, have the sea and winds to do with it? Moreover, those who follow Daniel, whether Enoch or Ezra or the N.T. writers (e.g. Acts 7.55f; Rev. 1.12ff—if Christ is meant here), either speak of ascent or an accomplished enthronement in heaven, but not of descent. See also J. A. T. Robinson's discussion in *Jesus and His Coming*.

Danielic scene is taken over, the Son of Man is just there—already part of the heavenly furniture, as it were; he does not descend. In the definitely post-Christian 4 Ezra the same tradition is carried on, and this time the Man of unknown origin rises from the sea to fly with the clouds. But again he does not descend at all.

The notion of ascent and descent was, however, familiar in the conceptions of the Hellenistic world, in which, as W. L. Knox wrote, "everything, including the souls of men, were in a continual state of ascending and descending between earth and heaven".[1] Philo, after subscribing to the doctrine that the air is full of incorporeal souls, and all parts of the universe filled with living creatures, goes on, "Now of these souls some descend upon the earth, to be bound up in mortal bodies. . . . But some soar upwards. . . . But others, condemning the body of great folly and trifling, have pronounced it a prison, and a grave, and, flying from it as from a house of correction or a tomb, have raised themselves aloft on light wings towards the aether, and have devoted their whole lives to sublime speculations."[2]

Specific instances of ascent are not far to seek. The cosmic Bull of Mithraism seems sometimes to have been thought of as going up to the sky after its death and somehow communicating to human souls the power of ascending likewise. Mithras himself similarly ascended through the seven spheres to the supreme heaven, and is represented as leading his worshippers by the hand. The same idea recurs in Mandaism, where Manda d'Hayye, the personified Gnosis, leads his own past the spell-binding planets. As we have seen, this was the function of the various *anthropoi*, who represent the drama of the soul escaping from the body. It was natural, of course, that a journey to heaven should be regarded as an ascent. The Egyptian king as Osiris was supposed to ascend to the sky on an ostrich feather.[3] Suetonius records the report of one who claimed to have seen the spirit of the Emperor Augustus soaring up to heaven through the flames of his funeral pyre.[4]

---

[1] *St Paul and the Church of the Gentiles*, p. 195.
[2] *De Somn.* 1.22, commenting on Gen. 28.12.
[3] Petrie, *Researches in Sinai*, pp. 183ff.
[4] Suetonius, *Augustus* 100.

Jewish saints also, from Abraham to the rabbis, were supposed to have ascended to Paradise.[1]

It is natural enough that the gods should have been thought of as descending if heaven is supposed to be somewhere "above". Thus the Olympians descended from their mountain on occasion to walk the earth in various forms and for various purposes. According to an early writing of the Hermetic class, called the *Kore Kosmu*, which describes the establishment of a sort of Egyptian golden age after human rebellion has been dealt with, Isis and Osiris came to earth to teach the arts of peace and so on.[2] Mention of Isis and Osiris reminds one of the goddess in the vegetation cults who descended to seek her consort: but this is a descent *ad inferos*.[3] Odeberg, however, points out that whatever may be true of *anabasis*, there are scarcely any "mystical" associations of *katabasis*.[4] For the following examples we must confine ourselves to sources which have been at least thought to contain non-Christian elements. The Corpus Hermeticum is generally regarded as free from Christian influence. In tractate 4.2 God sends down man, a mortal living being from an immor-

---

[1] Eccles. 3.21: "Who knows if the spirit of man ascends upwards and the spirit of a beast descends downwards to the earth?", is taken as the "first occurrence within Judaism of the idea of the ascent of the soul to heaven, apparently immediately after death . . ." (Rankin, *Israel's Wisdom Literature*, p. 138). See succeeding pages for the view that this whole teaching comes from "Chaldean astral religion permeated with Iranian elements" (Bousset, *Religion des Judentums*, pp. 522f; Rankin, p. 140).

[2] Frazer in his *Golden Bough* makes Osiris an earthly king to begin with. See also the summary of various beliefs in James, *Concept of Deity*, p. 33. Walter Scott remarked that this was the nearest approach discoverable to the Christian idea of the descent of the Saviour, though it really did not anticipate it at all (*Hermetica*, ii, p. 9).

[3] Those who stress the influence of Persian dualism in the Greek world are obliged to hold that the confluence of this with Greek dualism produced a view whereby *this* world became Hades (Rohde, *Psyche*, p. 403, n 75, held that the Stoics and Epicureans took up Empedocles' idea that this world is Hades). This is then supposed to have coalesced with the eastern vegetation cults and the notion of a descent *ad inferos* by the goddess in search of her consort. (In the Greek myths the idea of ascent is usually *from* Hades after a descent.) See Doresse, *Secret Books*, p. 217, for the descent into hell of the Mother to save Adam in the Secret Book of John.

[4] Odeberg, *F.G.*, p. 73.

tal, to be an ornament of the divine body, the cosmos.[1] In the next few paragraphs a Font of Νοῦς is sent down, and a herald is appointed to proclaim to the hearts of men: "Wash yourself if you can in this font, you who believe that you will rise again to him who sent down the font. . . ." (κρατῆρα μέγαν πληρώσας τούτου κατεπέμψε, δοῦς κήρυκα, καὶ ἐκέλευσεν αὐτῷ κηρύξαι ταῖς τῶν ἀνθρώπων καρδίαις τάδε· Βάπτισον σεαυτὴν ἡ δυναμένη εἰς τοῦτον τὸν κρατῆρα, ἡ πιστεύουσα ὅτι ἀνελεύσῃ πρὸς τὸν καταπέμψαντα τὸν κρατῆρα. . . .) The next examples are from Mandaism, and this complicates the problem, for here direct Christian influence is discernible.

In the Mandean literature ascents and descents are the order of the day. Manda d'Hayye, the chief messenger, is sent down to frustrate the creation planned by the three Uthras generated by the Second Life.[2] He does battle with Ruha (the Holy Spirit as a female demon) and her son Ur, King of Darkness. Then he ascends to the First Life. In another fragment is related the descent of Ptahil from the Second Life for creation. The three Uthras, Hibil, Sitil, and Anush, are created as Adam's guardians. In Right Ginza III 69.8–13, Manda d'Hayye addresses the Evil One Ur thus: "There comes one beloved son who was formed from the bosom of the splendour and whose image is preserved in its place; he comes with enlightening of life and with the command that his father commanded him; he comes in the garment of living fire and descended to thy world."[3] When this passage was quoted before[4] it was noted that it contains many Johannine words. In Right Ginza IV, Hibil-Ziwa, called the first-born son of Manda d'Hayye and the Great Life, descends to the "world(s) of dark-ness" by commission from his father (his mother is the feminine "Image" of the highest being, a notion which seems to be a com-bination of those in Poimandres that God loved his own Image and the Man his own reflection in nature). In his saving work of

---

[1] The story of the Fall of the Man in Poimandres through his love for the natural world is in contrast to this. It may be classed as a descent, and is indeed the classic descent of the gnostic Anthropos—the fall of intellect into matter.

[2] R.G. III, containing the story of creation. (See Odeberg, p. 75).

[3] Odeberg, p. 77.   [4] See above, p. 61.

freeing enslaved human souls from domination by the Prince of Darkness—a task which is described in terms drawn from the synoptic portrait of Jesus[1]—he has several descents and ascents through different worlds of darkness. He says, "I have descended to the Darkness, and have ascended to the worlds of light. I have come to you and am now sitting in your company."[2] There are seven descents in all in Mandaism. At the fourth the Prince of Darkness, Ur, is born. At the sixth he is put in fetters.[3] At the seventh Adam is created, his body from the seven planets and his spirit from the First World, the House of Life. Others that descend and ascend include "the Youthful Child, the Great Righteous Unique One".[4] He is identified also with Hibil, who besides being son of Manda d'Hayye is also son of Adam.

All the elements of the gnostic soul-drama are here. Adam and Eve get their spirits from Adakas, and this is his "fall"; before that they belonged wholly to the sphere of the Seven planets. This is the same sort of idea as that in Poimandres, where the Man as the personification of Intellect falls by becoming sexual and receives from the planets (creations of his brother the Demiurge) something of their nature which he must return before he can ascend to the Father. Empirical men in Poimandres also spring from a dual divine (intellectual) and astral (earthy) nature. There is no doubt that the language in which all this is couched is reminiscent of the Johannine tradition. But the central ideas are different. Odeberg errs when he describes the fall of Adakas to become the soul of man by saying that he "became flesh". Such use of Christian language to describe something different is tendentious. It is surprising in so careful a writer as Odeberg, but too common elsewhere.

The relation of Mandaism to the Fourth Gospel is a complicated question, which does not admit of a simple answer one way or the other. There are, on the one hand, the fundamental Johannine ideas: creation by the supreme Light, Incarnation by divine

---

[1] Hibil-Ziwa's descent recalls that of Simon Magus in Irenaeus and Hippolytus. He descended to save Helen (Ennoia) and was thought to have suffered in Judea but did not.

[2] Odeberg, pp. 79,81; cf. the Shekinah.

[3] Odeberg, p. 82.   [4] R.G., IX, 236.30.

intention and not by a fall, Redemption by a personal Redeemer and by love, not absorption or knowledge, which are original to Christianity and not borrowed. Moreover, the parody of Christianity which appears through the swirling mists of the Mandean tales—the Holy Spirit as a female demon,[1] Jesus Messiah as the baleful planet Mercury, who is unmasked by Anush-Uthra in the days of "Paltus" (Pilate) "king of the world", Hibil-Ziwa (or Manda d'Hayye) coming to Johana (John) for baptism—plainly derives from the gospels, and Burkitt thought he could show it was from the Gospel of Luke "as curtailed and arranged by Marcion".[2] On the other hand, the language of John and of the Mandeans is drawn in some important respects from a common source. Yet here again the matter is not so simple. Take the following passage from the Right Ginza XI, where the messenger who is called "son" of his father is judge because he is like his father and head of the tribe (of men): "Then the Primeval, First One, who is out of himself, established the three Uthras and blessed them and established them and established his beloved son the Discerner,[3] who was out of him [his father], and he said to these three Uthras, 'I blessed you with the blessing with which the parents blessed their children. Go out into that world, execute judgement and deliver from judgement the spirits . . . that are called and desired, and hear the voice of the life. . . . You shall go out victorious, when your work is finished.'" Here the appointment of the judge because he is head of the tribe of men recalls John 5.27, "He gave him authority to execute judgement" (κρίσις, i.e., discernment). He delivers those who are drawn by his Father and hear his voice, performs "works", says, "It is finished." It is hard in such a case not to suspect direct literary dependence one way or the other. In view of the date of the respective works, John has *prima facie* precedence. And this impression is confirmed by a comparison of the two passages. It

---

[1] "Spirit" is of course of feminine gender in Syriac and related languages, and play is made with this in Syriac theology.

[2] *Church and Gnosis*, p. 119.

[3] See Dalman, *Words*, p. 313, for the rabbinic teaching of Messiah who "discerns and judges". The idea of the First One being "out of himself" is typically gnostic: see the Gospel of Truth quoted above, p. 41.

is of course possible to produce a more edifying account from a less, as when the author of Genesis created the monotheistic Noah story out of the polytheistic account in primordial mythology. But the Mandean passage looks just what we should expect as a gnostic expansion of the Johannine texts in the light of typical gnostic belief, with the grammatical subject divided among several characters (Hibil, the Uthras). In view of the complexity of the problem it seems fair to leave the onus of proof with those who would urge the priority of Mandaism. What they usually offer, however, is simple assertion together with the denial of the possibility of sorting out the various strands of the web. And when it is held that Jesus himself taught doctrines more like the Mandeans than the synoptic account of his teaching (which has been brought into accord with "orthodox" Judaism) we are on the way to being bereft even of the touchstone of monotheism.[1]

A closer parallel to the Fourth Gospel is probably to be found in the notion of the descent of the Shekinah. We have already noticed that the words "tabernacling" with men in juxtaposition with the Glory suggests the Shekinah. The rabbis taught that the original abode of the Shekinah was with the *tahtonim*, i.e., men, but "when Adam sinned, it ascended to the first heaven. With Cain's sin, it ascended to the second; with Enoch's, to the third; with the generation of the Flood, to the fourth; with the generation of the Tower of Babel, to the fifth; with the Sodomites, to the sixth. With the sin of the Egyptians in the days of Abraham, it ascended to the seventh. Corresponding to these there were seven righteous men who brought the Shekinah down to earth again. These were Abraham, Isaac, Jacob, Levi, Kohath, Amram, and Moses."[2] At 1.14,18 John appears to be thinking of the descent of the Shekinah in the Word who is the Son of Man. Odeberg thought that 3.13, "No one has ascended but he that descended", was not concerned with the descent of the Shekinah because it was concerned with ascent. This strange mistake will appear presently.

Although the notion of descent-ascent occurs often in John— the angels of Nathanael, the ascending to see heavenly things and

---

[1] See the works already quoted by Pallis, Burkitt, Dodd, Kraeling.
[2] Gen. Rab. 19.7.

descending, the coming down of the manna—the impression must be corrected that there is a constant traffic in John between earth and heaven as in the Hellenistic notions canvassed above. On the contrary, John has a "high" doctrine of heaven: only the Son of Man has ascended thither. Odeberg maintained that "No one has ascended but he who descended" is directed against the apocalyptic theories of the ascent of saints to behold heavenly things—τὰ ἐπουράνια—and "coarse forms of experience-salvation". He wrote: "The whole context revolves on the idea of entrance into the Celestial World; and the subject is the question how a man can enter the kingdom of God, which is answered to the effect that if a man be born from above he enters the highest celestial realm."[1] John is opposing the idea that any, whether it be Enoch, Abraham, Moses, Elijah, Isaiah, or one of the rabbis, could ascend, implying that they never could, or at least that they could not except through Christ. But it is doubtful that John was thinking of ascending saints; for he speaks freely of Abraham seeing Jesus' day and Isaiah seeing his glory, which presumably implies some vision of the kind mentioned by Odeberg.

Other views would narrow down the possibilities. Thus Eph. 4.9–10 reads, "In saying, he ascended, what does it mean but that he had also descended into the lower parts of the earth? He who descended is he who ascended far above all the heavens, that he might fill all things." This, it is said, refers to Moses, and contradicts the belief that he won the victory and ascended.[2] This could fit the attitude to Moses in the Johannine Prologue and in the discourse about the manna.[3] T. W. Manson, however, connected the Ephesians passage with the conflict over the emperor-cult—"the God-become-man versus the man-become-god".[4] This probably catches the drift. In Isa. 14.13 "Lucifer" (the king of Babylon) tries to ascend to heaven to make himself like the most High. The temptation of Adam and Eve was to become as gods, and there may be a hint of this in the Philippians description of Christ who counted it not a thing to be seized at to be equal to God. In any

---

[1] *F.G.*, p. 95.
[2] Knox, op. cit., p. 223; see S-B in loc. Eph. 4.8.
[3] John 1.17; 6.32; cf. 50. [4] *Servant-Messiah*, p. 57.

case, the stress is on the uniqueness of Christ's ascension, and both in John and Ephesians the argument may be directed against no particular object. In the Acts of the Apostles it is David who "did not ascend into the heavens".[1] And so it is throughout the New Testament. In view of John's dependence upon the Wisdom literature, it is perhaps best to take 3.13 as the evangelist's triumphant answer to the Wisdom question: "Who has ascended into heaven and come down?"[2] The answer implied in Proverbs is "no one"; the divine alone belongs to heaven. This interpretation seems to do justice to John's intention.

Only thus can sense be made of the passage as it stands. It cannot be taken to imply that the ascent came first and then the descent. Is it to be imagined that Jesus is represented as telling Nicodemus that he has been up to heaven to see τὰ ἐπουράνια and then descended to tell men about them? Is this then the descent of the Incarnation, and in that case what could the previous ascent have been? Taken in context the saying makes it impossible to think that John was referring back to the Ascension at the end of the ministry, because it implies that τὰ ἐπουράνια were seen before the talk with Nicodemus. But these problems are only raised by a misunderstanding of the idiom employed in John 3.13. J. H. Moulton wrote, "We are familiar with the brachylogy—essentially akin to zeugma—which makes εἰ μή and the like = *but only*."[3] A close parallel to John 3.13 (one in which the meaning is unmistakable) occurs in Rev. 21.27. For purposes of comparison the two may be set side by side, thus:

Rev.   καὶ οὐ μὴ εἰσέλθῃ εἰς αὐτὴν πᾶν κοινόν...εἰ μὴ οἱ
           γεγραμμένοι ἐν τῷ βιβλίῳ τῆς ζωῆς τοῦ ἀρνίου.

John   καὶ οὐδεὶς ἀναβέβηκεν εἰς τὸν οὐρανὸν εἰ μὴ ὁ ἐκ
           τοῦ οὐρανοῦ καταβάς, ὁ υἱὸς τοῦ ἀνθρώπου.

If the former must be translated, "There shall in no wise enter into it anything unclean . . . but those will who are written in the Lamb's book of life", so the latter can be rendered "No one has ascended into heaven but one has descended." And this is the only translation which fits the actual circumstances. The sole and not

---

[1] Acts 2.34.   [2] Prov. 30.4. See Appendix B, p. 206.
[3] *Grammar of N.T. Gk*, i, Prolegomena, p. 241 (3rd ed. 1908).

very satisfactory alternative is to regard the verse as an explanatory comment written in the light of the (later) Ascension, entirely unrelated to the knowledge of τὰ ἐπουράνια which is the subject of the discussion with Nicodemus.

Thus the emphasis falls on the descent. The Ephesians passage declares that Christ, before his Ascension, descended first into the lower parts of the earth "that he might fill all things". Wherever the lower parts of the earth may be, on it or below, the suggestion is that the Ascension does not reverse the effects of the descent. So Paul tells the Romans: there is no need to go to heaven to bring him down or to Hades to bring him up.[1] He is referring to Deut. 3.12 and the accessibility of the Law; Dodd comments: "Christ is not an inaccessible, heavenly Figure (like the apocalyptic Messiah of Judaism), nor yet a dead prophet (as the Jews thought), but the living Lord of his people, always near."[2] John is making the point that of no one else but Christ could this possibly be true: "no one comes to the Father except through me". But he is also concerned with what follows, and the words found in some manuscripts may well be original: "No one has ascended but one has descended, the Son of Man *who is in heaven.*" The only-begotten Son is in the bosom of the Father. John retains the traditional idea of Ascension: "What if you see the Son of Man going up where he was before?" makes the "bread come down from heaven" credible. But that it is no question of a return to glory from the conditions of humanity is assured by the doctrine of the cross. "The divine was not diminished, it was raised to the highest degree in this impoverishment. When this event stands in the centre, the resurrection does not appear as a return from the lowliness and weakness of the purely human to the divine nature. Rather, the resurrection is the transition to the universal, divine outpouring of love in the preaching of the gospel to the ends of the earth; that is, God's continual descent with the gospel of the righteousness by grace into the depths of guilt from man to man until the end of the world."[3] He descended that he might fill all things.

[1] Rom. 10.6f.   [2] *M.N.T. Commentary on Romans*, p. 166.
[3] Wingren, *Theology in Conflict*, p. 32.

John's treatment of the subject is determined by the thought-forms of his day. The setting of the two worlds, above and below, which makes "descent" the appropriate mode of transition, is typically Jewish. The Deuteronomy passage referred to in Romans (above) is an example from the Old Testament: "Who will go up for us to heaven?"[1] Lucifer in Isaiah says, "I shall ascend into heaven."[2] In the New Testament St Matthew is especially fond of the contrast heaven-earth, and uses it where his sources apparently have something else.[3] And of course there are various "descents" in the synoptics. The angel of the Lord at Matt. 28.2 descends; in Matt. 3.16 and parallels (including John 1.32f), the Spirit descends; in Luke 9.54 the fire from heaven (lightning) also naturally descends. The precise way in which John thought may be inferred from his Wisdom background. Here as in some other places this is especially prominent. When Jesus says to Nicodemus, "Marvel not that I said to thee, You must be born anew (or "from above"); for except a man be born of water and the holy Spirit, he cannot see the kingdom of God",[4] the words recall Wisd. 9.17: "And whoever gained knowledge of thy counsel except thou gavest Wisdom, and sentest thy holy Spirit from the highest?"[5] But, more than this, the same Wisdom passage appears to provide the remarks, also made to Nicodemus, about τὰ ἐπουράνια and τὰ ἐπίγεια. Jesus says, "If I told you earthly things and you believe not, how will you believe if I tell you heavenly things?"[6] Wisdom has the prototype of the question: "And hardly do we divine the things that are in earth, and the things that are in the heavens who ever yet traced out?"[7] The Wisdom doctrine of the two worlds appears where Jacob is shown God's kingdom; he "sees the kingdom of God".[8] Otto wrote, "This passage refers to Jacob's vision of the ladder reaching to heaven. The kingdom of God is accordingly meant here, in the specific sense of the world above, the kingdom of heaven."[9]

---

[1] Deut. 30.12.   [2] Isa. 14.13.
[3] Kilpatrick, *Origins*, p. 21.   [4] John 3.7.
[5] The words "from the highest" occur elsewhere in the Book of Wisdom and recall John 19.11. See Appendix B, pp. 205f.
[6] John 3.12.   [7] Wisd. 9.16.   [8] John 3.3; Wisd. 10.10.
[9] *The Kingdom of God and the Son of Man*, p. 37.

John's dependence upon Wisdom here also is manifest: he has made use of Jacob and his ladder in the first chapter, where also the Word tabernacled with men as Wisdom with Jacob, and the reference to the kingdom of God is one of the very few outside the gospels as well as the only one in John.[1] Since Dalman's treatment in *Worte Jesu* it is customary to translate "kingdom of God" as "rule of God" in the synoptics generally; to "see the kingdom of God"[2] would then bear the sense "see that God is king". But John seems to identify the kingdom of God with "the heavenly things" as distinct from the "earthly things" in the same way as the Wisdom writer.[3] "The apocalyptist", wrote Otto, "wanders through this other world in his fantasies and dreams, measures its length and breadth, tells of the groups and activities of the angels who live there, rises from one heaven to another, and returns from them to earth. The simple man of religion knows nothing of such secrets. But he knows about the kingdom of God above, about a blessed heavenly world with God."[4] John may not be "simple", but he is a "man of religion" in this sense.

The setting of the two worlds, above and below, makes the theme of descent inevitable. The illustrations chosen are set against this background. Thus in 1.51 the angels ascend and descend as their forerunners did on Jacob's ladder. In 3.13 the Proverbs passage is probably in the background: "Who has ascended . . . and descended?"[5] At 6.62 and 20.17 the reference is to the Ascension, which is taken as fact in the same sense as it is in the synoptics. The numerous remarks about "coming down" in chapter six[6] are all based on the analogy of the manna which

---

[1] The only occurrences outside the gospels of parallels to the phrase "the kingdom of God" are "God's kingdom" (Wisd. 10.10 quoted above); "the kingdom of our God" (Ps. Sol. 17.4); and "the kingdom of the Lord" (T. Ben. 9.1). Despite the loose way in which the term is used by modern writers, it was evidently coined by Jesus. See Dalman, *Words*, pp. 91ff for the rabbis. Here the nearest approach is "the kingdom of your God". "The kingdom of the Lord" and "his (your) kingdom" also appear. Dalman thinks "the kingdom of heaven" was the phrase Jesus actually used, the evangelists being responsible for "the kingdom of God" out of respect for their heathen [*sic*] readers.

[2] John 3.3.   [3] Wisd. 9.16; 10.10.

[4] Op. cit., p. 37.   [5] Prov. 30.4.   [6] John 6.33,38,41,42,51,57f.

came down. It would appear that the notion of descent is forced upon the fourth evangelist by his world-picture, if he wishes to describe a transaction between the sphere of the divine and the not-divine. That this does not exhaust and somewhat distorts his thought upon the subject will be apparent. The Son of Man does not, for example, cease to be divine by "descending". Nor, apparently, does he begin to be human. The descent from "above" to "below" is not a simple passage from one sphere to the other, but the unification of the two. Jesus the Son of Man alone is heavenly by origin; no one has ascended, no one has seen the Father: as with apostolic Christianity in general, so with John, the kingdom of God no longer belongs exclusively to heaven. The Shekinah has come down; Nathanael is promised the vision of the two worlds united in the Son of Man. Odeberg writes: "The 'heaven open' of John 1.51 and the 'door' of John 10.9 refer to the same spiritual reality."[1] This is the gate of heaven, like Jacob's ladder which unites heaven and earth. And in connection with the Image of the Genesis Rabba comment which the angels unite with the empirical man, the same writer adds, "the unification of the celestial man and his appearance in the flesh is *eo ipso* a communion with the 'Father', under the aspect of the *anabasis*, and a revelation of the Father, under the aspect of the *katabasis*".[2] John mixes his categories because of the inadequacy of all spatial metaphors. When he speaks of divine sonship, as we shall see, he dispenses with spatial terms altogether.

The two worlds are expressed in the contrasts above-below, things in heaven-things on earth, the one from above-the one of the earth. But they also appear in expressions where the spatial metaphor is absent. Thus the contrast above-below seems to be the same as "of this world" and "not of this world" or spirit-flesh.[3] Presumably the "true vine", the "good shepherd", the "living water", "eternal life", and their opposites, fall on either side of the same division. Now we have already rejected the idea that John was a gnostic, that (in the words of Bultmann) he regards the universe from the standpoint of a "dualism to which

---

[1] *F.G.*, p. 323.   [2] John 14.9f; Odeberg, *F.G.*, p. 36.
[3] John 8.23; 3.12; 3.31.

everything earthly is falsehood and seeming".[1] Bultmann himself admits that the word "'flesh' only rarely occurs—except in the passages that speak of Jesus' coming 'in flesh'". As Schlatter wrote, "John does not share the dualist psychology. Who ever separated body and soul could never say that the Word became flesh."[2]

The Johannine dualism, however, presents a strong *prima facie* reason for examining the matter again from a different angle. John may not hold that the Incarnation was a fall, or even that the Son of Man descended into alien matter to rescue his own, but his view of the world may in fact be such and so unredeemed as to make such a theology the inevitable result of taking his thought to its logical conclusion, as indeed many teach or imply to-day.[3] It is not as though the issue was so clear-cut as to be obvious. In the same circles inconsistent ideas jostled one another. The descent of the Man in Poimandres is his fall; yet in the fourth tractate of the Hermetica God "sends down" man to be the ornament of the immortal cosmos, the "body of God".[4] Estlin Carpenter compares a passage from the Corpus Hermeticum, "the cosmos is the fullness of evil"[5] with its Johannine parallel "the whole cosmos lies in the evil one".[6] But like John again (according to one interpretation),[7] "the cosmos is the fullness of life" in Corpus Hermeticum 12.15. There is some evidence that the "dualist psychology" has tainted the New Testament itself. The writer of Jude exhorts his readers "to hate even the garment spotted by the flesh",[8] and St Paul himself is not entirely unambiguous in the matter. Whatever his eschatological expectations, 1 Cor. 7.1, "It is well for a man not to touch a woman",[9] reads very like the

---

[1] *New Testament Theology*, ii, pp. 7–11.   [2] *Der Evangelist Joh.*, pp. 22, 110.

[3] Cf. the constant suspicion in some modern writers that the real Jesus was simply an ordinary man—perhaps even a sinner, so that the scandal of the Gospel lies here! More than a trace of this appears in the writings of e.g. Barth, Niebuhr, and Tillich.

[4] C.H. 4.2.   [5] C.H. 6.4; *Johannine Writings*, p. 325.

[6] 1 John 5.19.   [7] See above, p. 28f.   [8] Jude 23.

[9] Sex is the touchstone in this matter of the flesh. It is to be noted that the gnostics did not reject it because it produced more humans to be ensnared in it (which is after all circular) but because of their horror of the flesh itself. The Mandeans like the Persians enjoined marriage; but like them again had a low view of woman. For a Jew to be unmarried was unusual.

heretical teaching put into his mouth by the apocryphal writers.[1] Whatever the distinction between σάρξ and σῶμα,[2] the two appear to be confused in Rom. 8.13: "for if you live after the flesh, you must die; but if by the spirit you kill the deeds of the body, you will live". Even our Lord is represented as agreeing that it is expedient not to marry.[3] It is difficult to assess the quality of the asceticism behind some of these passages, but we know that dislike of the flesh was firmly established in the first century. The body-soul distinction seems to have grown up in the sixth century[4] B.C. in Greek philosophical circles, of which the result was the sort of asceticism which receives naive expression in the *Phaedo*, e.g., "While we live, we shall, I think, be nearest to knowledge when we avoid as much as possible intercourse and communion with the body, beyond what is absolutely necessary."[5] That the causes were entirely philosophical may be doubted, though it is by no means clear how the disgust for the body reached the pitch it did from the dual starting-points of Greek and Iranian thought, neither of which are so extreme in isolation.[6]

But however the attitude arose, its effects were far-reaching. It has become the custom to draw a sharp distinction in this matter between Jewish and eschatological thought on the one hand and Greek and gnostic ideas on the other. But the distinction cannot be drawn with any firmness. Whatever be the provenance of the Testaments of the Twelve Patriarchs, the extreme modesty[7] of

---

[1] E.g. Acts of Paul and Thecla (James, *Apocryphal N.T.*, p. 273): "Blessed are the continent, for unto them shall God speak. . . . Blessed are they that possess their wives as though they had them not, for they shall inherit God. . . . Blessed are the bodies of the virgins, for they shall be wellpleasing to God and not lose the reward of their continence."

[2] See Quick, *Christian Sacraments*, pp. 226, 209, 31.

[3] Matt. 19.11ff. Plummer's comment is abundantly justified that Jesus is represented as referring to the remark about the inadvisability of marriage and not the previous one about its indissolubility. The Matthaean expansion is probably not authentic.

[4] James, *Concept of Deity*, p. 25. Heraclitus (c. 585–c. 475) could still hold that "the *dry* soul is best".

[5] 67A.

[6] See above, p. 114, n 3.

[7] E.g. "Engage not in much gossip with women. This applies to one's own wife; how much more to the wife of one's neighbour?" (Pirqe Aboth), and "A

the rabbis is far from the healthy robustness of the Old Testament. Moreover, the extreme dualism of the Gnostic writers has its analogue in the apocalyptists. Thus in 1 Enoch the righteous have

> hated and despised this world of unrighteousness
> And have hated all its works and ways in the name
> of the Lord of Spirits.[1]

Similarly, in the latest section (according to Charles) there are those "who have afflicted their bodies . . . longed not after earthly food. . . . And now I will summon the spirits of the good who belong to the generation of light, and I will transform those who were born in darkness, who in the flesh were not recompensed with such honours as their faithfulness deserved."[2] Mention of the dualism of the Enochic literature makes reference to the Dead Sea Scrolls inevitable. Speculation has been rife over the alleged gnostic elements in these writings, the dualism of light and darkness, the stress on knowledge. The "knowledge" that is meant is not that of gnosticism, as is shown by the fact that the word must be variously translated "mind", "interest", "obedience", "attention".[3] The New Testament is, however, saved from capitulation to the errors of dualism by the personalism of its faith. Jesus is the one who is known; he was a man, in the flesh. In the very place where Paul uses the equivocal expression, "likeness of sin's flesh", he also uses the words "in the flesh". Thus: ". . . God, sending his own Son in the likeness of sin's flesh . . . condemned sin in the flesh".[4] The "likeness" is to be added to the "sin" and not to the "flesh" in order to safeguard the sinlessness of Christ. Despite certain modern ideas to the contrary, St Paul, whatever he meant by, "He has made him to be

man should never walk behind a woman along the road, even his own wife. . . . whoever crosses a stream behind a woman will have no portion in the world to come. . . . A man should walk behind a lion rather than behind a woman" (b Ber 61a–Cohen, *Everyman's Talmud*, p. 98). One is not surprised to hear about the Pharisees who bumped their heads into walls through fear of looking up.

[1] Enoch 48.7.
[2] Enoch 108.7–11; cf. such writings as Jude and 2 Pet.
[3] Cf. Davies, *H.T.R.*, xlvi, 3; Bo Reike, *N.T.S.*, i, 2; Burrows, *The Dead Sea Scrolls*, pp. 252ff.
[4] Rom. 8.3.

Sin for us"[1] certainly did not mean that Christ sinned or became a sinner. John's dualism, springing from or coloured by his contact with Christ "come in the flesh",[2] is not that of flesh-spirit in the sense of the Testaments of the Twelve Patriarchs, the rabbis, or 1 Enoch, still less of the Gnostics; nor yet is it the dualism of the Dead Sea sect who identified light and darkness with different groups of human beings.[3] Contact with the Word-made-flesh has divided the world for John into the darkness of lovelessness and the light of love. His gnosis is that which consists in the knowledge of persons.[4] "He that hates his brother is in the dark, is walking in the darkness, and does not know where he is going, because the darkness has blinded his eyes."[5] It should be noted that this means more than the vague notion that "John's dualism is ethical", which could cover any number of things. It is what redeems John from the heresy typified in Manicheism.

It is beyond dispute that John used the words "below" and "of this world" derogatively. "You are from below. . . . You are of this world. . . . You will die in your sins."[6] But against this has to be set the ambiguity of the contrasts. The "world" for instance denotes human society or the cosmos as organized apart from God. Yet God "loved the world". The same ambiguity appears in the rabbinic use of the expression "the world", though the idea of God loving the world is absent.[7] For this reason each element in the Johannine dualism must be taken in context and not assigned to some previously decided scheme. The explanation appears to be that the attitude to the flesh in the Fourth Gospel is thoroughly Hebrew. The horses of the Egyptians are flesh, not spirit; all flesh is grass, and—our Lord's famous excuse for his disciples—the spirit is willing but the flesh is weak. It is possible

---

[1] 2 Cor. 5.21.   [2] 1 John 4.2.

[3] "Children of darkness" never occurs in the Johannine gospel and epp.; and "children of light" only occurs once. It also occurs in Luke and Eph.

[4] Cf. 1 Cor. 13.13 where Paul sets love above all mysteries and knowledge; also 1 Cor. 8; Rom. 14.

[5] 1 John 2.11.

[6] John 8.23–4. In D.S.D., where Brownlee translates "men of injustice" and Gaster "the base [sc. men]", the Hebrew seems to mean "the men from beneath" (אנשי מטה). See D.S.D. 11.2.

[7] Odeberg, p. 117.

to see this from a comparison of two passages in John. The Pharisees cry exasperatedly to one another as they watch the triumphal entry, θεωρεῖτε ὅτι οὐκ ὠφελεῖτε οὐδέν. In other words, they are ineffective.[1] The identical words of Jesus, ἡ σάρξ οὐκ ὠφελεῖ οὐδέν, presumably have the same meaning. The flesh is therefore genuinely neutral; Jesus' redemption is effective because it is from above. The other contrasts fit this well enough. Westcott's interpretation of ἐπίγειος as "what has its manifestation on earth" rather than "what partakes of the nature of earth" depends on whether the Lord is referring to the whole conversation or to the analogy of wind—and this in turn depends on the translation of πνεῦμα. If the earthly phenomenon is in question, ἐπίγειος refers to what is of the earth, but without moral judgement. And the man from above is later contrasted with the man of earth, in a passage which some have thought belongs to the Nicodemus episode.[2] In other places the notion of newness creeps in, as between the new birth and the old life,[3] the living water and the water of Jacob's well,[4] the true worship over against the worship of Mount Gerizim or Jerusalem,[5] the Law given by Moses and the grace and truth which came by Jesus Christ, or the manna of the Law given by Moses and the living bread which came down from heaven.[6] But the general idea is of effectiveness, fitness for the purpose in view, what is of use, genuineness in this sense, as opposed to the reverse. All the shepherds who came before the good Shepherd were thieves and robbers, says John, with an eye on the unworthy shepherds of Ezek. 34. Yet the main idea of the Shepherd analogy does not lie here. Many sermons and devotional essays have dwelt on the double meaning of the Greek καλός—good or fine—and we have even had the rendering "the beautiful shepherd". But the meaning is simply that of a shepherd who is good at his job, who knows his work and can do it. The true vine, in like manner, recalls the son of man vine of Ps. 80:[7] "the stock which thy right hand planted and the branch (Heb.

---

[1] John 12.19.   [2] John 3.31.   [3] John 3.6.
[4] John 4.7–15.   [5] John 4.20ff.   [6] John 6.32ff.
[7] Cf. the "noble vine of 'right' seed" in Jer. 2.21 as opposed to the "degenerate plant of a strange vine" in the same verse.

son) that thou madest strong for thyself",[1] and the vine of Ezek. 17, which "was planted in a good soil by many waters, that it might bring forth branches, and that it might bear fruit, that it might be a goodly vine".[2] In Sir. 24 Wisdom praises herself as a vine, and says, "Come unto me you that are desirous of me, and be filled with my produce. . . . They that eat me shall yet be hungry, and they that drink me shall yet be thirsty."[3] Elsewhere Wisdom invites, "Come, eat of my bread, and drink of the wine which I have mingled."[4] The bread and wine are of course paralleled by the flesh and blood in John; but words that are appropriate to Wisdom because of its very nature apply in an opposite sense to the rich food of Christ. "I am the bread of life", he says, "he that comes to me will not hunger, and he that believes in me will never thirst."[5] It is as the final word to men that Jesus is the "true" bread.[6] Jesus, not Law or Wisdom, is the living bread that finally satisfies.

Despite different overtones in particular instances the same idea seems to underlie the various contrasts, but it is neither that spirit is good while flesh is evil, nor the Platonic theory of the Idea seeking to impose its pattern on recalcitrant matter. Yet the concept of "flesh" (like that of "world") is ambivalent; it can either be "in touch" or "out of touch" with the divine life. Thus the difference between flesh and spirit easily becomes that between inward and external. Paul's "Though we once knew Christ according to the flesh"[7] and John's "You judge according to the flesh"[8] passes

---

[1] Ps. 80.15; cf. 17. Dodd points out that the connection between the "Son of Man" and the vine is clearer in the LXX.

[2] v. 8.   [3] Sir. 24.1,17,21.

[4] Prov. 9.5.   [5] John 6.35.

[6] John 6.32. Appasamy, *Christianity as Bhakti Marga*, pp. 145f, makes the point that for the Indian Bhaktas God is milky sugar-cane, nectar, luscious fruit, the finest delicacies; for John Christ is water, bread, the staple of human food. "What the Bhaktas desire is rapture, ecstasy, flights of emotion reserved for the few and that in extraordinary hours. What the fourth evangelist emphasizes is the moral strength which all men and women need to exercise every day of their lives." John contrasts in similar fashion to some extent with the Odes of Solomon, which in this respect sometimes distantly recall the Sufis, e.g. Rumi, but of course owe much to the Hebrew psalms.

[7] 2 Cor. 5.16.   [8] John 8.15.

over into a condemnation of externalism: "Now we know no one according to the flesh" and "Do not judge according to appearances, but judge righteous judgement."[1] This last remark is offered to those who have criticized the healing of a man on the Sabbath from a legalistic standpoint; and they judge Jesus by his birth and lineage.[2] But being Abraham's seed[3] does not make a true Israelite. Christians are not born of blood, nor of the will of the flesh, nor of the will of man, but of God.[4] So Nicodemus is offered a new life though he is old; the woman of Samaria is offered the water of a life which is unconcerned with whether she is Jew or Samaritan, man or woman, or where she worships. At the touch of God the flesh can become the vehicle of the life of God, of his manifestation; the Word became flesh and the opposition between spirit and flesh, upper and lower, is done away: the Son of Man unites heaven and earth. Thus the final contrast is between the flesh with its ingrained conventionalism and conservatism and the Son of Man; he is from above, they from below.[5] John's position is that of the author of the *Theologia Germanica*: "In truth, no creature or creature's work, nor anything that we can name or think of, is against God or displeasing to him; nothing is against God but only disobedience and the disobedient man."[6]

This is borne out by the fact that the flesh is the point at which Christ mediates himself to others. He gives his flesh as food. This is the bread "come down from heaven". It has often been pointed out that the idea of celestial food imparting immortal life is at least as old as Homer. The relation between food and life is indeed so obvious as to make it natural as a religious conception. In Jewish lore, the Messiah was to distribute heavenly food in the New Age. The rabbinic equivalent of a food from heaven is *parnasa*, sustenance, and it is often associated with manna, as in John 6. Here again the flesh appears as a stumbling-block. *Parnasa* sometimes means "the teaching of the Law", and the Law is also called "bread". Thus the "Jews" in John 6.27 think that "working for the meat that endures" means "working at the Law". The

---

[1] 2 Cor. 5.16; John 7.24. [2] John 7.41f, etc. [3] John 8.37.
[4] John 1.13. [5] John 8.23; cf. 8.15.
[6] Bernhart, ed. 1951, p. 142 (Gollancz).

imperishable food is teaching. In this they are wrong: Jesus is the true bread that came down from heaven. The "Jews" are scandalized at the proposition that he "came down from heaven", was of heavenly origin, and they want to know how this man can give his flesh for food.[1] This is quite modern. Many have wanted to know the same thing, and have taken the meaning to be that the heavenly food is Jesus' teaching. And it is true that in the Fourth Gospel Jesus gives himself in his words; this is the significance of the stress on "words". Teaching is one mode of communicating the divine life to man open to him who is the Son of Man. Jesus says, "The words that I have spoken to you, they are spirit and they are life",[2] and Peter says, "You have words of eternal life."[3] This is true in a general sense, and some have seized upon the absence of the article ἡ (or ὁ) in John 6.51, ὁ ἄρτος δὲ ὃν ἐγὼ δώσω ἡ σάρξ μου ἐστὶν ὑπὲρ τῆς τοῦ κόσμου ζωῆς,[4] to translate, "the bread which I shall give for the life of the world is my flesh", connecting ὑπὲρ τῆς τοῦ κόσμου ζωῆς directly with δώσω. This might be taken to mean that the "flesh" he speaks of is the "bread", the teaching in which resides his own personality, in contrast to the spiritual food of Judaism.[5] "True food" and "true drink" which some manuscripts read at 6.55 for ". . . food indeed . . . drink indeed" might be considered to bear this out.

The idea is true as far as it goes, but only because the teaching is the expression of the whole man. As Odeberg pointed out, the true reading of John 6.51 refers to the appearance of Jesus in the earthly world, to the fact that he has been born in an earthly organism, to his "historicity", to use Hoskyns' word. The Son of Man is the bread of life because as such he is in the form most readily assimilable by men. As the passage from the Odes of

---

[1] John 6.41,52.   [2] John 6.63.   [3] John 6.68.
[4] Instead of ἡ σάρξ μου ἐστὶν, ἡ ὑπέρ κτλ.
[5] Some MSS. actually read ὑπὲρ τῆς τοῦ κόσμου ζωῆς, ἡ σάρξ μου ἐστίν. Odeberg gives an Aramaic reconstruction of the accepted text to remove the difficulties of the Greek:

ולחמא דאנא אתניניה
בסרי הוא על חייא דעלמא

It is noteworthy that in this verse the words "flesh" and "world" occur together in their "good" sense.

Solomon puts it (from a slightly different point of view): "He became like me in order that I might receive him; he was reckoned like myself in order that I might put him on . . . like my nature he became that I might learn him, and like my form, that I might not turn back from him."[1] And communion with him is communion with God: "As the living Father sent me, and I live because of the Father, so he who eats me will live because of me."[2] But the earthly manhood of the Word is of a special kind. The life is given; the flesh is associated with the blood. So from "flesh" and "flesh and blood" as historicity, John passes to the flesh and blood of the eucharist. Some have denied this, but the mention of blood, together with flesh, bread, and Jesus, makes it almost inevitable. Confusion has been caused by the occurrence in the Received Text at 6.63 of "I speak" instead of "I have spoken": the "words I have spoken to you" are primarily the words of the previous discourse, culminating in the Johannine "words of institution", "This is my flesh"—a form which is found in the early liturgies, and perhaps implied in Ignatius and Justin Martyr also. Here the final word can be said on the contrast "the spirit makes alive, the flesh is of no avail". As Odeberg said of the whole question of flesh versus spirit in John: "What a modern, or else philosophical, mind would regard as the most immaterial of all, e.g., speculation upon 'absolute truths', 'pure thought', e.a., to John belongs to the sphere of reality described by the expression 'that which is born of the flesh is flesh'."[3] What then are we to make of the emphatic sentence, "The spirit makes alive, the flesh is of no avail"? It is a typical Semitic epigram, which in English would be rendered less absolutely: "The spirit makes alive, the flesh *only* is of no avail." As J. Jeremias points out, "it is characteristic of Semitic speech that the word 'only', which must be expressed in English, is very often omitted".[4] Mere reception of

---

[1] Odes Sol. 7.4,6   [2] John 6.57.   [3] *F.G.*, p. 269.
[4] *Parables of Jesus*, p. 28, n 35. He instances Matt. 5.18f,28,43,46; 11.13; 18.6,20,28 ; 20.12; 24.8; Mark 1.8; 9.41,42; 10.5; 13.8; 14.51; Luke 6.32,33,34; 7.7; 9.28; 12.41; 13.23; 15.16; 16.16,17,21,24; 17.10,22; John 10.33; 12.35 *et al.*, and adds, "Hence the addition of μόνῳ in Matt. 4.10 and Luke 4.8 to the quotation from Deut. 6.13, LXX, is actually correct. The observation is important for Rom. 3.28 and Gal. 5.6b."

the eucharistic elements is pointless; there must be union with their meaning, which is constantly reiterated in chapter six in the terms "flesh", "blood", "given for the life of the world".

In heart and mind I bear but thee.[1]

What matters is the *sort* of life we participate in, the life which is that of Jesus of Nazareth.

The connection of the bread of life specifically with the Son of Man may be traced to the Man-tradition in its Jewish aspect, though this is of course speculation. The Man is associated with Wisdom, as we have seen, and Wisdom is food and drink—in Philo manna, as in John, the "heavenly nourishment of the soul".[2] Like the manna, the Son of Man has "come down". And in rabbinic thought Adam is the Blood of the World and the Light of the World, another parallel with the one whose life is given for the world and who is its light. The life is the light of men,[3] and judgement comes by the rejection of the only-begotten Son of God, as of the light which men reject in favour of darkness, and so are judged.[4] Likewise, through his connection with life, "because he is Son of Man he can judge, sift, those who have it and those who have it not".[5]

The descent of the Son of Man in the Fourth Gospel, then, is no mythological descent, but enfleshment, the establishing of his means of communication with men. Jesus is thus both a "real" man, and the Image of God, Servant, and Righteous One, "truth nailed to a cross".[6] His relation to mankind is thus not abstract; he *draws* men by his love. Of course, in the Fourth Gospel as in the synoptics, the Son of Man exemplifies abstract principle—the principle of life through death, gain through loss. "He who loves his life loses it, and he who hates his life in this world will keep it

---

[1] Quoted Stevenson, *Max Joseph Metzger, Priest and Martyr*, p. 3.
[2] Quis Rer. 191. Cf. Sir. 15.3, "With bread of understanding shall she [Wisdom] feed him, And give him water of wisdom to drink."
[3] John 1.4.
[4] John 3.18ff.
[5] John 5.25ff. A. H. McNeile, *N.T. Teaching in the Light of St Paul's*, p. 265.
[6] "Truth nailed to a cross compels no one": the saying is Berdyaev's.

for eternal life."[1] Positively, the principle is "he that abides in love abides in God".[2] This is how he is related to humanity in general: "Abide in my love."[3] For his manhood is no abstraction, and his relation to empirical mankind is a personal relation. The Son of Man must be lifted up to draw all men to him, as the Servant is to "gather together into one the scattered children of God"; the seed must die in order that it may not remain solitary.[4] As Dodd has written, the Johannine conception of the son of Man

> challenges the mind to discover a doctrine of personality, which will make conceivable this combination of the universal and the particular in a single person. A naive individualism regarding man, or a naive anthropomorphism regarding God, makes nonsense of the Johannine Christology. Ancient thought, when it left the ground of such naive conceptions, lost hold upon the concrete actuality of the person. It denied personality in man by making the human individual no more than an unreal "imitation" of the abstract universal Man, and it denied personality in God by making him no more than the abstract unity of being. A Christian philosophy starting from the Johannine doctrine of Jesus as Son of Man should be able to escape the *impasse* into which all ancient thought fell, and to give an account of personality in God and in ourselves.[5]

Such a philosophy will have to take account of the fact that for John the Son of Man does not become personal at his descent or shed his glory, so that personality is not tied to earthly, finite existence.[6] In this way the status of the human person may be secured against attacks from opposite sides of atheistic "humanism" and absolutist theology.[7] Illumination may also be shed on

[1] John 12.25.

[2] 1 John 4.16.

[3] John 15.9.

[4] John 12.32. Cf. the "many sons" of Heb. 2.10,13, and "I and the children God has given me". Also Isa. 49.5, where the Servant "a light to the nations" (cf. the Light of the world) is to "gather Jacob together" to him. For the seed, see John 12.23f and cf. 15.8.

[5] *F.G.*, p. 249.

[6] We cannot accept Davies' judgement on Paul, that his doctrine of "pre-existence" is not intended seriously, as applicable to John.

[7] "How much then is a man of more value than a sheep?" (Matt. 12.12) is a question for which neither has an answer.

the problem of the relation of the impersonal and personal in our apprehension of the nature of God himself, which is raised in the Fourth Gospel itself by the use of abstract categories like "light" and "life" and the impersonal doctrine of judgement by self-exclusion from the light alongside the personal and anthropomorphic.

CHAPTER 9

THE WAY, THE TRUTH, AND THE LIFE

The purpose of this chapter is more limited than its title might suggest. We are concerned in this essay with the Christology of the Fourth Gospel and can only touch incidentally upon the wider question of the Christian life according to John. But in its narrower aspect the question is forced upon us by the attitude we have taken to the manhood of the Son of Man. If Christ as Son of Man is in some sense ideal Man, is he the "inclusive" Man who is himself the sum of believers? The later Gnostic Man, as for example in Manicheism and the Gospel of Truth, was "the All": the *pneumatici* were his members and this doctrine resembles at least two other doctrines which would be available in principle to the Johannine writer. Quispel quotes a passage about Adam from the *Yalkut Shimoni* on Genesis, para. 34: "He cast a soul into him and set him up comprising in him the universe."[1] The conception is a familiar one to students. Rabbi Meir said, "The dust of the first man was gathered from all parts of the earth." And Rabbi Oshaiah said in Rab's name, "Adam's trunk came from Babylon, his head from Eretz Israel, his limbs from other lands, and his private parts according to R. Aha from Akra di Agma."[2] The resemblance to Paul's doctrine of the Church as the Body of Christ, its "members" as his members, and Christ as the Head[3] is sufficiently clear. In the above quotation the head of Adam comes from the Eretz Israel. Whether the two doctrines are interdependent is a matter for discussion. Some have gone further, and declared that the manlike one of the Jewish apocalypses shows traces of an inclusiveness, at least with regard to the souls of the saints. Mowinckel includes this in his list of characteristics of the

---

[1] *The Jung Codex*, p. 77.   [2] Davies, *Paul and Rab Jud.*, pp. 53f.
[3] Cf. Col. 1.18; 1 Cor. 12.12 "for the body is one and has many limbs . . . so also is Christ". Also, "we are members one of another".

manlike figure to be compared with those of the Anthropos: "It seems, too, that at one stage, at least, of the history of the idea, there was a mystic connection between the Son of Man and the spirits of the righteous departed, so that they were thought of as identical with him in some way."[1] The hesitancy of this statement, manifest in its numerous qualifications, is however explained by the meagreness of the ground upon which it is based. This is an obscure passage in 1 Enoch that "in him dwells . . . the spirit of those who have fallen asleep in righteousness".[2] Mowinckel admits that "the reference here is not to the individual human spirits (in the plural) of the pious, but to the divine spirit (in the singular). The meaning can only be that the Son of Man is inspired by the same divine spirit of righteousness and piety which was active in the pious heroes, patriarchs, prophets, and sages of former times. . . ." He goes on to say, however, "In several parts of the east, including some Jewish centres, the Primordial Man was regarded as the Primordial Soul (or simply 'the Soul', *anima generalis*), in whom all other souls have pre-existence, and to whom they return at death",[3] and suggests that the passage in 1 Enoch reflects a survival of this idea. The foundation seems a slender basis for the edifice constructed upon it. In the absence of further evidence and in view of the remoteness of the connection between the manlike one and the Anthropos,[4] it will be best to suspend judgement. If there is any doctrine of the inclusiveness of the Son of Man in the Fourth Gospel, it does not come from here any more than from the Gnostic Man. The connection with the Adam teaching or Paul's doctrine of the Church is scarcely in any better case. Adam does not appear in the Fourth Gospel,[5] nor is the doctrine of the Son of Man discernible there

---

[1] Mowinckel, *He That Cometh*, p. 430.

[2] 1 Enoch 49.3; Mowinckel, p. 377.

[3] He refers to Murmelstein in *W.Z.K.M.*, xxxv, 1928, pp. 261ff.

[4] On the Anthropos see above, ch. 7.

[5] Thornton's exegesis of "in him was life" as Eve (life) present in Adam as his rib seems fanciful. In the *Apocryphon Johannis* the supreme God sends Adam a helper, the Epinoia of light called Zoe, which is hidden in Adam so that the archons might not know of it. This is the sort of way in which gnostic fancy parts company with a true theology.

closely related to the Adamite speculation. And the only possible reference to the Church as the Body of Christ appears in the saying, "Destroy this Temple and in three days I will raise it up. . . . He spoke of the Temple of his Body." Nevertheless, Christ is the Vine and we are the branches, a metaphor which expresses a profound relationship. "Apart from me", says the Johannine Christ, "you can do nothing." We are reminded of the Pauline "I live, yet not I—Christ lives in me" and his doctrine of ἐν Χριστῷ. The followers of Christ are to be with him where he is;[1] they are to know him as the Father does;[2] they are to be "taught of God" even as the Son is;[3] the risen Christ calls them "brothers" and speaks of "my Father and yours".[4] Dodd writes: "The community of life between Father and Son is reproduced in them at every point."[5] "Beloved, now are we God's children—and it is not clear yet what we shall be! But we know that when he appears we shall be like him, for we shall see him as he is."[6] John could scarcely express a higher opinion of human possibilities.

Dodd has therefore contended that all this points to a doctrine of inclusiveness which, together with John's teaching upon the *anabasis* of the Son of Man, shows affinities with the Hellenistic ideas of an ascent of man in union with the heavenly Man from this earth-bound life to heaven. He would probably point out that the promise to Nathanael[7] is set in the future, and implies, not a future realization of Nathanael's own, but a future event, the cross in fact. By his death the Son of Man is to draw all men to himself,[8] to gather together into one the scattered children of God;[9] and the children become one thing as the Father and the Son are one thing. Dodd points out that "to be uplifted" probably means "to be exalted" and that this word is used in the New Testament for the Ascension of Christ. He connects John 3.13, "No man has gone up into heaven but he that came down from heaven, the Son of Man" with 3.14, "And as Moses lifted up the serpent in the wilderness even so must the Son of Man be lifted up", and writes: "The ascent of the Son of Man is here equated with his exaltation.

---

[1] John 14.3. [2] John 10.14f, 27. [3] John 6.45 ; 8.28.
[4] John 20.17. [5] *F.G.*, p. 195f. [6] 1 John 3.2.
[7] John 1.51. [8] John 12.32. [9] John 11.52.

John conceives the 'uplifting' of the Son of Man as making possible for men that union with him by which they too ascend to the Father."[1] He calls in the Image teaching as we have done but says that this makes "I, if I be lifted up, will draw all men to me"[2] imply the drawing up of men to Christ in his exaltation, which is his being "lifted up" on the cross. But this is also his ascension, so it is the ascension of men also.[3] This is how John relates the world below to the world above.

The argument is attractive, for the notion of the ascent of the soul is a perennial element in Christian spirituality.[4] But it breaks down under the evidence. As we have seen, John relates the two worlds in Christ by their unification, which the descent of the Son of Man effects, and not by an ascension from one to the other. Jesus himself is the Image, or rather, the Word that became flesh in him is the Image, and the Genesis Rabba passage which Dodd quotes in connection with the Jacob's ladder reference at John 1.51 points to the idea of the unification of the Image with the empirical man. John 3.13 "no one has gone up into heaven" is obviously to be taken with the preceding verse, "how will you believe if I tell you heavenly things?" and not with the following. The translation offered above, "No one has gone up, but one has come down, the Son of Man" is obviously the only satisfactory one; otherwise verse 13 must be regarded as a parenthetic comment on the Ascension, made by the evangelist, and therefore as unrelated to the context. But this is unnecessary. That the lifting-up and the Ascension are distinct is shown by the fact that, in keeping with the tradition represented by the synoptics, the Jesus of John appears only to the disciples. John 6.62, therefore, "What if you see the Son of Man ascending . . . ?", is addressed to the disciples. The previous verses, 60 and 61, expressly say as much. John then maintains a distinction between the "Jews" and the disciples at least in this respect, however much he may be inclined

---

[1] *F.G.*, p. 247.   [2] John 12.32.   [3] *F.G.*, p. 376.

[4] For a modern example, cf. H. P. Liddon (quoted E. Herman, *Creative Prayer*, p.14): "Prayer is the act of the whole man [*sic*], detaching himself from the embarrassments of sense and nature, and ascending to the true level of his destiny."

to put the same idiom into all mouths. But 8.28, "When you have lifted up the Son of Man, then you will know that I am he", is not addressed to the disciples. It is addressed to the "Jews", the Pharisees in fact, as verse 13 of the same chapter makes absolutely clear. It cannot therefore satisfactorily be referred to the Ascension, but to something different. Speaking more generally, if John "spiritualizes" the concept of the Ascension at all, it must be by suggesting that this ascension was complete in the whole event of the Word becoming flesh (in Odeberg's words, "the *katabasis* is *eo ipso* the *anabasis*"): in any other sense the implication is inescapable that Jesus in his lifetime ascended to another level of being, a divine level. This would virtually amount to adoptianism, of which there is no trace in John. In the New Testament in general it is not Man as such which ascended but Christ.[1] This is also the case with John who also maintains that Christ as Son of Man is eternal and descended.

"His incarnation is not a gradually ascending process, but a fall;[2] 'He who was rich yet for our sake became poor, that we through his poverty might be made rich.' Here is John's picture of the bread of life which came down from heaven." So wrote George Matheson in the days when evolution was in the air.[3] And apart from this particular theory Dodd would of course agree. In the final discourses, though there is much talk of "going" to the Father, the word for "going up" is carefully avoided. ἀναβαίνω πρὸς τὸν ἀποστείλαντά με is what we should expect John to put into Jesus' mouth; but in fact this is the farewell of the angel in Tobit 12.20. What the Johannine Christ says is ὑπάγω πρὸς τὸν πέμψαντά με.[4] We should almost imagine that the neutrality of the language was deliberate, if we did not remember that the whole question is irrelevant. The meaning of the Ascension in John is identical with that of the synoptics. Dodd obscures this to

---

[1] See J. Burnaby, *E.T.* Apr. 1959, p. 203—a review of J. G. Davies' *He Ascended into Heaven*.

[2] The word "fall" in the quotation from Matheson is his own; it is to be understood in the non-technical sense of "descent".

[3] The quotation is from a small book by George Matheson, *St John's Portrait of Christ*, pp. 44f.

[4] John 16.5; cf. 7.33; 13.36; 14.5; and ἀναβέβηκα in 20.17.

some extent because he is inclined to divorce the passion and resurrection narratives from the theology of the gospel[1] and so presumably the words: "I have not yet ascended to my Father";[2] though on his own showing the risen Lord, at the beginning of his talk with Thomas, is not yet "in the eternal world".[3]

It is in fact doubtful if the notion of a way to God is to be taken as more than a passing metaphor. Hort spent some time upon this and wrote:

> St Thomas in the question which he interposed had clung literally to the figure. The conditions of locality which the Lord used freely and discarded freely, as symbols of a truth which could be only symbolically conveyed, became to the disciple the entire reality. In his eyes the journey must be like one from land to land or, as we might say, from planet to planet. It was certain that neither he nor his fellow-disciples knew to what spot of space the Lord was going: how then, he asked, could he or they know the road, the way, by which he would have to travel? He detached the single phrase from all that led up to it and illustrated it. The words of encouragement which he had heard uttered in the same breath went for nothing. He had no ears for the faith that was to calm down the trembling of heart, or even for the promise of reunion.[4]

And again:

> To the unbelieving Jews he had spoken of his "going"; and once to the officers sent by the chief priest and Pharisees to catch him, that they might expel him from the world, he had said, "Yet a little while I am with you, and I go unto him that sent me." But this idea of a return home from a mission abroad is changed for another now when he is speaking peace to his own disciples. The character in which he speaks is not that of an envoy but of a Son; and the earth itself is no longer a distant or foreign shore, but lies within the heavenly precincts: the interval remains, but it is subordinated to a mightier comprehension. He calms the tumult of the disciples' hearts by pointing to the wide compass of his Father's house. In one of its "mansions", its abiding-places for the stages of the journey, he and they are reclining and speaking. His departure would be only to another abiding-place within the same vast house; or at least to what would be to them another abiding-place though the word should cease to be appropriate as applied to himself. He speaks not of another place to which he is going, but of going his way that he might prepare a place for them, that where he

---

[1] *F.G.*, pp. 426ff.   [2] John 20.17.

[3] *F.G.*, p. 443. See Dodd's note 2 to this page; what is urged above must not be taken as implying that the Ascension was a "movement in space"!

[4] *The Way, the Truth and the Life*, p. 15.

is they also may be. Thus in what he says of his own journey he keeps out of sight all distinct images of locality; and even when he refers to their journey to come, he at last resolves the place to be prepared for them into a simple sharing of his presence.[1]

Once more we reach the same position. The Hellenistic Man is essentially a messenger, an envoy; for the Son such a metaphor is partial, and like all half-truths misleading if pressed. The "going" is indeed in another sense the "coming".[2] Thus in John the salvation of men is not effected by their going up, though it is by their seeing the lifting-up of the Son of Man and their being "drawn" to him. The word "ascend" is never used of the disciples.[3] They are simply to be kept from evil.[4] The contrast with Hellenistic salvation is complete.

"What must I do to inherit eternal life?" asks the lawyer in the preamble to the Lucan parable of the Good Samaritan; and in Mark the rich man asks the same question.[5] It was the question of the age, asked by Jew and Greek alike. Jesus' answer is typical of the Jew, set in moral terms; but for both Jew and Greek it was the *quality* of the life which guaranteed its eternity: the devotee of the mysteries found his unity with the divine in the not-necessarily moral feelings evoked by his identification with the deity in ritual drama. But John practically makes the expression "eternal life" his own special property; and in his writings the idea for which all were groping stands out in all its clarity. Life is a theological conception, and like light and love could stand as a Johannine "definition" of God, defining God's relationships rather than his being. Thus the idea of love is moved from the periphery to the centre of the picture. In the Corpus Hermeticum, where light and life figure prominently as descriptions of the highest God, love has no place—at least not in the Christian sense. Jesus again gives a thoroughly Jewish contribution when he puts the highest duty in terms of love for God and one's neighbour. So in John the

---

[1] Ibid., pp. 13f. Dodd made the point in a review of the article on ὁδός in Kittel's *Wörterbuch* that for Hebrew thought the way is more important than the goal. *J.T.S.* new series *V*, 1954, p. 246.

[2] John 14.3. [3] John 3.13; 6.62; 20.17.

[4] John 17.15. [5] Luke 10.25; Mark 10.17.

presence of God is the presence of love: where love is, he is. This is practically identical with the statement that God is light, and that we must walk in the light; which, according to the writer of the First Epistle of John, is the summary of Jesus' message.[1] God, that is to say, is pure love, with nothing of the darkness of evil in it. The "dualism" of John is on this level, the darkness that the world lies in is the darkness of lovelessness, for to hate is to be blinded.[2] In this loving relationship morality has its place and its fulfilment: "If you love me, keep my commandments."[3]

This eternal life becomes actual in Jesus: he is himself Resurrection and Life,[4] the fulfilment of what man should be. In him is contact with life, for he lives because of the Father: he is the divine Word in whom is life.[5] To live with Christ is "to live 'eschatologically'— i.e., in the realm not of means but of ends, or as St Paul puts it 'in the heavenlies'".[6] Hence the factor of *Imitatio Christi*. This is easily misunderstood, and is often nowadays regarded with suspicion; but it is inseparable from the New Testament teaching. In the synoptics to "follow" or "go after"[7] Christ involves a break with past life[8] and a taking up of one's cross, the denying of self.[9] The call to follow is echoed in John, from 1.37 to 21.19. Paul wishes his converts to "imitate me as I Christ";[10] they have become "imitators" of the apostles and of the Lord.[11] The word "example" is used in 1 Pet. 2.21,[12] where we are to "follow his steps", and it occurs in the Fourth Gospel itself. After the feet-washing Jesus says, "You call me Master and Lord, and you say well, for so I am. If I then the Master and the Lord have washed your feet, you ought to wash one another's

---

[1] 1 John 1.5. [2] 1 John 2.9,11. [3] John 14.15.
[4] John 11.23–5. [5] John 6.57; 1.4.
[6] Raven, *Science and Religion*, i, p.33, n 2.
[7] Aramaic for "follow".
[8] Mark 1.18; 10.28.
[9] Mark 8.34; Matt. 10.33; Mark 14.68.
[10] 1 Cor. 11.1.
[11] 1 Thess. 1.6.
[12] The Syr version uses "blessing" for "grace". Have we here an explanation of the various renderings, "grace", "reward", "to excess" in the Lucan and Matthaean versions of the Sermon? Cf. my note on "Reward" in Matt. 5.46 (*E.T.*, Apr. 1956, p. 219).

feet."[1] Perhaps we have here a hint of why John connects eternal life and the giving of it with Jesus as Son of Man. The old idea of Jesus as an ideal for humanity has often been branded, in the last fifty years, as a modernization, a reflection of the humanistic ideal.[2] The notion however has been revived in a more realistic form by T. W. Manson, who held that "the Son of Man" for Jesus was a corporate idea which Jesus expected the disciples as the Remnant, the new Israel, to fulfil in their own persons. When this expectation failed and all forsook him, he fulfilled the rôle on his own. Whatever may be thought of this "corporate" idea, Mowinckel has recently insisted that the idea of an "ideal" man, which "at first sight seems to be a modern, European idea", "when rightly understood is seen to be connected with the thought of the ancient east".[3] The term "the Righteous One", he goes on, "denotes first and foremost the most essential quality of man, when he is what he ought to be: the 'right' man, the ideally pious and moral person".[4] As we have seen, the Johannine Christ, like the Christ of the synoptics, reflects the character of the Righteous One of Wisd. 2: he is actually called "the Righteous One" in the First Epistle. Now the Righteous One is characterized by his suffering, and when we examine the places in the New Testament where Jesus is held up as an "example" to be "imitated", it is this factor which seems to be in question. Thus in 1 Peter, "hereunto were you called: because Christ also suffered for you, leaving you an example, that you should follow his steps . . .". The feet-washing in John is an obvious acted parable of the death of Christ. The disciples are thus taken up into the supreme moment of the divine action. And in Eph. 5.1f we are to be "imitators of God, as beloved children, and walk in love, even as Christ also loved you and gave himself up for us, an offering and a sacrifice to God". Our relation to God is to be that of the only Son. The relation between Father and Son is expressed in fully personal

---

[1] John 13.14.

[2] E.g. Baldensperger, *Das Selbstbewusstein Jesu in Licht der messianischen Hoffnungen seiner Zeit*, pp. 178f.

[3] *He That Cometh*, p. 384.

[4] Ibid., pp. 383f; cf. Pedersen, *Israel*, i–ii, pp. 336ff.

terms. The Father loves the Son because he lays down his life,[1] and the cross displays the love of the Son for the Father.[2] He lays down his life on the principle enunciated also in the synoptics, that "the one who has lost his life will find it", and, laying down his life, he takes it again, glorified as the seed is glorified which, after it falls into the earth, is no more solitary but fruitful.[3] This was the principle grasped by the Church at Pentecost in opening its membership even to the Lord's murderers: the personal lives by growth, dies by restriction into "safety". The children become one thing with the Father as the Father and the Son are one thing, for the glory given to them is the glory which the Father gave the Son, that which he had before the world was.[4] Christ is thus the "Way" because he is also the "Truth". In the life, death, and resurrection of Jesus Christ "the Christian sees . . . the way God is for ever going in his world".[5] He is the Way in the sense that he is the whole background against which action must be performed, the atmosphere in which life must be lived. He is the "Life" when men come to him, see him, believe in him, live by him as he lives by the Father. It is characteristic of Christianity that it should thus see the "Way" not as a set of rules to be followed or even as a way of life to be followed (as in the Old Testament) but *as a person*. The One who began with the disciples as *Maran*, "our Master" (or simply "sir" since *Mar* cannot stand without a personal suffix) is seen to be the heavenly Lord; the personal relation with him as teacher, rabbi, becomes the pattern of relationship to the ultimate, the "Way", in fact, for the universe itself.

Such, according to John, is the stature and dignity of man. As things are, it is possible for a man to be a child of the devil,[6] for unity with God is a matter of will and love and mutual knowledge. Hence the need for rebirth, to be "born of God".[7] There must be an inner change; our worship must be "in spirit and

---

[1] John 10.17. The notion in Poimandres that ὄντως γὰρ καὶ ὁ θεὸς ἠράσθη τῆς ἰδίας μορφῆς is poles apart. (C.H. 1.12).

[2] John 14.31.   [3] John 12.28.   [4] John 10.30; 17.22,5.

[5] E. L. Allen, *Studies in Christian Social Commitment*, p. 46.

[6] John 8.44.   [7] John 1.13; 3.3,7.

truth"; his worship must be the spirit of our life. The use of the
word "children" not "sons" for the disciples emphasizes their
distinctness from the only Son, who is "perfect among the sons of
men". Such a conception of salvation by believing, knowing,
loving, excludes that of salvation by absorption, and the notion of
an "inclusive" Son of Man must be read into the Fourth Gospel
before it can be found there. There is only one true Man, who as
such is Son of God; other men are drawn into the status of children by love for him. The method is as in the Odes of Solomon:
"Because I love him who is the Son I shall become a son."[1] This
explains why some have seen a resemblance to the paradoxical
Stoic belief in a divine element in all men and the possibility of
its realization only by choice.[2] Thus the Christian's relation
through Christ to God illumines the relation of the Son to the
Father. It has been said that the dictum "God is love" tells us
more about love than about God, and so the use of human analogies for the relation of Christ to God has resulted, historically, in
an enrichment of human relationships. But, on the other hand,
John's language suggests that he proceeded in the opposite direction and interpreted Jesus' unity with the Father in the light of
that fellowship with God into which Jesus had initiated the
believers. Christ the Way for his followers is the Way he himself
took. Thus the whole meaning of the gospel is contained and
summed up in each episode because each is an encounter with
him, the significance of which can be expressed in a series of "I
am" clauses: I am Messiah, I am bread, I am light, I am the good
shepherd, I am resurrection and life, I am the way, the truth, and
the life, I am Son of God, I am he, before Abraham was, I am.[3]
Christ is thus no mere mediator, no go-between; his relation to
God is what he comes to enable in men. "The Father himself
loves you"; "you will be taught by God" even as the Son is.[4]
Christ stands aside that the Holy Spirit may come to initiate the
believers into the fullness of their inheritance, which is Christ

[1] Or, "In order that I may love . . ."; Odes Sol. 3.7.
[2] For this see Knox, *Church of the Gentiles*, p. 224; Dodd, *F.G.*, p. 42.
[3] John 4.26; 6.35; 9.5; 10.11; 11.25; 14.6; 10.36; 8.58; 18.5,8.
[4] John 6.45; 8.28.

himself. This is the language of direct communion. "If a man keeps my commandments, my Father will love him, and we shall come to him and make our home with him."[1] Thus the developed doctrine of the Trinity is foreshadowed: all are equally concerned in the work of salvation; all make contact (even) with the individual soul.

[1] John 14.23.

CHAPTER 10

THE SON OF GOD

In the Fourth Gospel the Son of Man alone is spoken of as descending and ascending; only at 20.17 may it be inferred that the Son of God is being spoken of as ascending, and he never descends. Descent is the prior idea in any case, and ascent is spoken of in connection with it and as complementary to it. The Son of Man is the being of divine origin who descends in order that he may become an earthly figure. That the conception of descent is not applied to the Son of God can only mean that the spatial metaphor is not applicable to him: his sonship is

> to him, all one
> If on the earth or in the sun.[1]

The descent adds something to the divine humanity which it does not add to the divine sonship as such. The personal Word who is Man by his descent becomes an earthly human being; his relationship to the Father and to men is therefore changed. The Son of God, on the other hand, does not change.

Even on the earthly level the analogy of sonship, of family relationships, is perennial, outgrowing the analogies drawn with ephemeral forms of government and philosophy. In the New Testament our Lord's teaching is particularly rich in the exploitation of the conception of the Father and his children, and he evidently stressed it because of all relationships this alone is indissoluble. The Prodigal remains a son despite his wanderings and what he has done, and even despite what he believes he deserves. When the son in the parable says, "I am no more worthy to be called your *son*", his father brushes it aside, gives him all the honour of a son, and describes him to the Elder Son as "your brother". But the very universality of the conception leads to its

---

[1] Browning, *The Boy and the Angel.*

149

appearance everywhere in mythologies of all sorts. Babylonian, Egyptian, and Greek religion abounds in gods who are sons of other gods. In the semi-philosophical systems which grew up in John's day the various subordinate creators and powers are called "sons" of the supreme deity. In Poimandres the supreme God is Nous, life and light, and his three sons are Logos, Demiourgos, and Anthropos. The Logos, on the analogy of discriminating Reason, separates the elements; the Demiurge makes living beings other than man; the Man is the incorporeal aspect of man personified, who produces empirical man by union with nature. Dodd explains the analogy by taking the Logos to be the offspring of Nous in the same sense as Reason in man is the offspring of his mind.[1] Popular religion is, however, seldom philosophical, and in Hellenistic times masterful "men of destiny" were often regarded as in some sense divine. This is true of such various characters as Julius Caesar and Apollonius of Tyana. Hermes Trismegistos himself was sometimes thought of as having once been a man. Of another Plutarch wrote: "When Cleomenes was impaled the report of a portent at the time of his death gave rise to the popular rumour that he was a hero and child of the gods."[2] This is near enough to the crucifixion story to give pause. Egyptian influence doubtless had much to do with the trend of deifying kings. Alexander's attitude to kingship was profoundly altered by his encounter in 332 B.C. with the Egyptian priests who hailed him as a child of God. To the more discerning, however, it was apparent that character had a lot to do with the matter, and so for Epictetus the wise man is a son of God.[3] This is nearer to the developed Jewish manner.

The analogy of sonship has been pressed into service in ways which are not so familiar to us as these, and especially in regions where the language spoken was Semitic. We can still understand the expression which makes a man "son" of his city-state or country,[4] as our semi-poetic terms "fatherland" and "mother-

---

[1] *F.G.*, p. 39.
[2] Plutarch, *Cleomenes* 39.823c. See Philostratus, *Life of Apollonius* 5.24.10.
[3] Ep. I, 9.6.
[4] Moulton-Milligan, *Voc. of the Gk Test,*, p. 649.

land" show. In the Bible the inhabitants of Jerusalem are "sons of
Zion". But Semitic idiom goes much further. We should not
naturally call easterners "sons of the East".[1] It takes a certain
effort of mind to realize that the familiar "son of man" simply
means "a man". In Aramaic the phrase is one of a series of stereotyped expressions which have almost become compound nouns.[2]
In Galilean Aramaic the following occur: "son of a day (year)"
for one day (year) old; "son of the house" for servant; "son of
slavery" for slave; "son of freedom"[3] for freeman. Syriac produces ecclesiastical coinages also: "sons of the Church" are
clergy; "son of nature" means consubstantial; a "son of the
(religious) life" is a monk.[4] The Old Testament is full of similar
idioms. A "son of the house" is a slave here also;[5] a "son of
death" is a condemned person;[6] "sons of Belial (= wickedness)"
are wicked men;[7] "sons of the captivity" are exiles;[8] "the sons of
the prophets" are their organized disciples. "Sons" of Bashan are
rams from there;[9] "sons of the quiver" are arrows;[10] a "son of
oil" is a source of oil, apparently an olive tree.[11] A branch is called
a "son": "Look down from heaven and behold and visit this vine,
and the stock which thy right hand planted, and the *son* that thou
madest strong for thyself."[12] "Sons of God" are rulers or angels.[13]
This latter usage recalls the demiurges of Hellenistic pseudophilosophy, and may indeed have contributed to the notion. The
"sons of God" who shouted for joy at the creation in Job 38.7
occupy much the same place, though they do not fulfil the same
function.[14] So again the "sons of God" who took wives of the
daughters of men and begot heroes, after the fashion of the
Olympian gods who fathered Hercules and his like upon human
women, and who played such a part in later apocalyptic writings,

[1] Gen. 29.1.
[2] Stevenson, *Grammar of Palestinian Jewish Aramaic*, p. 24.
[3] Odeberg, *Short Gram. of Galilean Aramaic*, § 348 and p. 174.
[4] See Payne-Smith, *Compendious Syr. Dict.*, pp. 53f.
[5] Gen. 15.3.   [6] 1 Sam. 20.31.   [7] Judges 19.22.
[8] Ezra 4.1.   [9] Deut. 32.14.   [10] Lam. 3.13.
[11] Isa. 5.1; Zech. 4.4.   [12] Ps. 80.15.   [13] Ps. 82.6; Dan. 3.25.
[14] The angels who assisted at the creation are combined with the demiurges in
some Gnostic systems.

have their counterpart in the Gnostic systems.[1] One special use
of the term "son of God" is important. Israelites are sons of God,[2]
or sons and daughters of God,[3] or are called collectively "the son
of God": "Israel is my son, my first-born."[4] The Wisdom literature carries on the usage: "Upon the destruction of the firstborn
they confessed the People to be God's son."[5] The question
whether or not the Messiah was called Son of God does not press
upon us here, but the theocratic king is son of God: "I shall be
his father and he will be my son",[6] and 4 Ezra (unless the passage
is a Christian interpolation) speaks of the Messiah thus: "My son
will be revealed with those that are with him, and will remain four
hundred years."[7] In the gospels the high Priest identifies "the
Christ" with "the Son of the Blessed",[8] Peter identifies him with
"the Son of the living God",[9] and Nathanael hails Jesus as "Son
of God, King of Israel".[10] Moreover, and this is important for our
purpose, the gospel writers show that they know the meaning of
the Semitic analogy of sonship; thus we read of "son of light",[11]
"the son of peace",[12] and "the son of perdition".[13] This last is
from the Fourth Gospel and shows that John was acquainted
with the idiom. It will appear presently that it influenced his whole
thought about the sonship of Jesus.

The phrase "son of God", then, in Jewish usage, signifies a
being which in some sense shares God's nature, whether it be an
angel or a righteous man; or else some being for which God has
special concern, either the nation or an individual: and the two
senses of course may coalesce. The idea of a loving relationship is

---

[1] The legend occurs in Philo and the D.S.S.
[2] Deut. 14.1f.   [3] Deut. 32.19.   [4] Ex. 4.22.
[5] Wisd. 18.13; cf. 16.26.   [6] 2 Sam. 7.14.
[7] 4 Ezra 7.28. "Jesus" is omitted as an obvious Christian gloss.
[8] Mark 14.61.   [9] Matt. 16.16.   [10] John 1.49.
[11] Luke 16.8; John 12.36; also 1 Thess. 5.5; cf. Eph. 5.8, "children of light".
"Sons of light" occurs often in Mandaism for celestial beings and in the D.S.S.
for the enlightened.
[12] Luke 10.6.
[13] John 17.12; cf. 1. Sam. 20.31, בֶּן־מָוֶת, worthy of death. D.S.D. 9.16,22;
D.S.C. (Zadokite Doc.) 8.12, "sons of the pit" is not a clear parallel. The identical
phrase of John is used for the uncircumcised in Jub. 15.26 and at Jub. 10.3 for
those who perished in the Flood, the "sons of destruction".

present, as the following passage from the Pirqe Aboth shows: "Beloved is man, for he was created in the image of God; but greater was the love in that it was made known to him that he was created in the image of God, as it is said, For in the image of God made he man.[1] Beloved are Israel, for they were called sons of God; but greater was the love in that it was made known to them that they were called sons of God, as it is said, You are children of the Lord your God."[2] But the loving relation may be absent and then the two senses are separate. This produced controversy. In the commentary on the words quoted in the Aboth passage above, "You are the children of the Lord your God", the Talmud states the conflicting opinions of two rabbis. One says that Israelites are only children of God when they conduct themselves as children should. The other rabbi says that Israelites are children of God even when wayward and sinful: the Father's love is even to the undeserving. For does not the Scripture speak of "sottish children"[3] and "children in whom is no faith".[4] This is the distinction which we have designated "ethical" and "ontological": the former being represented in the New Testament by "Love your enemies and you will be sons of God"[5] and the latter by the parable of the Prodigal Son. The first attitude is represented in the psalm where Israel is identified with "such as are of a pure heart" and in the Testament of Levi: "The most High has heard your prayer, to separate you from iniquity, and that you should become to him a son, and a servant, and a minister of his presence."[6] This is the view that John makes his own. "We know that God hears not sinners."[7] As the First Epistle puts it: "In this is made clear the children of God and the children of the devil: everyone who does not do righteousness is not of God, nor is the one who does not love his brother."[8] There is only one Son of God; even his own

---

[1] Aboth 3.15(18); Gen. 9.6.   [2] Deut. 14.1.
[3] Jer. 4.22.   [4] Deut. 32.20; b Kid 36a.
[5] "Your Father in heaven" (Matt.) and "the most High" (Luke) leave no possibility of choosing between them since both expressions are favourites with the respective evangelists.
[6] T. Levi 4.2.   [7] John 9.31.
[8] 1 John 3.10. Cf. 4.15, "Whoever confesses that Jesus is the Son of God, God abideth in him, and he in God."

are only "children" not sons, because he alone is the Righteous
One.[1] Although men are presumably related to the Son of Man
through his manhood they are not automatically even children of
God; they may become children of the devil.[2]

This unique sonship of Jesus is expressed in the Fourth Gospel
in the first place in terms of dependence and knowledge. Jesus is
not independent of God, as he would be if he set up as a second
god. To the "Jews" who accuse him of making himself "equal
with God" in this sense[3] he answers, "The Son can do nothing
of himself, but (he does) what he sees the Father doing."[4] Elsewhere "My Father", he says, "is greater than I am."[5] This recalls
the subjection of the Son to the Father in the Pauline apocalypse,[6]
an idea which Cullmann regards as the key to all New Testament
Christology. To the doctrine of equality used by Paul and the
author of Poimandres[7]—his acquaintance with which is proved
by the "Jews" accusation—John prefers the ideas of unity and
mutual indwelling. Jesus and the Father are "one thing" because
the Father is in him and he is in the Father. This is partly a matter
of action, as we shall soon see, but it is expressed first of all and
essentially as mutual "knowledge". This sort of knowledge is far
from the gnosis with which it has been confused. The noun does
not appear, and the verb stresses the idea of personal intercourse.
This is specially Hebrew. "The ox knows his owner, and the ass
his master's crib", says Isaiah;[8] the Johannine Christ says, "I am
the good shepherd, and know my own and am known of mine."
Sexual union in the Bible is called "knowing".[9] The insight
surely is that this too in its essential meaning is personal.[10] The
Qumran texts afford additional evidence that in later Judaism
"knowing" had the non-intellectual meaning we find in the

---

[1] 1 John 2.1.   [2] John 8.44.   [3] John 5.18.
[4] John 5.19.   [5] John 14.28.   [6] 1 Cor. 15.28.
[7] Phil. 2.6; C.H. 1.12.   [8] Isa. 1.3.
[9] Gen. 4.1, 17 of the man; 19.8 of the woman.
[10] We find a modern writer on *The Psychology of Sex* saying "love is essentially
an act of cognition" (Schwartz, p. 20; this writer is influenced by Berdyaev). It is
the anonymity of prostitution that gives it its peculiar distastefulness and barren-
ness. G. Quell, dealing with love in the O.T., says that it is "rooted in the sex
life" (Art. in Kittel; *E.T.* by J. R. Coates, p. 3). Of course even the Greek
ἀγάπη is not always free from sexual implications: see L & S sub v., and cf. M.M.

Bible. "Knowledge" has to be variously translated as "mind", "interest", "obedience", "attention".[1] From the Fourth Gospel the psalmist's dictum "In Jewry is God known"[2] cannot be expunged: Salvation comes from the Jews. Knowing, loving, believing, go together in John. To know God is eternal life,[3] as is walking in the light and love which are God. Even when "believing" is intellectual ("that you may believe that . . ."), E. F. Scott was surely right to admit that "the act of belief to which the evangelist attaches a paramount value is the summing-up in an intellectual judgement of a previous religious experience. Assent is demanded not merely to a bare fact, but to the claim of a person, and it therefore partakes in some measure of the character of trust". This "knowledge" of the disciple can, *mutatis mutandis*, be transferred to the Master. As his disciples are to enter the New Covenant of Jeremiah 31 and be taught of God,[4] so the Son also is taught: "I do nothing of myself, but as the Father has taught me, I speak these things."[5]

That John was not the first to apply these categories to Jesus is shown by the existence of the synoptic saying, "No one knows the Son except the Father, nor does any one know the Father except the Son, and he to whom he wills to reveal him." Dalman said: "When Jesus testifies that all things are delivered unto him by 'his Father' and adds that only 'the Son' and 'the Father' are mutually known to each other, the statement can be understood as a reference to a real relationship which exists universally as between a father and a son, and thus finds also an application as between Jesus and his Father."[6] Such a generalization is, however, entirely inadequate. It is not the relationship of *any* son to *any* father which is in question; if it were, it would scarcely merit special utterance. Nor is it really apposite to find here, with Bultmann, Hellenistic influence where the notion of mutual knowledge appears. In the last resort no sharp distinction can be drawn between Jew and Greek in the matter; even the "knowing" of

---

[1] Cf. the articles referred to above: Davies in *H.T.R.* and Bo Reike in *N.T.S.*
[2] Ps. 76.1.   [3] John 17.3.
[4] John 6.45; the ref. is to Isa. 54.13, but cf. Jer. 31.33f.
[5] John 8.28.   [6] *Words*, pp. 193f.

Philo and the Corpus Hermeticum is not entirely intellectual.[1] And in any case, "I love them that love me"[2] is a Wisdom principle, and the "No one knows the Father" saying is in a chapter which shows Wisdom influence, at least in Matthew, where the "comfortable words" which follow seem to be a paraphrase of Sir. 51.23ff. John needed to go no further than the Righteous One of Wisd. 2.12ff to find a type of his own Righteous One: they both claim to have God for their Father and to have knowledge of God. But it is unrealistic to find the matter as well as the form of the Johannine doctrine in such sources. J. E. Davey, in his criticism of Dodd's treatment of the dependence of Christ in the Fourth Gospel, said that "by his denial in the main of a mystical element in the Johannine picture of Christ, this dependence remains for him largely an external matter of doctrine".[3] The chief reason for this impression is, however, that in the course of exposition the fact of Christ's own life with God is laid aside— more, or less, according to the individual writer's aim at the moment or his general predilection. In the last resort the writers of the gospels were drawing upon such insight as they had into the actual relation of Jesus to his Father, and no lesser assumption will hold water.

The metaphor of sonship in the Fourth Gospel thus shows itself first of all in the personal relationship of Jesus with his Father. This is the inner significance of the mutual indwelling of Father and Son. But it is also a matter of action, as Aquinas asserted of the presence of God. The Son does the works. In this sense Cullmann's dictum that the Son is God "insofar as God reveals himself in his saving acts"[4] applies to the Fourth Gospel. The second aspect of the metaphor of sonship, to which attention has already been directed, was that it emphasizes the likeness of son to father. To this John attaches great importance. He lays down what he expects from children: they will resemble their father. And they will not merely resemble him. In our expressive

---

[1] Dodd, *F.G.*, p. 27, etc., and 65.
[2] Prov. 8.17.
[3] *The Listener*, i, no. 1289.
[4] *Die Christologie des N.Ts*, p. 300.

idiom, they will "take after" him, have the same ways, will their father's will, and if children of God will love the Son.[1] That is to say, sonship involves the sharing of character, and this is stressed in respect of the "children" in the First Epistle.[2] The Son of God, therefore, "takes after" his Father, shares his character. On this idea turns some of the deepest teaching of the Fourth Gospel, which is also some of the most misunderstood. This concerns the "signs" which is the Johannine word for Jesus' miracles, and the "works" which include the signs but are also more than these. Anderson Scott was expressing a common opinion when he wrote that the "works" are the "exercise of divine authority with little recognition of their function as a reflection of character".[3] It is astonishing that such views have so long held the field. A casual comparison with the way in which the word "works" is used in the Book of Revelation (where it occurs some score of times) suffices to show the difference in John. In the Fourth Gospel the works are closely associated with the manifestation of the character of God. John in fact stresses that like produces like and that only the good produces the good, so that good works reveal God.[4] The signs are there "that you may believe that Jesus is the Son of God",[5] yet searching for signs of the wrong sort is deprecated as vigorously in the Fourth Gospel as in the synoptics. The crowd is rebuked because it seeks Jesus not because of the true meaning of the signs but because its members ate the loaves—a touch reminiscent of the synoptic Temptation story[6]—while later their call for a sign is ignored.[7] The courtier is brusquely accused of being one of those who will not believe until they see "signs and wonders";[8] and the episode with Jesus' brothers suggests that the "works" in John are not evidences to be publicized at all—by thinking that they were the brothers showed that they "did not

[1] John 8.39ff.
[2] 1 John 2.29; 3.2,6,9; 4.7; 5.1,18.
[3] *Living Issues in the N.T.*, p. 99.
[4] John 3.2; 9.16; 14.10.
[5] John 20.30f; cf. 2.11.
[6] Which is the epitome of the synoptic teaching on signs.
[7] John 6.26,30; for the Temptation, Matt. 4.3f.
[8] John 4.48.

believe in him".[1] The works make a simple appeal to moral insight: "Many good works have I shown you from my Father; for which of these do you stone me?"[2] The works of God are made manifest in the healing of a blind man.[3] Is it not a greater thing to make a man's body every whit whole on the sabbath than to perform the sacred rite of circumcision, which is after all a mutilation?[4] This appeal to moral judgement runs throughout. If God were their Father, they would love the Son.[5] Those who believe not have not the word, the love, of God in them.[6] Those who will God's will know where the teaching is from;[7] the "Jews" only fail to recognize Jesus because they do not know God when they see him.[8] Some of them do see and say, "God listens to the man who does his will; how can a man that is a sinner do such signs?"[9] "Can a devil open the eyes of the blind? These are not the sayings of a devil."[10] In "Q" the Son of Man is a sign to his generation as Jonah was to his.[11] John takes his stand on the same principle as that used by Jesus, "Go and tell John what you have seen and heard . . . and happy is he who finds no stumbling-block in me".[12] It is also the principle enunciated by Wisdom: "Surely all men are vain by nature who are ignorant of God and could not know the One Who Is from the good things that are seen: neither by considering the works did they acknowledge the craftsman."[13] Jesus and the Father are one thing on the basis of the identity of works.[14] Quick wrote, "It is clear that the deepest purpose of Christ's mighty works themselves is to be

---

[1] John 7.1–5. Perhaps it is relevant at this point that Jesus makes light of Nathanael's wonder at his clairvoyance and points instead to a different sort of sign in the future: the vision of heaven and earth united in the Son of Man.

[2] John 10.32.   [3] John 9.3.   [4] John 7.23.

[5] John 8.42.   [6] John 5.38,42; cf. 47.   [7] John 7.16f; cf. 9.31.

[8] John 7.28f.   [9] John 9.31; 9.16.   [10] John 10.21.

[11] It is ironical that, whereas the central point of the Book of Jonah is the recognition by the most unlikely people (the Ninevites) of the truth of Jonah's preaching, the book itself has come down to posterity as the classic example in the popular mind of wonder-working and miracle-mongering.

[12] Luke 7.22.

[13] Wisd. 13.1; cf. D.S.D. 4.2 where the language shows traces of the Wisdom passage.

[14] John 10.30,37f.

signs, i.e., to have the value of words, revealing his relation to God."[1] And, as we should expect from this, the words are confused with the works: "The words which I say to you, I speak not from myself; but the Father dwelling in me does his works."[2] So, since there is nothing that the Son does "of himself",[3] he can make the claim, "I said, 'I am Son of God': and if I do not do my Father's works, do not believe me; but if I do, and you do not believe me, believe the works, that you may come to know and be convinced that the Father is in me and I am in the Father."[4] This believing in the works is not a second-best faith, but a stage on the way. It is God who does all good, and the beginning is to recognize good when you see it. In the synoptics the unforgivable sin is that of attributing the good works of the unorthodox to Beelzebub;[5] John also records that Jesus was charged with being possessed.[6] "There is only one who is good"[7] might be taken as his watchword. This stress on God's character is essential to true religion, for how a man thinks of God determines all the rest, as Father Kelly said;[8] and as C. E. Raven put it, "the Johannine theology is in fact the finest and most satisfying attempt ever made to express the *kerygma* in terms of the character of God revealed by it".[9] The earliest proclamation of the *kerygma* included the simple statement that Jesus "went about doing good", and W. L. Knox protested against the idea that the first Christian converts could have long been satisfied with the "bare facts" of his life and death.[10] This was in fact the first impetus towards the composition of gospels, and the motive is explicit in John.

The basis of all this is the conviction that Jesus came in his Father's Name, that is, not of his own accord but to seek the glory that comes from the only One.[11] This glory is connected with the works. To glorify the Name of God is a Semitism which suggests

---

[1] *Doctrines of the Creed*, p. 110.
[2] John 14.10; cf. 8.28. [3] John 8.28; 5.19,30.
[4] John 10.36ff; for the translation, see Bernard, in loc.
[5] Mark 3.22. [6] John 8.48f. [7] Mark 10.18.
[8] Quoted W. Robinson, *Whither Theology?*, p. 42.
[9] *Gospel and Church*, p. 52.
[10] *Sources of the Synoptic Gospels*, i: *St Mark*, p. 5.
[11] John 5.19,30,43,44.

revealing the glory of God's character as much as making his reputation glorious. God's name is his dignity, his presence, his manifested character, himself as known.[1] So Jesus says in John, "Father, glorify *thy name*.... I have glorified *thee* on the earth ... glorify me *with thine own self*.... I have *manifested thy name*."[2] Jesus in fact almost *is* the divine Name. The glorification "means the establishment of God's *heavenly glory* on earth in the Shekinah (= Jesus ...). The complete unification of the *kabod* and Shekinah will be demonstrated to all in the Passion of Jesus and his lifting-up in the experience of the believers."[3] Those who love him and keep his commandments will see his manifestation, because it is all on the level of insight into the character of God. When the "other" Judas asks, "Lord what has happened that thou wilt manifest thyself to us and not to the world", Jesus answers, "If a man *loves* me, he will keep my word, and my Father will love him, and we shall come to him and make our home with him."[4] This is the answer to the problem of the Parousia as well as of the Resurrection. Jesus reverses the pagan notion of a future revelation of a *different kind*:[5] as Nels Ferré says, God cannot have "more" glory in the sense that his glory is now limited. He "has and wants no glory except the glory of his own love", and that glory "is in the fact that he has so made us that we are free to stand over against him and withhold such understanding and praise".[6] Hence when Judas goes out and it is dark, Jesus says, "Now is the Son of Man glorified, and God is glorified in him."[7] "Why", asks Dodd, "does John, with his prevailing interest in the heavenly glory of Christ, keep out of the Resurrection narratives all such obvious suggestions of divine majesty as we find in Matthew, and

[1] Ex. 23.31; Deut. 12.5 and 11; 1 Kings 8.29; etc., and see above, pp. 38f.

[2] John 12.28; 17.4ff.

[3] Odeberg, *F.G.*, pp. 334f; this quotation does not, however, imply full agreement with Odeberg's interpretation of the lifting-up.

[4] John 14.22f; cf. Wisd. 1.2.

[5] Cf. McIntyre, *Christian Doctrine of History*, p. 83: "It cannot be repeated too frequently that the Christ who shall appear at the Parousia is that same Christ who has already sojourned among men. ... The First Coming of Christ into the world was as much the judgement of the world as the Second."

[6] *The Christian Understanding of God*, p. 112.

[7] John 13.31.

emphasize the element of human feeling?"[1] Not (as Dodd suggests) because the cross has as it were exhausted the glory and nothing is left but a resumption of relations with the disciples, but because this is where we should expect the glory, though, John implies, it would not really be the glory which comes "from the only God". Throughout the earthly life, where only the humanity is evident to the outward eye, the glory must be brought out by constant iteration; but the glory of the Resurrection is the revelation of the true meaning of the wounded side and nail-pierced hands.[2] Throughout the Fourth Gospel, "the idea of a divine glory that shines and dazzles is kept in the background": the evangelist "wishes to direct his reader's attention to a far deeper meaning underlying the divine glory. In other words, the incarnation is not a concealment but an unveiling of the divine glory, though in the appearance and figure of Christ no bright light shone around him."[3] This is an idea which has found wide recognition; thus Quick: "St John's gospel conveys the impression that in his inmost being the Son of God, though truly incarnate, and truly suffering and dying, had yet in a sense never left the Father's side. The repeated and solemn use of the present tense by Jesus when speaking of his own essential life and being cannot be accidental."[4] The sense in which it is true is that the Father and the Son always shared the same character, the same glory.

Here then is the Johannine doctrine of the divine sonship. Abraham's children do Abraham's works.[5] "Whoever is begotten of God does no sin."[6] The devil's children do *their* father's

---

[1] *F.G.*, p. 441.

[2] John 20.27. But note the possibility of μὴ πτόου at v. 17 for μὴ ἅπτου, a restoration for which Bernard (pp. 670f) makes out a good case.

[3] Rigg, *F.G. and Its Meaning for Today*, p. 52. For a modern parallel see W. James, *Varieties of Religious Experience*, p. 210. I quote part: ". . . as I was walking in a thick grove, unspeakable glory seemed to open to the apprehension of my soul. I do not mean any external brightness, nor any imagination of a body of light, but it was a new inward apprehension or view that I had of God . . ." The Shekinah too from being a cloud of glory comes simply to stand for God's presence.

[4] Op. cit., p. 110.

[5] John 8.39.   [6] 1 John 3.9.

works.[1] The devil is the father of the lie; Jesus, on the other hand, speaks the truth,[2] and not only so but "does the truth". Divine sonship is almost defined as sinlessness: "Everyone who commits sin is the slave of sin. The slave does not live for ever in the house, but the son does."[3] The argument as it stands is somewhat confused, for the slaves of sin are apparently also and at the same time slaves in the household of God. The Son does not abide for ever in the household of sin! But the drift is clear: "Which of you convicts me of sin?"[4] Thus "we beheld his glory, the glory as of the only Son of the Father, full of grace and truth".[5] Paradoxically, this is why the Son stands for judgement. The Father has left all judgement to the Son because he is Son of Man.[6] Man was formed to judge in uprightness of soul.[7] The Messiah was to judge not after the sight of his eyes or the hearing of his ears but righteously.[8] The idea is of an impartial order of truth set up in which judgement comes to light. In the same way neither Son nor Father judge in the accepted sense.[9] But the Son testifies against the world that its works are evil because of what he is, the eternal life and light in human terms,[10] and those who do not believe in his name, that is, recognize his character, are judged already.[11] They choose darkness because their works are evil; they have rejected the eternal life that is in him. Jesus does not judge superficially but bears witness to the light, to himself;[12] his judgement is primarily upon his own mission. But this is what creates division among men.[13] Thus the judgement really is God's, because Jesus judges by the witness of his works, which are the works of God.[14]

We may thus see how near and how far from the Chalcedonian

---

[1] John 8.40 and 44; cf. 1 John 3.8.

[2] John 8.44ff; and 40f.

[3] John 8.34f. D omits "of sin" with b Syr sin and Cl.

[4] John 8.46.

[5] John 1.14. We are obliged to translate thus: again no general relation of *any* father to *any* son is intended. Contra, Moulton, *Proleg.*, pp. 82f.

[6] John 5.22 and 27. [7] Wisd. 9.2f.

[8] Isa. 11.3f; cf. John 7.24, "Judge not according to appearances, but judge righteous judgement".

[9] John 8.15. [10] John 7.7; 1.9; 9.5.

[11] John 3.18. [12] John 8.18. [13] John 7.43; 9.39.

[14] John 5.36. So that even God obeys the injunction "Judge not"!

theology is the Fourth Gospel. Jesus is Man as God intended him; he lives the life God intended and as such is Son of God: because he thus lives, signs appear which reveal his glory, his relation to God. The Son then is son in the only true sense—the sense in which John uses the word "true":[1] he shares his Father's character. This is no more than to say that he is true Son of Man. As we have seen, the idea of the manhood of the Son of Man was not absent from the earlier tradition, even in its apocalyptic form. It may also be that there is some significance in the fact that Luke traces the genealogy of Jesus back to Adam "the son of God"[2] and it was to a man that, according to the synoptic account, God said, "You are my only Son; in you I have found satisfaction". This is the level at which John's story begins: the "Son" (or "chosen one") is he who baptizes in holy spirit—here still neuter.[3] When Nathanael acclaims him Son of God in the sense of "king of Israel",[4] Jesus, as at the Confession of Peter in Mark, sets this aside in favour of "the Son of Man". According to the preferred text, Jesus asks the man born blind, "Do you believe in the *Son of Man?*", not, as the Received Text has it, the Son of God.[5] But, along with the others, John has seen more than mere manhood in Jesus. "In the last resort", wrote S. L. Frank, "faith is the *encounter of the human heart with God,* God's manifestation to it."[6] John has met God in the Son of Man: he has seen the glory of the only Son, and recognizes it as the glory he must have had before the world was.[7] It was something seen in Jesus himself and his life with God which implied not only the subordination inherent in sonship ("My Father is greater than I") but also a wider background than this life could provide. This is a great deal more than *Ich war, sprach der Poet, bei dir.* The Son is not merely

---

[1] See above, p. 129.

[2] Luke 3.38. In the Greek the sonship of Adam to God is on the same level as the rest of the genealogy, but the Syr changes: "son of Adam, who was of God". Here later reflection is seen "correcting".

[3] John 1.32ff.   [4] John 1.49.

[5] John 9.35–7. "Son of Man" B D W syr sin and now P⁶⁶. The alteration to "Son of God" can easily be explained, but not the other way round.

[6] *God With Us,* p. 20 and see ff.

[7] John 1.14; 17.5.

the most righteous of men, the "perfect among the sons of men",[1]
temporarily possessed by the divine Spirit. The eternity of the Son
of Man, i.e., the personality of the Word, implies an eternal relationship of Son to Father. None of John's doctrines are mutually
exclusive. Indeed, the very analogy of personal relationships used
implies the permanence of that relationship. Here the generalized
argument, out of place with the "Agalliasis utterance", is permis-
sible.[2] As Temple Gairdner put it, "even on earth a man does
not become—is not—a father until his son is in being".[3] On the
saying, "Abraham rejoiced to see my day",[4] Westcott, Burney,
Billerbeck, and Odeberg all quoted the reference to Abraham's
visions of coming events,[5] with its accompanying formula,
"When he saw . . . he rejoiced." In John Moses and Isaiah are
represented as having similar prevision.[6] Burney assumed that
"my day" is thus "the Day of the Son of Man".[7] But as Odeberg
objected, the "Jews" take it as a claim that Jesus and Abraham
have met, and this must have been in the "timeless" world.[8] In a
widely-read novel Kagawa made his Christ say, forseeing his
Resurrection, "Can you find the end of that which has no beginning?"[9] John, looking back, remembers his saying, "Before

[1] Wisd. 9.6.

[2] Matt. 11.27 and parallel.

[3] Quoted P. Hartill, *The Unity of God*, pp. 49f.

[4] John 8.56f.

[5] Abraham was supposed to have seen future events in the vision mentioned in
Gen. 15.8ff. See Westcott, op. cit., on John 8.56; Burney, *Ar. Or.*, p. 111 n;
Billerbeck, ii, pp. 525f; Odeberg, *F.G.*, p. 306. In the T. Abraham mentioned
above in connection with the same chapter (ch. 8) p. 94 above, Abraham ascends
to heaven; throughout this tract there is a season, an "hour" for things, as in
John. Some authorities at John 8.57 have "has Abraham seen thee?" Mrs Lewis
included the first hand of Vaticanus, and connected the passage with the experience on Mount Moriah (*Light on the Four Gospels*, pp. 154f) which may have
influenced John's "only-begotten" (see above, pp. 46f).

[6] John 5.46; 12.41.

[7] Op. cit., 11 n (on p. 112).

[8] *F.G.*, p. 307. Mowinckel (op. cit., p. 371) is apparently referring to John 8.58
when he says, "Thus, as early as the time of Enoch (long before Abraham, as
Jesus said) the Son of Man was." But there is more of the Abraham legend than
the Enochic in the *F.G.* As we have seen, Box thought that by this time the former
had ousted the latter.

[9] *The Two Kingdoms*, p. 114.

Abraham was, I am." The only Son, like the Father, is the One Who Is,[1] and so the word "Father" is usually substituted for "God" in his relation to Jesus because here there is no distinction between God and not-God.

[1] So in Wisd. 7.22, as has been pointed out, the μονογενές Wisdom is the "craftsman" as God is at 13.1 where he is also the One Who Is.

CHAPTER 11

THE FACT OF JESUS OF NAZARETH

In previous chapters the interpretative element in the Fourth Gospel has been fully recognized, and the assumption has been freely made that substance as well as form owes something to the evangelist. We have however constantly come up against the fact that John is concerned basically with something far more unyielding than the exigencies of theological speculation. John is in fact concerned to emphasize with all the power at his disposal that he is speaking of a man who actually lived and of events which actually took place. "What we have seen and heard declare we unto you", as the First Epistle puts it. The problem raised by this has been one of the thorniest in New Testament scholarship, and its urgency has never been more fully recognized than in recent years. Thus Hoskyns wrote of the Fourth Gospel, "The place of life and judgement, the place where the final eschatological decision is made, is no transcendental, mystical, supernatural activity of the Son or Word of God. The place of decision is the flesh of Jesus, his audible words and his visible death,[1] in fact, the historical event of his mission."[2] The "historicity" of the narrative is essential to the theology of the gospel. What has percolated through to the popular writer as the critical orthodoxy of a generation ago, that "It is less Christ the Man than Christ the theological figure that interests the fourth evangelist",[3] represents a false distinction. The Man *is* the theological figure for John; he stresses the manhood, not in any abstract sense, but in relation to one who actually lived. His name was Jesus of Nazareth the son of Joseph, and men wondered how he could in fact have

[1] John 12.31ff; 19.30.
[2] *F.G.*, p. 300.
[3] Bertrand Russell, *A History of Western Philosophy*, p. 346.

"come down from heaven".[1] His brothers figure naturally in the story.[2] He felt tiredness and thirst and could do nothing of himself.[3] He was a Jew, was called "a prophet" and "rabbi" and "Messiah".[4] And all this was necessary of course as part of John's anti-gnostic polemic, apart from its inclusion by way of ordinary reminiscence. If the stories John recounts about Jesus were myths, either made up by himself or taken over from others, it would have undermined his whole attack. The notion that he would in fact oppose docetism by exteriorizing his own religious experience or that of his circle argues a credulity which is frankly incredible. In view of his strong theological interests, the very gospel-form which he gives to his work argues for his "historical" leaning. For him Jesus is the Word, the visible presence of God, the Shekinah and Glory, the Bearer of the Name, the Image. He is the sinless Son of God, the embodiment of God's character and doer of the works. A theophany like that in Poimandres would have served the purpose of a peg upon which to hang theological truths. Yet John prefers the form of the gospel, because what he has to say, like the whole Christian proclamation, must be told in the form of a tale about what happened, about a man who actually was, and was like *this*.

The same point emerges from the briefest of comparisons with Philo, with whom John shows many similarities in language. If John followed Philo in his use of symbolism, if, that is to say, he allegorized as Philo allegorizes the Old Testament, this in itself would show that he was dealing with existent material, since Philo did not invent the stories he so treated. But in fact John does not use allegory in the way Philo does. When the latter tells of the Migration of Abraham, the "land" Abraham leaves means the body, his "kinsfolk" the senses, and his "father's house" is speech. There is nothing of this kind in John. For John, if there is a deep symbolism to be discerned in the events, the events mean something in themselves. If the healing of the blind man provokes the reflection that Jesus enlightens the spiritually blind, it is still

---

[1] John 6.42.   [2] John 7.1–5.   [3] John 4.6f; 19.26; 5.19.
[4] See the quotations from Dodd on pp. 7of above, and the whole discussion on the Messiah in ch. 5.

true that Jesus did both heal the blind and enlighten the spiritually blind. If the death on the cross is the symbol of the love of God, so it is for all Christendom, and so in fact Jesus did love men. And the method of symbolic interpretation is in any case applied in a curiously half-hearted manner; full interpretations are only given after the Feeding of the Five Thousand, the Healing of the Blind Man, and the Raising of Lazarus. The other incidents are more or less left to take care of themselves.

Possible criteria for distinguishing the factual from the interpretative element are, however, disappointing. It might be thought, for instance, that if John were a Jew writing for Greeks we could skim off the Greek element and leave a residue of fact. But the whole foregoing study has been based on the assumption that John was not an intellectual amphibian of this sort but one who moved in circles where Greek and Jewish elements were inextricably blended. The belief is in fact gaining ground that the rabbis themselves were less free from Greek influences than was formerly supposed. Even to abstract those features which are recognizably Johannine might do more than is intended, for a comparison of the "Q" sayings in Matthew and Luke do not always speak for the originality of those with the highest Palestinian flavouring. Again, the notion that the vivid impression of reality conveyed by some of the Johannine accounts attests their authenticity breaks down under the pressure of fact: John describes in this manner scenes at which no observer was present, the conversations with the woman at the well of Sychar and with Pilate in the judgement hall. If the alternative here is to regard John as "one of the most consummate realists in fiction" then it must be accepted, though it is to be observed that the word "fiction" begs the question. There are, however, features in the Johannine account which at least seem to stand on a different footing. Some of these harmonize readily enough with what appears to have been the situation in which Jesus lived and worked. Scholars dealing with the various episodes have often pointed to details which are best explained on the basis of apparently contemporary customs. An instance from the writings of David Daube will explain what is meant. W. Bauer was unable to discover the significance of the detail in the story of the Samaritan woman that she "left her waterpot".[1] Daube points out that the pot was left for Jesus to drink out of, and that this was a far more serious thing than mere contact with "an Am-Haaretz, a Jew careless about the rules of cleanness".[2] This may of course mean nothing more than that John was a Jew writing for Jews who would not need to be told; but the fact that he does not explain may also be because the story springs from an early tradition where no explanation was necessary. There are other features of this sort, as when the demand of the crowd for a sign greater than that of Moses seems to reflect current messianic expectations[3] and the saying of Jesus at 7.37 seems to require the setting of the water-ceremony in the Feast of Tabernacles. The same applies, and with more force, to the various topographic details which would be irrelevant and unintelligible in Ephesus or Alexandria or wherever the gospel was written. Dodd writes: "All attempts that have been made to extract a profound symbolical meaning out of the names of Sychar, the city of Ephraim, Bethany beyond Jordan, Aenon by Salim, of Cana and Tiberius, or again, of Kedron, Bethesda (or Bethzatha), and Gabbatha, are hopelessly fanciful; and there is no reason to suppose that a fictitious topography would in any way assist the appeal of the gospel to an Ephesian public."[4] For all we know the same significance attached to many other things which John leaves to chance, such as the six waterpots of stone at Cana, the information that Judas kept the box, the number of fishes in the resurrection story, or Nathanael's fig-tree— apparently so significant yet unexplained.[5] Certainly the symbolic interpreters have been no more fortunate with these. Again, the term Son of Man early fell into desuetude and its meaning was

---

[1] *Das Johannes evangelium*, 2 ed., pp. 68f.

[2] *The N.T. and Rab. Jud.*, p. 374.

[3] See Bernard, p. 194, and quotation from Lightfoot, *Biblical Essays*, p. 152.

[4] *F.G.*, pp. 451f; see his notes there on Siloam *et al.* J. Jeremias has written in *E.T.* for May 1960 on the identification of Beth Esda in the Copper Scroll from Qumran. Cf. also for the evidence of recent archaeology A. M. Hunter in *E.T.*, March 1960, p. 165.

[5] John 1.48,50. Cf. however the theory of A. Guilding, *The F.G. and Jewish Worship*, that John based his "facts" on details from the current lections in the Jewish triennial cycle.

apparently forgotten even by Semites.[1] Yet John shows that he knew the underlying Aramaic. Paul also assumes the etymology of his ἄνθρωπος, but he admittedly belongs to an early tradition. These examples are varied and somewhat incongruous but they are sufficient to show the drift of a piecemeal argument for a factual element in John.

Other information is introduced unobtrusively into the narrative which it seems possible either to check from outside sources or to regard as historical in a quite strict sense. Thus the date of Christ's ministry appears in the story of the Cleansing of the Temple. The "Jews" say that it has been in process of building for forty-six years. Josephus[2] says that it was begun in the eighteenth year of Herod the Great, which was 20/19 B.C.;[3] so Jesus would be, as Luke avers, about thirty when he began to teach.[4] And this although John elsewhere makes the "Jews" say vaguely, "Thou art not yet fifty years old." Again, John is either more aware of, or less inhibited against writing about, the political factors which conditioned Jesus' ministry. He stresses the messianic question as a political issue, and agrees with the synoptists when they represent Jesus as preferring the title "Son of Man" to that of "Messiah".[5] It is here that details of a strictly historical character begin to creep in. John is as certain as the synoptists that the course of events is controlled by God; the Prince of this World also takes a hand, as do the powers of darkness in Luke.[6] But for John it is clearly the political charge which ensures Jesus' death; the taunt to Pilate about not being Caesar's friend was just the thing to influence the man from what we know of his character; Caiaphas' counsel, "the Romans will come and take away our place and nation", fits the historical situation; the political significance of Jesus' withdrawal after the feeding of the five thousand men is in startling contrast to the mystical interpretation of the miracle which occurs immediately after. In these respects John has

---

[1] See above, p. 108. [2] Ant. XI, xi, 1.
[3] See, e.g. Oesterley and Robinson, *A History of Israel*, ii, p. 376.
[4] John 2.19f; Luke 3.23. [5] John 1.49,51.
[6] Luke 22.53. For recent work on the history in John and his relation to the synoptists see A. M. Hunter in *E.T.*, April 1960, p. 219.

access to a tradition which is more intelligible to the modern mind than those represented by the synoptics. Other features of a non-political but similar nature appear, as for example, the explanation of the sudden decision of the first disciples to follow the Lord by the account of a previous meeting by the Jordan.[1] They are isolated instances, however, of little value from the point of view from which the gospel was written, and we have not lingered over them because they do not concern the Christology. But they do serve to show why it is that belief has never died out that John was dealing with fact.

It nevertheless remains that the only other records which we have to compare with the Fourth Gospel are the synoptics and we must go on to show how the comparison works. Here it must be said at once that a great deal depends on whether John was or was not acquainted with the synoptics or the tradition which underlies them. That he was is no longer the dogmatic assumption it once was[2] though it is difficult, without more knowledge than we possess of how the traditions circulated, to say whether John could have been entirely isolated from such traditions. The Fourth Gospel then, has the same general form as the synoptics: a long account of the Passion preceded by stories of the ministry. Dodd gives a rough parallel table of the earlier parts showing how they can be made to correspond.[3] There are sayings in the Fourth Gospel which appear to be variant forms of sayings known from the synoptics[4] "and at other times to have been moulded upon patterns of which the synoptics also have examples. These are all the more significant when we find a run of such sayings, having some similarity to the sequences of sayings in the synoptics

---

[1] G. Matheson suggested that a Judean ministry preceded the Galilean, and explained the suddenness of Christ's bursting on the scene in the synoptics by this previous work and recognition: "He has begun by what he considers small wonders—recognitions of character by clairvoyance; but he declares these to be only preliminary to the vision of an open heaven, and of a communion between heaven and earth." (*St John's Portrait of Christ*, p. 11.) One is reminded of the beginning of Samuel's work. This is typical of what could be done in the way of harmonization of the gospel accounts.

[2] Dodd, *F.G.*, p. 449. [3] Ibid., p. 448.

[4] Howard gives a list, *F.G.*, App. F.

which some would regard as representing a very early stage in the transmission of the sayings of Jesus (prior to comparatively voluminous collections of sayings such as the hypothetical 'Q'). Such sequences, for example, seem to occur in John 4.32–8; 12.24–6; 13.13–20."[1] Not only sayings but the same issues appear. To take a few at random: it is not enough merely to be Abraham's children;[2] Jesus refutes criticisms of his healing on the sabbath on the ground that they are mere legalistic quibbles;[3] the "signs" are nearer to the synoptic mighty works than is sometimes recognized,[4] and they are likewise accompanied by a refusal to work wonders in true synoptic fashion.[5] The Jesus of John is also the teaching Christ of the first three gospels: his words are of vital importance.[6] If in John the person of Jesus is central not only in a theological sense, so it is in Mark. "And he went out of the house and did not wish anyone to know, but he could not escape notice."[7] It is plain that in this sense throughout the gospels "a city set on a hill" could be a Christological dictum; if the disciples for Matthew are the "light of the world", John is justified in claiming the same for their Master. In Mark "all men seek thee": in John the burning question is, Will he come up for the feast? The Pharisees said among themselves, "Behold how you prevail nothing; the whole world is gone after him".[8] The fourth evangelist brings out with great force the effect of Jesus' personality on his contemporaries. As in Mark, so here, some think him possessed, but the crowd says, "These are not the sayings of one possessed",[9] and the police sent to arrest him return with the simple excuse, "No man ever spoke like this."[10]

On some essential points of doctrine which have seemed

---

[1] Dodd, *F.G.*, pp. 451f.

[2] John 8.37; Luke 3.8.

[3] John 7.24 and prec. vv.; cf. Mark 7.10–13, and Burkitt, *Gosp. Hist. and its Transmission*, p. 241.

[4] See above, pp. 157f. For those who have reverted to the view that the synoptic miracles are not expressions of Christ's compassion but proofs of divinity the position is entirely reversed.

[5] John 4.48; 6.30.

[6] John 5.38; 8.37; 8.31; 12.48; 14.24; 15.3; 17.14.

[7] Mark 7.24.   [8] John 12.19.

[9] John 10.21.   [10] John 7.36.

characteristic of him John appears on the contrary to share a tradition which goes back beyond the earlier strata of the synoptists. It is of the essence of the Gospel that it appeals to faith: "Repent and believe in the Gospel." It is in full accord with this that Jesus refuses to perform "signs" of the kind required by the Pharisees. In the Temptation story he sums up the position in the words of Deuteronomy: "Thou shalt not tempt the Lord thy God." But that he did not refuse signs of a different order is clear from his reply to John the Baptist: "Go and tell John what things you hear and see . . . and happy is he who is not offended by anything in me." The Pharisees ought to be able to read the signs of the times as they read the signs of the sky. The pure in heart see God. The devil cannot be divided against himself. If the Pharisaic doctors do not heal by Satanic means (and how could they?) then "If I by finger of God cast out demons, the rule of God has come upon you." The Son of Man himself is to be a sign as Jonah was, in that the truth of his mission should be apparent to all.[1] John, as we have seen, follows a strictly similar line. For him the works or signs of Jesus reveal the character of God and therefore the unity of the Son and the Father. But the principle is of wider application. Men are judged by their recognition of the true signs, their acceptance of the Son of Man. This strain of teaching about judgement is progressively overlaid in the gospels as we have them. Thus, "Everyone who acknowledges me before men, the Son of Man will acknowledge him before the angels of God" (or before my Father in heaven),[2] becomes "Whoever is ashamed of me and mine (or, my words) in this adulterous and sinful generation, the Son of Man will be ashamed of him when he comes in the glory of his Father with the holy angels".[3] In Matthew the conventional words from Proverbs are added: "He will render to every man according to his deeds." Elsewhere, however, the drift is clear enough: the judger is judged, the unforgiving unforgiven, the foolish shut out, the unloving brother shuts himself out. So also in John. Those who love the darkness turn from the light, and this is the judgement. This is given as the symbolic explanation of the saying, "He who does not believe is condemned already,

[1] Luke 11.32.   [2] Luke 12.8; Matt. 10.32.   [3] Mark 8.38.

because he has not believed in the Name of the only Son of God".[1] Judgement in John, as in the synoptics, is by refusing the signs, and the chief sign is the Son of Man himself.

The question of John's contact with an early strain of eschatology is somewhat similar. The characteristic of Christianity in this regard appears in the teaching of Paul of the New Age which has begun already, of the Epistle to the Hebrews that we have tasted the powers of the Age to come, of the synoptics that "the kingdom of God has come upon you"; and this despite the fact that we still live in this evil Age and even await the coming of the kingdom of God in some sense. So in the First Epistle of John "the world lies under the evil one" and in the Fourth Gospel the "Prince of this world" is abroad, and "the hour is coming when all who are in the tombs will hear his [the Son of Man's] voice, and come forth: those who have done good to the resurrection of life, and those who have done evil to the resurrection of judgement".[2] Yet life eternal is available here and now: "Look at the fields: they are white already for harvesting, and sower and reaper rejoice together."[3] The repetition of the phrase "the hour is coming and now is" expresses such insight into the nature of the whole problem that it may well go back to Jesus himself. There is a strain of eschatology in Luke 17 and elsewhere which is very like this, in which the whole world does not die with the Redeemer but the decisive centrality of the Son of Man and his coming is emphasized as like that of Noah and Lot, who did something and the ends of the world were upon men. In John too there is no static timeless situation: here too the course of events moves towards an hour,[4] a time,[5] which must come— a "time" which is as much within history as beyond it because the Son of Man is present in the flesh.

At times also, the common elements seem to show that John is in contact with more primitive reminiscence. A comparatively trivial instance is that of the "cup" which appears to have occu-

---

[1] John 3.18. [2] John 5.28f. [3] John 4.35f.
[4] John 2.4,23; 5.25,28; 7.30; 8.20; 12.23,27; 13.1; 16.2,4,21,25,32; 17.1.
[5] John 7.6,8; cf. John 8.28, "When you have lifted up the Son of Man, then you will know that I am he", etc.

pied Jesus' thoughts in his last days. It is difficult nowadays wholeheartedly to accept the view that John was juggling with Marcan texts, altering their position and import to suit his own ends; yet the cup which appears at the Last Supper as the symbol of Jesus' death, is mentioned to James and John ("Are you able to drink the cup I shall drink?"), and causes Christ to shrink in the Garden of Gethsemane, occurs later in John: "Shall I not drink the cup my Father is offering me?" Again, it is clear that Jesus prophesied the downfall of the Temple.[1] In the synoptics several symbols are associated with this. The parable of the fig-tree in Luke concerns the people of God, the Jewish community. Here it is getting a second chance. In Mark it is cursed. Faith as a grain of mustard-seed will remove this fig-tree. And in another form the saying concerns the fig-tree[2] or else the mountain, which is "the mountain of the Lord's house".[3] The parable of the Mustard Seed refers directly to Nebuchadrezzar's kingdom which overshadows the fowls of the air, here the Gentiles or outcasts of Israel. That Jesus intended to replace Judaism is so obscure in the synoptics that some have been able to maintain that he had no such intention, that he did not intend to found a Church. Yet it would seem from the above sayings that the kingdom of God is to replace Judaism.[4] So John says: "Neither here nor at Jerusalem will you worship the Father." But further: the account of the cursing of the fig-tree in Mark is bisected by that of the Cleansing of the Temple, and it is here that John inserts the saying, "Destroy this Temple, and in three days I will raise it up." In Mark this is made into a charge of witchcraft against Jesus at his trial[5] and it is thought that John is trying to obviate this by his interpretation: "He spoke of the Temple of his body." But Jesus' mind appears to

---

[1] Mark 13.2; Matt. 24.2; Luke 21.6.

[2] Luke 13.6ff; Mark 11.12–14, 20–5; Luke 17.6 (Sycamine = mulberry-tree = fig-tree; the Aramaic words did service for all).

[3] Isa. 2.2 = Mic. 4.1; Matt. 17.20.

[4] Cf. Luke 23.26–32, "If they do this when the tree is green, what will happen when it is dry?" and Matt. 21.43, "The kingdom of God will be taken away from you and given to a nation producing the fruits of it". Note the unusual form "kingdom of *God*" in Matt.

[5] See below on the significance of this, pp. 183f.

have run on the thought of "three days". That the threefold prophecy of resurrection in Mark "on the third day" is not a *vaticinium ex eventu* appears from the more obscure forms the idea takes, for example in Luke 13.31ff where Jesus says, "Tell that fox, I cast out demons and do healings to-day and to-morrow, and the third day my life is completed",[1] and Luke 17.22ff where the "days of the Son of Man" and "his Day" are likened to those of Noah and Lot, and in each case "days" are followed by "a Day".[2] The point is not that the three days everywhere mean the same thing, but that the image was present to Jesus' mind in a way that was unclear to the earliest recorders of his sayings. John's interpretation of the saying about the three days in the Temple foretells the replacement of the Temple by something else, cryptically called his Body. This probably means the Church, if it does not refer to something more abstract,[3] but there is no reason why it should not refer also to the resurrection, in John's characteristic style. But this is the connection which seems to exist in the various "days" sayings in the synoptics, and it appears to go back to Jesus: the destruction of the holy Place, the resurrection, and the replacement of the material Temple with one "not made with hands".

Other cases of links with an earlier tradition are somewhat different. One such is the interpretation of the Feeding of the Multitude. As Daube points out, the miracle in Mark is also "treated as a parable, and though there are important disagreements with John, four similarities at least are worth observing. In the first place, no mention whatever is made of eating and being filled. The miracle consists in the remains alone—no matter precisely what significance may be attached to them in these passages. In the second place, it is definitely only bread which remains. The fish is entirely suppressed. In the third place, it is the disciples who

---

[1] The next sentence reads, "Nevertheless I must go my way to-day and to-morrow and the next day". As Black points out (*Ar. Ap.*, p. 152), the Peshitta gives, "I must *work* today and tomorrow, and the next day pass on (i.e., die)".

[2] See Glasson, *The Second Advent*, p. 85.

[3] Bernard, in loc., quoted Justin (*Trypho* 86) and the Epistle of Barnabas to prove that the Lord's earthly body was not intended. It seems doubtful whether the Church was intended either in the latter place; the words refer to "our habitation within us" which is "a spiritual Temple built for the Lord". (Ep. Barn. 16.7ff).

are supposed to have taken up the fragments, not the people at large. And in the fourth place, the remains are thought of as a σημεῖον, a visible sign. This we may infer both from the position of the episode, which directly follows a demand by the Pharisees of concrete evidence, of a σημεῖον,[1] and from the fact that the disciples themselves are represented as "of little faith".[2]

The contradictions and contrasts between John and the synoptics must not be minimized. At times we may be glad of the corrective which the synoptics administer. The limited concern exhibited by the Good Shepherd as distinct from the synoptic shepherd is a case in point. The fact that the Johannine idiom by its very existence prevents contact with the actual words of Jesus, and so with the man as he was, is a matter for regret—and on John's own premises. It remains that most of the episodes in John are different altogether from those in the synoptics; Nicodemus, Nathanael, and Lazarus are new figures who appear nowhere else; teaching about the Holy Spirit is almost wholly different. The conception of the kingdom of God in John is of a realm above; in the synoptics it is the rule of God in heaven or on earth. Not that the discrepancies are all insuperable. John the Baptist is minimized in the Fourth Gospel in a way which suggests later controversy and contrasts with the praise Jesus lavishes on him in Matt. 11.7–11. Yet verse 12 cannot be ignored: the least inside the kingdom of God is in fact greater than the prophet outside. The problem of reconciling the supposed chronologies does not now excite the interest it once did, since it is seen that exact chronology is quite irrelevant to the purpose of the gospels. It has long been recognized that the visits to Jerusalem which were once supposed to disturb the "Marcan scheme" can be fitted into such "scheme" as there is; and it has often been pointed out that, though Mark explicitly[3] mentions only one visit, he implies that Jesus knew the district and had made arrangements about the colt and the last

---

[1] Matt. 16.1ff; Mark 8.11ff.   [2] *N.T. and Rab. Jud.*, p. 46.

[3] T. W. Manson placed Mark's Cleansing of the Temple at the Feast of Tabernacles (*Bul. of Jn Rylands Lib.*, xxxiii, 2); it is remarkable that on Carrington's calendrical hypothesis his placing happens to agree. Burkitt long ago connected the cry "Hosanna" with the Aramaic word for the palm-branch used in the feast of tabernacles.

supper.[1] Luke as well as John supplies the information that he had
friends at Bethany,[2] and he and Matthew quote him as saying to
Jerusalem, "*How often* would I have gathered thy children
together as a hen gathers her chickens."[3] That the Ascension took
place on the day of resurrection could be inferred from Luke as
well as from John, though the former is our only authority (in his
second work) for placing it forty days later.[4] The apparent contradiction over Jesus' home-country in John 4.43f seems to be due to
a simple misunderstanding on the part of critics.[5] The difference
between the synoptic parables and the Johannine "allegories"[6] is
not in the same class since it concerns the whole question of the
different idiom of the Fourth Gospel, but it is worth noting that
Hoskyns and R. H. Lightfoot have pointed out that there is
affinity of purpose. In the synoptics "the whole visible panorama
of nature and the whole visible business of human behaviour bur-
geons with a mighty secret yearning to be made known: and in
his parables Jesus does manifest this secret or *mystery*, thereby con-
ferring upon the smallest and most insignificant occurrences the
supreme dignity of the revelation of God". So also in the Johannine interpretation of the Feeding of the Five Thousand, "the
essential meaning of eating and drinking is examined, and at once
the hope of food that will satisfy eternally instead of merely satisfying for a day becomes the issue . . . is now seen to point to Jesus
as the ultimate answer to men's hunger . . .".[7] In fact, "the way
in which, in the first three gospels, the Lord explains the nature of
the kingdom of God by teaching that it is like this or that, should
be compared with the way in which, in St John's gospel, he com-

---

[1] Mark 11.1ff; 14.13ff.   [2] Luke 10.38ff.

[3] Luke 13.34; Matt. 23.37. E. Stauffer, *Jesus and His Story*, uses the Johannine
chronology and fits the synoptic material into it.

[4] Acts 1.3. Paul stretched the period to include the "appearance" on the
Damascus road. See, for the forty days, Moule, *E.T.*, lxviii, no. 7.

[5] Hoskyns confidently affirmed that John 4.43f showed that the evangelist
thought Jesus belonged to Judea. But see R. H. Lightfoot, *F.G.*, pp. 26ff and esp.
pp. 44f.

[6] It is a mistake to say that there are no true parables in the F.G.: the remarks
in 11.9–10, about walking in the light and the dark, are a true similitude into
which the interpretation does not creep.

[7] Davey, intro. to Hoskyns' *F.G.*, p. 59, and Hoskyns in loc.

pares himself to some aspect of the natural world, such as bread or light or a vine".[1]

On this question of John's departure from the synoptists, the episodes which seem to have caused most trouble to the modern mind are the raising of Lazarus and the turning of the water into wine. This is not simply a question of John versus the synoptists, but also of the nature of the miracles themselves. Our scientific generation gives immediate publicity to anything that appears to run counter to the "laws of nature", but it must be remembered that in the world of those days tales of marvels and omens, rivers running blood and stones gushing out water were of everyday occurrence. The histories of Herodotus and Bede stand on a better footing now than formerly, despite their wonders. The "tremendous miracle" of the raising of a dead man would not be such a sensation to a first-century writer as to necessitate its inclusion by Mark; Luke's widow of Nain and her son are tucked away into a corner. The significance attached to the incident may of course be mistaken;[2] there is room for mistakes. Yet on the other hand the circulation of such a story would explain the enthusiasm of the Triumphal Entry,[3] which the synoptics give nothing to account for[4] (assuming that there were previous visits to Jerusalem). It may even give point to the question on the resurrection in Mark[5] as well as to the hostility of the hierarchy (as opposed to the Pharisees); for there is no evidence that the Temple trade was connected with the priests.[6] The view, once popular, that the Johannine

[1] R. H. Lightfoot, p. 45.

[2] See Dunkerley, *N.T.S.*, v, no. 4, p. 326, who points out that John's account may presuppose a considerable interval between the raising of Lazarus and the development of the final crisis, and suggests that this may separate the two things in significance also.

[3] The difficulty is already overcome for those who see in this only a token ceremony staged by the Galileans.

[4] Bernard, p. clxxxii.

[5] Mark 12.18ff. T. W. Manson, *Servant-Messiah*, p. 83, says only that the question was "doubtless meant to explode his pretensions to be a teacher in Israel". See Raven, *Jesus and the Gospel of Love*, p. 211.

[6] Manson, *Servant-Messiah*, p. 82. But see Stauffer, *Jesus and His Story*, pp. 61f. The hierarchy of course disbelieved in the resurrection of the dead. Dunkerley, in the article referred to above, argues that the parable of Lazarus is based on the incident lying behind the Johannine account of the Raising of Lazarus.

miracle story grew out of the Lucan parable of Dives and Lazarus has little to be said in its favour. The same is true of the contention that the Turning of the Water into Wine is an elaboration of the parable of the new wine and skins.[1] The latter is, however, an even greater difficulty to moderns, for whom it seems pointless to use such powers to save a couple from embarrassment, and the sort of wonder-working that does not accord with God's ethical nature. Once again, however, it cannot be assumed that a first-century writer would share our point of view and reject the tale as it originally came from the servants in the way we should.[2]

Generally speaking, these stubborn factors which make the Fourth Gospel more than mere romance have never been absent from the minds of exegetes. The difference in recent years has been that their whole setting has changed in such a way as to emphasize their importance and therefore the "historicity" of John. The nineteenth-century scholars rightly saw that the Johannine account formed a unity bound together by interlocking themes, themselves integral to a deeply reflective theology and distinctive idiom[3] which made it difficult to isolate separate incidents. On the other hand it appeared that a historical basis could be abstracted from the synoptics. The synoptic miracles in particular lent themselves more to "rationalization" and those which did not could be ignored. But the position is now seen to be more complicated. The dictum "We must not ask whether John's record is *true*, but what it *means*" was after all a confession of failure; the suggestion sometimes offered that John wished his work so to be approached is quite without foundation. Moreover, it has been increasingly seen that the synoptics are more theological than was once supposed. The Marcan introduction, "The beginning of the Gospel of Jesus Christ" leaves little doubt about

---

[1] Mark 2.22.

[2] Though of course the attempts to "explain" it have been singularly unconvincing, e.g., that the guests were drunk (μεθυσθῶσιν, John 2.10) and did not know the difference between wine and water, so that Jesus could ironically serve them with the latter; or that his discourse was so sparkling that it intoxicated all present.

[3] C. K. Barrett in conversation likened this to the music of Bach with its suspensions and unresolved chromaticisms.

what is to follow. R. H. Lightfoot put it startlingly: "Theologically he (John) would seem to stand nearest to St Mark, for in the first as well as in the last of the gospels the Lord's Person is of vital significance."[1] This only does injustice to Matthew and Luke. The themes which John shares with Paul appear: Jesus is the Son of God, the crucified Servant who dies for the sins of men; the risen Saviour; the way to life is through death. That these themes reappear in John—a writer whose whole idiom is different—itself argues for the essential authenticity of his material. Again, few are now disposed to engage in the business of showing how the miracles could have been dressed-up versions of events attributable to purely natural causes. In the first place they are part and parcel of the Gospel proclamation, signs of the kingdom of God. In the second place the issue is not whether they are marvels but whether the act of God can be discerned in them. Schweitzer had carried his *Quest of the Historical Jesus* to its logical conclusion. Jesus was not the End, but only a messenger of the End; when he tried to be more the wheel of history turned and crushed him. Dodd coined the term "realized eschatology" to express his conviction that Schweitzer's "thorough-going eschatology" was not "thorough-going" enough. So far so good: what "realized eschatology" implied for Christ was a step in the right direction. But still the Christological question was shelved: the kingdom still occupied the place reserved in the gospels for the Christ. John forces the question on our attention. Dodd once more, referring to an admonition of A. J. Carlyle, has delivered himself of the following opinion: "I believe that the course which was taken by *Leben-Jesu-Forschung* ('The Quest of the Historical Jesus', according to the English title of the most important record of that 'Quest'), during the nineteenth century proves that a severe concentration on the synoptic record, to the exclusion of the Johannine contribution, leads to an impoverished, a one-sided, and finally an incredible view of the facts—I mean, of the *facts*, as part of history."[2]

[1] Op. cit., p. 42.
[2] Op. cit., p. 446. On Bultmann's reduction of historicity and Christology see P. Althaus, *The So-called Kerygma and the Historical Jesus*.

The problem of historicity in John cannot in fact be divorced from the whole problem of history in the gospels. And it is here that a new approach is most evident. Historians are now less confident of their ability to separate "brute fact" from interpretation: indeed, the interpretation is part of the facts to be analysed. As far back as 1916 T. R. Glover in his famous *Jesus of History* quoted E. A. Freeman to the effect that even a false anecdote may be good history.[1] In the middle of the nineteenth century Westcott wrote, "What is called pure 'objective' history is a mere phantom. . . . The subjectivity of history is consequently a mere question of degree. . . . The truthfulness of the historian as a narrator lies therefore in his power of selecting those details so as to convey to others the true idea of the fact which he has himself formed. . . ."[2] He instances the Old Testament prophetic historian whose "aim is to reveal this life to others through the phenomena which the life alone makes truly intelligible to him".[3] This writer's prophecy, "There is undoubtedly at present a strong feeling in favour of realistic, external, history; but it may reasonably be questioned whether this fashion of opinion will be permanent...", has now been fulfilled in some quarters with a vengeance. Not, however, that it has all been gain. The older critics, as Dodd pointed out,[4] excised those elements in the synoptics themselves which seemed to them reminiscent of the Fourth Gospel; the newer, finding them to be integral ingredients of the synoptic tradition, fear that, as the credit of John increases, that of the earlier records correspondingly diminishes. The bogy of historical relativism haunts certain types of modern thought.[5] Knowledge is impossible if the writer's account simply reflects the conditions and needs of his own day and circle. There is no logical brake on this showing to the process whereby it becomes simply a reflection of the writer's own psychological make-up. Such

---

[1] Different pagination in various eds. Cf. J. Robinson, *A New Quest of the Historical Jesus*, p. 99, n.

[2] Op. cit., p. lv.

[3] Ibid.

[4] P. 446, n 2·

[5] In our time history has become a catchword: the totalitarians have been able to justify anything in its name.

scepticism would remind one of William James' agnostic "who should shut himself up in a snarling logicality and try to make the gods extort his recognition willy-nilly, or not get it at all" so that he "might cut himself off forever from his only opportunity of making the gods' acquaintance".

The notion behind this modern historical relativism is expressed in Collingwood's conception of metaphysics as the fundamental assumptions of particular societies.[1] It reflects on John's status as a historian that he would have rejected such a position *toto coelo*. His view of truth is absolute. Yet as we have had cause to see, it is also factual: the Son of Man is no abstract manhood, nor is his "theory of ideas" *fort metaphysique*. His notion of the "true" follows upon this. The shepherd is good at his job, the bread feeds and does not poison or leave hungry still; similarly the living water and the true Vine which give life and the ability to act. Here we are close to the "real" world in the every-day sense. The idea that is given credence in the writings of R. Niebuhr, that delusion is necessary for good in history would have got short shrift from the writer of the Fourth Gospel.[2] And not only so. John's emphasis on the flesh, albeit the flesh quickened by the Spirit, guarantees an interest in fact. The shepherd could have been an eternal Idea instead of a living Pastor; the life could have been an aristocratic spirituality instead of the product of a personal relationship; the bread could have been lofty doctrine instead of a body broken. The Resurrection was a fine oppor-tunity for ethereality to one so given. But John keeps close to fact because he believes that these facts are real and so creative: creative in those who work to fulfil their meaning in their own portion of history, which itself is shaped by what makes these facts real.

Yet the problem raised by positivistic historiography cannot be dismissed. The interpretative element in the records cannot reduce the basis in actual happening to nothing. If the Pharisees

---

[1] Collingwood himself vigorously attacked Dilthey on the grounds that he reduced history to psychology: *The Idea of History*, p. 173. Cf. T. M. Knox's comments (ibid. xiii and also xvii).

[2] Cf. Niebuhr, *Moral Man and Immoral Society*, p. 277. For Niebuhr's view of the historicity or otherwise of the cross itself see Alan Richardson, *Christian Apologetics*, p. 171, n.

and the disciples had compared notes on the threat to destroy the Temple or on the healings which the former likewise attributed to witchcraft, they would have reached some measure of agreement; and on the same showing so would a modern observer, if, *per impossibile*, he had been present. On the Aristotelian principle ὃ πᾶσι δοκεῖ τοῦτ' εἶναι φαμέν we might discount the prejudices of all concerned and arrive at a basis of "fact".[1] In this sense what remains as "the facts" might not square with theological requirements, and this possibility has to be faced. Modern theology, beginning in the Marburg tradition which lay behind both Barth and Bultmann, reinforced by the discovery of Kierkegaard, tended to fear that the facts if discovered might undermine the faith.[2] The Jesus thus discoverable would be the Jesus who belonged to the world of the flesh, of "psychic, historical perceptibility", and we are no longer to know Christ "after the flesh". Theology must be made independent of the contingent: it cannot be based upon verifiable data. But this flies in the face of essential Christianity. The "ends of the world" have come upon us because we have met God in the flesh. We indeed no longer know Christ "after the flesh", but this in itself implies the importance of knowing who he was in the flesh. He who denies that he has come "in the flesh" is anathema. If we may so put it, God became subject to the ambiguities of history while not ceasing to be God: the Word "became flesh" and so "overcame the world". If therefore it were possible to show that Jesus was not in fact such as to be congruous with this claim, our faith would be in jeopardy. There is no security from this possibility on Christian premises. It is itself part of the setting for the "existential" decision.

This is being urged now by those who cannot be accused of conservatism. J. Robinson writes, "how can the indispensable historicity of Jesus be affirmed, while at the same time maintaining the irrelevance of what a historical encounter with him would mean . . . ?"[3] And again, "Is not an incarnation beyond Jesus'

---

[1] Cf. on this e.g. the discussion of socio-economic prejudice in McIntyre, op. cit., pp. 27f.

[2] Cf. D. M. Baillie, *God Was In Christ*, pp. 53f.

[3] Robinson, op. cit., p. 88.

historical existence . . . an absurdity?"[1] That Christianity is historical means something more than that it "makes sense" of history. The Incarnation is more than a symbol for the impact of God upon a group of men through the coincidence of various doctrines (such as the suffering of the Servant and the coming of the gnostic Redeemer) with the desolation and conviction of sin produced by the death of a man of God. Jesus is more than the locus of such an impact. When he acted, God acted; his character is God's character; what he is, that in some sense God is also. So John insists. And theology must constantly grapple with his thought in the matter. When Jesus becomes unknowable or not worth knowing, then Christianity becomes a myth, a mystery of salvation, a witness to the irruption of "mystic forces" into the life of mankind, but not a meeting with God in the flesh. As Robinson says again, "a myth does not become historical simply by appropriating the name of a historical personage".[2] He quotes Erik Sjöberg: "Even if Jesus was a historical person, but we could know nothing about his historical person, then the Jesus preached in the Church and portrayed in the gospels is nevertheless actually a mythological figure. For then he has nothing in common with the Jesus of history, who remains unknowable to us, except for the name. Here the New Testament message is much more radically mythological than is presupposed in the contemporary discussion about 'demythologising' the Gospel."[3] The writer of the Fourth Gospel is faced with a similar problem in docetism: he plainly believes that Jesus is knowable and the study of his pages disabuses the mind of the tendency to find transcendental doctrine divorced from the flesh of Jesus: ἐὰν μὴ φάγητε τὴν σάρκα τοῦ υἱοῦ τοῦ ἀνθρώπου . . . The Johannine position may be fairly put in the words of D. M. Baillie: "If it is true that 'no man can say, Jesus is Lord, except in the Holy Spirit', it is equally true that no man can say it in the truly Christian sense, except through a knowledge of what Jesus actually was, as a human personality, in the days of his flesh."[4]

[1] Ibid., p. 91. G. Bornkamm: Jesus of Nazareth represents the new approach from the Bultmann school.
[2] Robinson, op. cit., p. 89.   [3] Ibid., p. 88, n 4.   [4] Op. cit., p. 52.

Faith depends on the sort of person Jesus was. The cross itself is meaningless if it is simply an accidental death or the result of a miscarriage of justice. At bottom, and stripped of its facility of method and rigidity of presumption, this was the significance of the original Quest. The same conditions obtain to-day. "The fact of the mere *existence* (*Da*sein) of a man to whom the kerygma appeals as 'legitimation' does not free modern man, who is all too aware of the possibility of apotheosis in the history of religion, from the doubt that Christian faith too perhaps owes its existence to human presumption. If on the other hand it could be shown that the application to Jesus of originally mythical categories of interpretation has its thoroughly justifiable point of departure in his historical *kind* of existence (*So*sein), then this would be a decisive pastoral aid."[1] This is the Christological problem in its contemporary dress. The older way of solving it was to appeal to the attraction of Jesus for modern men: as such its value was notoriously difficult to assess. Burkitt, as will be remembered, found the Johannine Christ in some respects "positively repellant". What is now required is the assurance that the records present a figure of sufficient stature to substantiate the claims made for him. This is the original significance of the Johannine signs, whatever their appeal for us. Moreover it is required that the challenge made on his behalf should be that which he intended himself. "For if it is the Primitive Church which is the first to apprehend Jesus Christ as fulfilment, and if such a conception is projected back into the mind of Jesus Christ by the New Testament writers, then the conclusion follows that Revelation is something that happens in the Primitive Church and in the writers of the New Testament, but not in Jesus Christ. Further, the Revelation of which we are speaking becomes a Revelation *concerning* Jesus Christ and is not Revelation *in* Jesus Christ."[2] Here the most we can ask is that John and the synoptics agree. Even Bultmann accepts as authentic Jesus' answer to John's embassage, as the form which the proclamation took in Jesus' own preaching. If we put this alongside the Johannine scheme we find that the two

[1] Hans-Hinrich Jenssen, quoted Robinson, op. cit., p. 13, n 6f.
[2] McIntyre, op. cit., p. 47.

tally. Matt. 11.4ff reads, "Go and tell John the things you hear and see: the blind receive their sight and the lame walk, the lepers are cleansed, the deaf hear, the dead are raised up and the poor have the Gospel preached to them: and blessed is he who finds nothing in me to put him off." Alongside this we can put the healing of the blind man, the restoring of the cripple at the pool Bethesda, and the raising of Lazarus. Even the form of presentation is similar.

The gospels have in this way met this problem (*sc.* of engineering a meeting with Jesus in his sayings and actions), not only by placing the kerygma on Jesus' lips, but also by presenting individual units from the tradition in such a way that the whole Gospel becomes visible: At the call of Levi, we hear,[1] "I came not to call the righteous but sinners"; at the healing of the deaf-mute, we hear,[2] "He has done all things well, he even makes the deaf hear and the dumb speak." Thus such traditions become kerygmatic, not by appropriating the traditional language of the Church's kerygma, but in a distinctive way: They retain a concrete story about Jesus, but expand its horizon until the universal saving significance of the heavenly Lord becomes visible in the earthly Jesus.[3]

But this is precisely what we have been accustomed to find in John, where every episode is salvation because Jesus is present in it. To be sure, the total picture is in different focus. The poor and outcasts are conspicuous by their absence. But this is where the interpretative element enters in, to bring the changed approach into line with the whole vision: God so loved the world—the whole world, as the First Epistle makes plain.

The Fourth Gospel is thus best understood as a complement to the others not in the sense that it interprets them but that it shows us how to interpret them.[4] They give the past as it exists in reminiscence: John carries on their work in a different idiom and in a way which in some ways recalls Jesus as he was more clearly, while at the same time distorting the actual tones of the Master. In other words, he overwrites the tradition with comments incorporated into the text. The presupposition of those who have concerned themselves with the "historical Jesus" has been always the same, that if we could get back to the facts we should discover

[1] Mark 2.17.   [2] Mark 7.37.   [3] Robinson, op. cit., p. 95.
[4] See Howard, *Christianity*, p. 178, for the assumption by the F.G. of the earlier tradition.

something radically different from that which inspired the Church's proclamation, whether it were a winsome teacher stripped of the miraculous or a fanatic who would offend our modernity and religious sense, a madman who would destroy the whole edifice we have built for ourselves. But the first disciples saw him as he was, and it led them to formulate the kerygma— not only Easter, because it was not just the rising of *anyone*, but of *this* man. John realizes that he cannot make his readers see him thus ("Sir, we would see Jesus")[1] by using the idiom natural to the synoptics, indeed this idiom is not natural to himself; so he tries in the blend of Jewish and Hellenistic elements which comprises the thought-background of his circle. By this means and by his interpretative method he produces a Picasso-like effect[2] by which one sees not only the profile but at the same time the thoughts going on in the Master's mind.[3] His final question is the same as theirs: Do you then believe? "This is written that you may believe. . . ." Once more it is plain that John intends at least to write history, which after all is the most we can ask of a historical source. This does not, of course, absolve us from the duty of examining each story on its merits, but it is something to understand how John could write as he did if he really wanted to describe actual events.

In the last resort the test must be whether the history is representative.[4] That it is so in the gospels is a large claim, but one which the facts substantiate. The reading of the gospels brings us into contact with a world of fact, a world in which matter and the flesh have their normal and earthy place, a world of real problems, of disease and decay and death, in a way which no other religious literature does. Here is no never-never land, but the world as it always is, real, mysterious, only partly intelligible, and

---

[1] John 12.21. The Galilean disciples with Greek names combine to bring the question of the Greeks to Jesus.

[2] I have borrowed this image from Robinson, p. 86, who uses it in a different connection.

[3] An example is the prayer at the raising of Lazarus: "I thank thee that thou hast heard me. I know that thou always hearest me, but I said it for those who stand around."

[4] Cf. Althaus, *The So-called Kerygma and the Historical Jesus*, pp. 69ff.

containing God. Of course some knowledge of the conditions of
the day is necessary: that is part of the historical reality of the
record; but no more than the ordinary Christian is capable of.[1]
One needs but scratch the surface and the substance of all history
stands bare. We are obsessed by our modernity and the peculiarity
of our predicament; we imagine that no one was ever like us and
that even the gospels must be reduced to the bloodless categories
of contemporary so-called philosophy (whether positivistic or
existentialist) as modern physics was once supposed to have
reduced the rich world of the senses to a world of shadows,[2] as
though we were not born and did not die, did not have children
and parents, did not suffer from disease and worry and supersti-
tion, and did not desire a better country.[3] To have achieved the
ability to set the things of life in true perspective is to have
achieved the ability to write history. John has this in sufficient
measure. He shares the ability to tell the story as the first three
evangelists did, to recall this real slice of the real world's history
as it was; as such he distinguishes himself totally from the
apocryphal writers and accredits himself as a historian.

John's attitude to history, however, in common with that of
Christians in general, goes deeper. The events he describes, rather
than being judged by history, themselves judge history. More
accurately, the Man is the judge. As Christ claimed to be the
"sign" for his own generation, so he is the sign to all generations.
In this sense a "sign" is not an artificially constructed proof but
recalls those events in the life of an individual which, even if
inexplicable in themselves, illuminate the rest. In this way
Christianity may be said to have created history. In the ancient
world the art was chiefly a rhetorical exercise, *opus oratorium
maxime*, as Cicero put it. For the early Christians the relation
between events was primarily due to the action of God, as, for
instance, in the history of the Jews. Other kinds of history were
products of human convenience or ingenuity. But Christian

---

[1] The extent to which one must become a "first-century Jew" to understand
the gospels is much overdone at present.
[2] See Eddington's *Nature of the Physical World*.
[3] Heb. 11.16.

eschatology produced world history, with purpose and intelligibility. Together with this went the interest in facts born of the Incarnation which rivalled that of Thucydides. John's essential historicity lies in his conviction that he is mediating an encounter with the Truth, not merely with a presupposition for some sectarian viewpoint. Truth is its own criterion, but it is not in the last resort amenable to the methods of scholarship. It has been asked why we could not take ἀγάπη, Christian love, instead of worry, as the really significant "existential": this is what John does. "He that does the works (i.e., keeps the commandment of love, and so enters into the 'works' of Christ) will understand whether the teaching is from God." "By this shall all men know that you are my disciples, if you have love one for another." "What we have seen and heard declare we unto you, that you may have fellowship with us, and our fellowship is with the Father and with his Son Jesus Christ." Here is the verification. What we know elsewhere of altruism and of doctrines of loving-kindness in God only serves to illuminate that, if we are true to history, here in the person of Jesus is indeed the fullness of time.[1] And the divine love made effective in history ensures the continuity of the authentic tradition by its presence among the believers. "A servant is not greater than his lord, neither is one that is sent greater than him that sent him. If you know these things, blessed are you if you do them. . . . He that receives whomsoever I send receives me, and he that receives me receives him that sent me." The risen Christ bears in his body the marks of the historical cross.

[1] Ferré, *Christian Understanding of God*, pp. 185f.

CHAPTER 12

CONCLUSION

It is sometimes said that the Gospel according to St John appeals to the twentieth-century mind. If this is true in fact, it is because John approaches universalism in his religious language, and because, despite the emphasis upon the person of Christ and upon his concrete manhood, he yet gives an impression of affinity with Greek abstract thought, which is the basis of our own way of thinking. Thus alongside and in illustration of the Son's status and function as judge is the teaching of judgement by light and self-exclusion from it which sounds like a timeless doctrine divorced from any specific Judgement Day. Likewise the impression is given that a particularist religion becomes in John an eternal religion of the spirit: the time is coming when you will neither worship the Father here nor at Jerusalem, but in spirit and truth. This appeal of John to the Greek in us obviously betokens some affinity between him and those people, whoever they were, from whom he borrowed his religious vocabulary. For, as we have seen, this was no invention of his own genius, but was the possession also of a host of other writers in greater or less degree, ranging from the orthodox of the Wisdom literature to the fantasy-spinners of Mandaism. The difficulty is not now to find parallels to the Johannine style, often of a quite striking kind, but to decide which parallels come closest to his thought—although it must be conceded that even the nearest do not greatly resemble it. It must be granted also that the writer of the Fourth Gospel, however he may be able to deduce the abstract and universal implications of what he describes and however he may seize upon sayings and incidents which afford an excuse for discourse or meditation, is in the line of the biblical tradition in his ability to tell a story and to value it as the source of his meditations. Moreover, it cannot really be denied that he finds the story rooted in the tradition that "salvation is of the Jews". Significant for this is the fact that it is being increasingly realized that Greek thought as well as Greek words had penetrated to the schools of Palestine itself, so that possession and use of such words and ideas need not label a writer as out of the main stream of that Hebrew-Judaic tradition which it has been customary to differentiate sharply from Hellenism. It is noticeable, however, that in this concrete, historical, non-metaphysical (however we may put it) style of thought the Greek ideas taken over are treated in a crudely practical and almost mythological fashion. An example of this is the way in which God is represented as using the Law as his blueprint for the creation.

The reflection that the writer of the Fourth Gospel has affinities with this concrete Hebraic type of thought would suggest that his "metaphysics", such as it was, would take the same line. Thus he might have reflected that the Word was the expression of God's mind or that to find the word for anything is to make it known, but it would be more congenial to him to find such divine self-expression in events or actions (or in a person) than in any universal Reason or abstract Idea. Though then we with our pure Greek background might interpret this "truth" as "reality" and find comfort and illumination therein, John himself may not have intended this at all. We may recall Odeberg's remark quoted on page 133 above, that what *we* consider the most "spiritual" of all, speculation upon absolute truths, belongs for John to the sphere of reality described as "that which is born of the flesh". The universalism is there; but it does not consist in a generalized statement about human nature. Rather it is the relation of every man to the Son of Man who is himself God's word to every man as a man. Here then is the "purified but firm Anthropomorphism" which von Hügel declared "essential to the full vigour and clear articulation of Religion".[1] But John is at one and the same time less aware than we are of the metaphysical distinction—because metaphysics scarcely rises above his horizon—and more conscious of the figurative character of the inevitable language, as his constantly-changing metaphors show. Bread, light, flesh, blood,

[1] *Letters*, p. 37.

a vine, all can stand for the divine and stand for Jesus also. And thus to say that "God is light" is more than to use a simile, God is like light. It is to use a symbol which can have a primeval religious significance and be grasped without being understood. But the oneness of Father and Son is more than such metaphor; it is the basic datum. That John thought of this in terms of a Judaic "theory of ideas" would seem to be the best available explanation of his thought, though here of course we enter the realm of speculation. With John at a certain depth there is an anonymity, an opaqueness, absent from St Paul, which renders guesswork inevitable. He never defines except in terms of results and relationships, so that, as has been remarked, love and life and light are more descriptive of our "experience" of God than of God's own being. This of course is biblical, but John goes further. He never uses the names of some of the conceptions he employs, such as the Image, the Servant, the Shekinah. In the same way Jesus' manhood is never explicitly affirmed, though it is hard to see how anyone ever doubted that John believed in it passionately; and his divinity is never defined, though this has been obvious to all.

The elements then of later orthodoxy are present in the Fourth Gospel. Jesus is God and Man. But the writer seems to have thought of Jesus' manhood as well as his divinity as concurrent with the fact of his being the Word, one might say as being inherent in it. It is only the Son of Man who descends, and he descends to become flesh, not man. Before Abraham was, he was; he had glory with the Father before the world existed. If he is the Name or the Shekinah, the manifested Presence of God, he is also the Image, the concrete embodiment of the divine and the true Man at one and the same time.[1] Strangely enough, then, it is as Son of Man and not as Son of God that Jesus is "pre-existent", and we are justified in attributing this to the Jewish predestinarianism for which everything, from the souls of men to the Name of the Messiah (in the Jewish sense of "Name") existed beforehand in the mind and purpose of God, and existed in such a way that they could be transferred to the world when it appeared

---

[1] The Image of Israel in the Gen. Rab. passage on Jacob's ladder is "engraved on high"; the Image of Hibil-Ziwa in Mandaism is "preserved in its place".

as the puppeteer places his dolls on the stage. If John is not so crude as this the illustration serves to show that he is no nearer to some other types of thought which his may at first seem to resemble. Thus, for instance, John's idea appears to resemble Leontius' *enhypostasia* as interpreted by H. M. Relton,[1] that personality in God includes that in man. This is an attractive idea, though it does not seem to have been Leontius' own; moreover in context and to-day it is easily confused with Apollonarianism and Monophysitism.[2] It would in fact be more congruous with the Logos doctrine of Philo or Justin than that of John. The evangelist in fact moves in a different world of thought: a notion difficult to assimilate even when once grasped. He does not speak in metaphysical terms because he does not think in them: he is a religious man, thinking as well as worshipping "in spirit and in truth", which for him is a relationship with the living Father through Jesus the Son.

An essential point about the theology of the Fourth Gospel is that the centre of the picture is not Jesus but the Father. The Fourth Gospel and First Epistle are the great theocentric tracts of the New Testament. The Johannine Christ takes every opportunity to point to the Father as the source of all his significance and effectiveness: he is to the Father as his Name or Presence or Glory are to God, and this is the language of strict monotheism. In more personal terms he is the Image or Servant or Son. As we have seen, it is not the Son who descends to become flesh. The Son of God is ever in the bosom of the Father. Here, as our modern jargon would have it, there is a "tension" between John the monotheist and his conviction of the divinity of Jesus. But it is not a tension between the Manhood and the Godhead. The sonship to God is not in contrast to the manhood. It consists in the relationship which exists between Jesus and God. This relationship is expressed in the works, the signs, which express the unity of essential being in the unity of love, of will and of character. "If

---

[1] *A Study in Christology.* Dorner, Ottley, and Relton held that for Apollinaris himself the Logos was the prototype of human personality; but the view has not won general assent.

[2] The doctrine reappears in Berdyaev.

you do not believe me that I am in the Father and the Father is in me, believe the works." That the eternal Son of Man is the Word of God is expressed in terms of his sonship to God, because in this aspect he embodies and so reveals the divine character. This too, like some other things in John, has appealed to a type of modern thought. Truly, it is said, John does not think in terms of person and substance. He merely thinks of the Man who embodies the will or kingdom of God, who is still a man but so related to God as to be his son. True, as far as it goes: but for John the Man *is* the divine Word, and this involves his obedience and likeness to the Father. He was, as the Word who is Man, before the world was. This is not indeed the language of substance and person; but it contains the germs of the later doctrine, if perhaps of other doctrines also. Alexandria and Antioch have not yet been reached.

The essential Jewishness of John's thought comes out again in that he clinches his argument with a quotation from the psalms, used in rabbinic fashion. The judges to whom the Word of God came were called "gods"; Jesus is the sanctified and sent one, therefore he is Son of God. Which of you convicteth me of sin? The Son remains in the Father's house for ever. And the word of God did not merely *come* to the Son of Man: he *is* the Word. Aphraates, the Syriac Father, produced an argument which is closely parallel in several points to the Johannine, and follows the same Jewish line. It occurs in his "Homily" no. XVII, entitled "Of the Messiah that he is Son of God". I quote for convenience Burkitt's summary:[1]

> "Though we truly hold that Jesus our Lord is God the Son of God, and the King the Son of the King, Light from Light, Son[2] and Counsellor and Guide and Way and Saviour and Shepherd and Gatherer and Door and Pearl and Lamp; and by many Names is he called. But now we will show that he is the Son of God and that he is God who from God hath come."[3] For the name of divinity has been given to just men, as for instance to Moses, who was made a God not to Pharaoh only but also to Aaron,[4] and though the Jews say God has no son, yet he called Israel his First-born;[5] and Solomon his son.[6] David also says of them: I have said, Ye

[1] *Early Christianity Outside the Roman Empire*, pp. 41ff.
[2] Cf. Isa. 9.6.   [3] § 2.   [4] Ex. 6.1; 7.1; § 3.
[5] Ex. 4.22f.   [6] 2 Sam. 7.14; cf. Heb. 1.5.

are Gods and sons of the Highest all of you.[1] God gives the most exalted titles to whom he will: he called impious Nebuchadnezzar King of Kings. For man was formed by him in his own image to be a Temple for him to dwell in, and therefore he gives to man honours which he denies to the Sun and Moon and the host of heaven.[2] Man of all creatures was first conceived in God's mind,[3] though he was not placed in the world till it was ready for him.[4] Why should we not worship Jesus, through whom we know God, Jesus who turned away our mind from vain superstitions and taught us to adore the One God, our Father and Maker, and to serve him? Is it not better to do this than to worship the kings and emperors of the world, who not only are apostates themselves but drive others also to apostasy?[5] Our Messiah has been spoken of in the prophets even to the details of the Crucifixion.[6] We therefore will continue to worship before the Majesty of his Father, who has turned our worship unto him. We call him God, like Moses; First-born and Son, like Israel; Jesus, like Joshua the son of Nun; Priest, like Aaron; King, like David; the great Prophet, like all the prophets; Shepherd, like the shepherds who tended and ruled Israel. And us, adds Aphraates, has he called sons and made us his Brothers, and we have become his Friends.[7]

Burkitt commented: "Nothing less than the full abstract here given does justice to Aphraates' style and method. It is surely most surprising and instructive to meet with work animated by this spirit in the middle of the fourth century. For my own part, I feel it follows too closely the lines of our Lord's answer to the Jews for me to venture to brand it as unorthodox."[8] We are not concerned here with the orthodoxy but only with the style and method. Many of the Johannine features seem to spring from independent reasoning on similar lines and with the same collection of symbols. Similar reasoning is employed in the proem to the Epistle to the Hebrews, the Christology of which so closely resembles that of the Fourth Gospel.[9] Some of these symbols are used by a much wider circle of writers; such as the Guide[10] and the Way, the Shepherd, Door, Gatherer,[11] Pearl[12] and Lamp. Thus in

[1] Ps. 82(81).6; § 4.   [2] Deut. 4.17; §§ 5,6.   [3] Ps. 90(89).1,2.
[4] § 7.   [5] § 8.   [6] §§ 9,10.
[7] §§ 11,12.   [8] Op. cit., p. 43.   [9] See above, pp. 77, 92, etc.
[10] See Gaster above, pp. 21f, for guide= teacher in the D.S.S. The word is used of the Holy Spirit in John.
[11] Cf. John 11.52.
[12] Cf. the "song of the pearl" in the Acts of Thomas (probably of Syriac origin).

Aphraates man is in the Image[1] of God; first conceived in God's mind and placed in the world when it was ready for him, to be a Temple[2] for God to dwell in. Jesus is the great Prophet[3] and the Shepherd.[4] He has made us Brothers[5] and Friends,[6] and is Son of God because he shares God's character: as such he is more worthy of worship than the kings and emperors of the world.[7] Aphraates argues in Jewish fashion; he has access to the symbols and language which John shares with the Odes of Solomon and the Syrian tradition generally. It seems that over two hundred years before, the writer of the Fourth Gospel thought along similar lines.[8]

The reflection upon the historical problem is that there is no insuperable contradiction between thought which moves along these lines and belief in Jesus as a real man who really lived. The problem of the history is therefore half solved by the anthropology. Manhood is no compound of gross matter and intellectual spark of supreme Being; it is practically defined as the ability to love. To have the word or love of God in one's heart is to be drawn by the Father to the only Son and thus to come to the true life. Those who are thus drawn into one—the scattered children of God—and partake of the flesh of the Son of Man are in fact the Church, but the Church is considered in its ideal aspect as the new humanity. The Son of Man is thus related to other men not as the abstract to its embodiment or even as the pattern to its copy (though this enters in) but as a person to persons. It has often been said that a personal relationship cannot be defined except in terms of itself. Such terms are themselves the result of centuries of reflection along Christian lines. At a time when they were entirely unavailable, it was the achievement of the fourth evangelist to

[1] See above, pp. 55–61.

[2] In John, the Temple is probably Jesus' own person as well as the Church.

[3] See above, pp. 71–8.

[4] John 10.1ff.

[5] See above, pp. 73ff, 78, 139.

[6] John 15.15; cf. Wisd. 7.27. See above, pp. 19, 24, etc., for the "names" of Jesus.

[7] Cf. the taunt to Pilate, "Thou art not Caesar's friend", and the thorn-crowned King of Truth.

[8] It is noteworthy, however, that in John the Spirit is not feminine, as in the Syrian tradition.

express the idea behind them and so to contribute to their invention. He did this by telling the story, telling it in a way which recalled the facts, and by so doing revealed the truth of man at all stages of history. To meet the Christ as he walks through the pages of the gospel is to meet him as he goes throughout the ages. But more than this it is to be assured of meeting him as he is now and of having part with him, being where he is, in the eternal world.

CHRIST AND THE OTHER ADVOCATE

It was fashionable quite recently to declare that the New Testament writers made no distinction between Christ and the Holy Spirit. Thus Streeter: ". . . they felt themselves, both as a community and as individuals, to be possessed by a spiritual power or presence. This they described indifferently as 'the Holy Spirit', as 'the spirit of God', as 'the spirit of Jesus', or simply as 'Christ'."[1] This fitted in with a dislike of precise definition in religion, with the feeling of the divine as an influence or force rather than as a person. Paul and John were both called in as witnesses. In the final discourses the Johannine Christ says, "He (the Spirit) dwells with you and will be in you. I shall not leave you orphans; I come to you."[2] This, then, it was said, is the sense in which the "going" is the "coming". "The Spirit was not yet because Jesus was not yet glorified."[3] Therefore A. H. McNeile wrote: "It [sic] 'did not yet exist' till Christ had been set free by death to the fulness of his glory."[4] "The Spirit was Christ himself in the full and free activity into which he entered by the liberation of death." As the perfume from the broken flask filled the house, so, it was imagined, the death of Christ released his spirit throughout the world. More recently both Hoskyns and Dodd have shown themselves inclined to the exegesis that the words at the cross, "He handed over his spirit"[5] refer to Jesus' bequest of the Holy Spirit to the world or to the faithful standing below.

The dislike of definition sprang from the insight that

---

[1] *The God Who Speaks*, p. 109.   [2] John 14.17f.   [3] John 7.39.
[4] *N.T. Teaching in the Light of St Paul's*, p. 299.
[5] John 19.30. Also Barrett and Lightfoot. It is worthy of note that this "Origenesque" interpretation did not occur to Origen or any of the commentators whose work was available to M. F. Wiles: see his *The Spiritual Gospel*, p. 67.

Christianity began with actual encounters and experiences and not with speculation or dogma. The doctrines to be found in the New Testament itself were merely inadequate attempts to express the truth in earthly language. But the conclusion that distinctions were impossible was hasty. "If we . . . ask whether there is any difference between having God's presence with us, having Christ dwelling in us, and being filled with the Holy Spirit, we are bound to answer that the New Testament makes no clear distinction." So wrote D. M. Baillie. But he went on to say that "it is not that no distinction is made between the Father, the Son, and the Holy Spirit; but all three come at every point into the full Christian experience of God".[1] In John the Father is also to come: "We shall come to him and make our home with him"[2] refers to the Son and the Father both indwelling the believer. Yet this does not imply that no distinction is to be made between Father and Son. Why then blur that between Son and Spirit?

Moreover, a writer who believed (if we have rightly argued above) that the Word was eternally Man, who asserted that the Word was made flesh, and who in accordance with this laid emphasis upon the personal, would be likely both to distinguish the Spirit and to stress the continuity of the Manhood. This in fact we find. Whether or not we accept the separation of the five Paraclete-sayings as performed by Hans Windisch,[3] the most natural reference of "I shall see you again and your heart will rejoice and your joy no one takes from you"[4] is to the resurrection,[5] after which Jesus is still Master and Brother.[6] Likewise, we find that the expectation that personality would be stressed in the doctrine of the Spirit is fulfilled. John emphasizes the personality of the Spirit more obviously than the other New Testament writers. The personal pronoun "he" is used in speaking of him;

[1] *God Was in Christ*, pp. 153f. It is arguable that to connect the Spirit exclusively with the Son is to fall into the danger of "Jesus-worship": see Raven, *The Creator Spirit*, p. 20.
[2] John 14.23.
[3] See W. F. Howard, *Christianity acc. to St John*, pp. 74f.
[4] John 16.22.
[5] Cf. John 20.20, "Then were the disciples glad when they saw the Lord".
[6] John 20.16f.

he is distinguished from Christ as "another Paraclete".[1] Despite the Johannine emphasis upon "love" as the bond of fellowship, there is no hint of the Augustinian notion of the Spirit as bond between Father and Son.

"The Spirit was not yet because Jesus was not yet glorified" does not imply that the Spirit did not yet exist. Apart from the stress on personality, it is unlikely that one steeped in the Wisdom literature would be unaware of the Spirit's activity before Christ.[2] We may suspect a Semitic mode of language as in the fourteenth psalm, where the wicked (foolish) say that "there is no God". Commentators are at pains to point out that this is "not a denial of the divine existence, but of his presence and interposition".[3] In connection with the Johannine passage Bernard[4] quotes Acts 19.2, "We have not heard whether there is a Holy Spirit" and suggests the complement "in operation". "Available" might be better, but something is needed in view of the improbability that these disciples of John the Baptist had never heard of the Holy Spirit.[5] That the Spirit came specially into operation after the Resurrection, at the beginning of the Messianic Age, was part of the early Christian experience—recorded in the Acts and borne out by the teaching of St Paul. The Spirit becomes available. He comes into full operation through the death of Christ, when "the

---

[1] John 14.16; cf. 1 John 2.1, "We have a Paraclete with the Father, Jesus Christ . . .".

[2] The Spirit is often connected, sometimes identified, with the divine Wisdom in the Wisdom books, which carry on and develop notions characteristic of the O.T. As in Joel, so in Proverbs, the pouring-out of the Spirit is promised (Joel 2.28; Prov. 1.23): in the Wisdom literature elsewhere the Spirit is life (Job 32.8; 34.14f; Eccles. 12.7), and connected with this is the renewal of all things (Ps. 104.27,29,30, "Thou sendest forth thy Spirit and they are created; and thou renewest the face of the earth": see Wisd. 7.27, where Wisdom "renews all things"). As the Spirit brooded over the primeval chaos to bring order from it, so Wisdom is the origin and supporter of Nature (Prov. 8.27–31) and, as the Spirit gave skill and genius (see Ex. 35.30–5), so Wisdom gives knowledge of the manifold works of God in creation (Wisd. 7.17–22). As we have seen, the expression Holy Spirit occurs also in the Tests. of the XII Patriarchs and in the D.S.S

[3] C. A. Briggs, *A Crit. and Exeget. Comm. on the Book of Psalms*, i, p. 77.

[4] *St John*, p. 284.

[5] The Spirit, according to the synoptics, figured in John's teaching (Mark 1.8 and parallels).

Son of Man is glorified, and God is glorified in him ".[1] By looking at the cross the disciples are healed;[2] they are clean because of the word which Christ has spoken to them—presumably the word that he is going away.[3] Henceforth the Spirit will be able to convict the world in respect of sin, and of righteousness, and of judgement: the world crucifies its own true manhood and righteousness goes the way of the cross; the world's victory is already the blackest form of defeat.[4]

[1] John 13.31.   [2] John 3.14f.
[3] John 15.3; cf. 13.10; 7.33 and 8.21; 13.33.   [4] John 16.8–11.

THE WISDOM BACKGROUND OF THE FOURTH GOSPEL

In the foregoing study the dependence of the fourth evangelist upon the Wisdom literature and the Wisdom school in general has been stressed. It will be convenient to collect in short compass the parallels between the Fourth Gospel and the Wisdom books of the Old Testament and the Apocrypha. To turn to these is to turn to a source upon which John actually drew, from which he actually quoted words and phrases, and in which it is possible to single out ideas which he developed from germ. Dealing with a different subject-matter and in a different manner, John approached his task with a mind so stocked with Wisdom ideas and turns of phrase that some of them appear almost incidentally. The following examples are taken more or less at random.

In John the Logos enlightens every man and through him all things were made. In the Wisdom literature Wisdom is the principle of creation, especially man's, and God possessed her "in the beginning" of his ways.[1] The Logos-doctrine is not developed in these books, but all things are made by the Word,[2] which is momentarily personified as leaping down from heaven;[3] Wisdom comes from God's mouth,[4] and in one place Wisdom and Word are practically identified by the parallelism of the clauses.[5] Moreover, in Proverbs the career of Wisdom resembles that of the Word in the Johannine Prologue.[6] And Wisdom is the true light,[7] the "only-begotten",[8] and the agent of revelation.[9] She

---

[1] John 1.3f; Sir. 24.10ff; 42.21; Wisd. 7.21; 9.2; cf. 1.6; John 1.1.

[2] Wisd. 9.1; Sir. 42.15.

[3] Wisd. 18.15; that this passage influenced the N.T. is shown by Eph. 6.17; Heb. 4.12.

[4] Sir. 24.3.   [5] Wisd. 9.1f.   [6] Prov. 8.22; and 1.20–end.

[7] Wisd. 7.10,26,29; cf. John 1.5.   [8] Wisd. 7.22.   [9] Wisd. 10.10.

forestalls those who desire to know her, making herself first known, even as, according to the First Epistle of John, we love because God first loved us.[1] Them that love her the Lord loves: and in the same mood the Johannine Christ says, "He that loves me will be loved by my Father."[2] The principle of reciprocal love also appears: "I love them that love me."[3] Love of Wisdom is obedience to her laws: the Johannine Jesus says, "He that loves me is he who keeps my commandments."[4] Various Johannine themes occur in the Wisdom writings. Thus the serpent episode in Num. 21.8f is considered, and the idea deduced from it is that God's Word heals all things; in John the incarnate Logos is to be lifted up like the serpent.[5] Wisdom is symbolized by bread and water, and, after the reference to Wisdom "tabernacling" with Jacob which recalls the Shekinah and John 1.14, by a vine;[6] those who eat her will yet hunger, those who drink will yet thirst.[7] But the one who comes to Christ will never hunger, never thirst.[8]

Special attention must be drawn to the remarkable passage in the second chapter of the Book of Wisdom, in which a suffering Righteous One is depicted.[9] It is a passage which sounds very "Johannine" and has influenced the New Testament writers. It is quoted above. In it the Righteous One vaunts that God is his Father, professes to have knowledge of God, and claims he is the son of God—all of which recalls passages in the Fourth Gospel.[10] Moreover, he makes himself servant of the Lord,[11] and his ways are "different".[12]

The germ of certain Johannine doctrines also appears in the Wisdom literature. In Prov. 15.29 God hears the prayer of the righteous one (cf. John 9.31; 11.42). This is a typically Jewish idea, but it chimes in well with the fundamental idea of the Book

---

[1] Wisd. 6.13; 1 John 4.10. [2] Sir. 4.14; John 14.21.
[3] Prov. 8.17. [4] Wisd. 6.18; John 14.15.
[5] Wisd. 16.12; John 3.14. [6] Prov. 9.5; Sir. 24.8,17.
[7] Sir. 24.21. [8] John 6.35; 4.13f.
[9] Wisd. 2.12ff; cf. 1 John 2.1.
[10] Wisd. 2.16; cf. John 5.18; Wisd. 2.13; cf. John 8.55; Wisd. 2.18; cf. John 10.36; 19.7.
[11] Wisd. 2.13; cf. John 13.1ff. Isa 53 is pursued further in Wisd. 5.
[12] Wisd. 2.15; cf. John 7.6f; 15.18f.

of Wisdom, that God created all things good and created not
death; that judgement occurs because like associates with like,
those who love the light with the light; and so the ungodly made a
covenant with the poison of destruction, calling death to themselves (Wisd. 1.13f). This is very like "In him was life", or, to
punctuate differently, "What came to be in him was life" in John
1.4, and the "God is light" of 1 John 1.9—the Johannine doctrine
of "God's innocence". Compare also the remarks about the man
born blind.[1] It is also like the Johannine notion of judgement by
light and by self-exclusion from it.[2] Closely allied to this doctrine
in John is that of "works" which reveal God; and Wisdom provides the germ of this too: "Wisdom . . . knows thy works . . .
and what is right according to thy commandments." "Surely all
men are vain by nature who are ignorant of God and could not
know the One Who Is from the good things that are seen;
neither by considering the works did they acknowledge the
craftsman."[3] In John it is the "works" of Jesus which reveal the
character of the One whom no man has seen at any time. It is
interesting too that elsewhere[4] Wisdom herself is the craftsman,
in the place where she is called "Only-Begotten", and is one
therefore with him who is called the "One Who Is". For the
writer of the First Epistle of John writes of "That Which Was
from the beginning", and the Christ of the Fourth Gospel
declares, "I am."[5] This notion that God created all things good
and that like associates with like is of course Platonic; for that
matter it seems also to have been Sadducean. Perhaps it explains
the difference between John's Good Shepherd who is only concerned with the ninety-nine and the synoptic shepherd who seeks
and saves what is lost. And incidentally the image of the shepherd
is used in Eccles 12.11 where wise words are given by the "one
shepherd", and in Sir. 18.13, where the Lord deals with "all
flesh" as a shepherd with his flock.

Certain other Johannine reproductions of Wisdom ideas and
turns of phrase are striking. In the Book of Wisdom power is
given to kings "from the highest"; the Johannine Christ says to

---

[1] John 9.3. [2] John 3.19. [3] Wisd. 9.9; 13.1.
[4] Wisd. 7.22. [5] 1 John 1.1; John 8.58, etc.

Pilate, "Thou wouldest have no power over me if it were not given thee from above."[1] And a passage in the Nicodemus story so resembles one in Wisdom as to suggest that the translation of ἄνωθεν may after all be "from above". Jesus says, "Marvel not that I said to thee, You must be born anew (or, from above); for except a man be born of water and the Holy Spirit he cannot see the kingdom of God."[2] The Wisdom passage reads, "And whoever gained knowledge of thy counsel except thou gavest Wisdom, and sentest thy Holy Spirit from the highest?"[3] The same Wisdom passage seems to contain the origin of the Johannine references to the "earthly things" and the "heavenly things"—likewise in the Nicodemus story. Jesus says, "If I told you earthly things and you believe not, how will you believe if I tell you heavenly things?" Wisdom has the contrast already stereotyped: "And hardly do we divine *the things that are on earth*, and *the things that are in the heavens* who ever yet traced out?"[4] Once more Jesus says to Nicodemus, "No one has ascended into heaven but the one who descended out of heaven"; and the sage, this time in Proverbs, has provided the idea: "Who has ascended into heaven and descended?"[5]

And there are other reminiscences of the Wisdom books scattered throughout the Fourth Gospel. The light-symbolism is less prominent in the former: see Job 24.13 and Sir. 17.26 for its typical form. But religion is friendship with God just as the Johannine Christ says, "I have called you my friends."[6] "Convicts" is used in Wisdom as it is in John.[7] The same applies to the notion of God bearing witness.[8] Jesus says in the Fourth Gospel, "You will seek me and not find me"; Wisdom says, "They will seek me . . . not find me".[9] Wisdom ordains man to "execute judgement"; so Christ has authority to "make judgement" "because he is son of man".[10] As the Son of Man has overcome the world in John and been given authority over all flesh, so Wisdom

[1] Wisd. 6.3; John 19.11.
[2] John 3.7.
[3] Wisd. 9.17; cf. John 3.5–8.
[4] John 3.12; Wisd. 9.16.
[5] John 3.13; Prov. 30.4.
[6] Wisd. 7.14,27; John 15.15.
[7] Wisd. 1.3; 4.27; John 16.8.
[8] Wisd. 1.6; John 5.32.
[9] John 7.34; cf. 13.33; Prov. 1.28.
[10] Wisd. 9.3; John 5.27.

gave the first-formed man the strength to get dominion over all things.[1]

And there are other echoes. "Signs and wonders";[2] "as thou knowest not the way of the wind";[3] Elijah's word "burning like a torch";[4] all these occur in John. "He gives not the Spirit by measure" recalls "upon all flesh by measure, but without stint to them that love him".[5] The idea of Prov. 26.12 reappears at John 9.41—that there is more hope for one who acts in ignorance than for one who says he knows. The writer of the First Epistle of John declares that "he who does the will of God abides for ever"; that is to say, "the righteous live for ever".[6]

Here then is the actual origin of some of the Johannine phrases and ideas albeit in a less developed stage. But unlike Philo, the Corpus Hermeticum, Mandaism, and the like which also resemble John, this is an actual source from which he borrowed. Many features of these other writings also are attributable to Wisdom influence.

---

[1] John 16.33; 17.2; 1 John 5.4; Wisd. 10.2.

[2] Wisd. 8.8; cf. 10.16; cf. John 4.48.

[3] Eccles. 11.5; cf. John 3.8.

[4] Sir. 48.1; cf. John 5.35.

[5] John 3.34; Sir. 1.10. The doctrine of John 14.23 reflects that of Wisd. 1.2, "(He) is manifested to them that do not distrust him".

[6] 1 John 2.17; Wisd. 5.15. Other references will be found above in the text; those given here have not been intended to be exhaustive.

INDEX OF BIBLICAL REFERENCES

OLD TESTAMENT

NEW TESTAMENT

INDEX

CITATIONS FROM OTHER LITERATURE

APOCRYPHA AND PSEUDEPIGRAPHA

DEAD SEA SCROLLS

RABBINIC WORKS

CLASSICAL, HELLENISTIC, AND EARLY CHRISTIAN WRITINGS

GENERAL INDEX

Freeman, E. A., 182
Fridrichsen, A., 88

Gairdner, W. H. T., 164
Gaster, T. H., 20, 21, 128, 196
Gayomart, 50, 100, 101, 111
Gillet, L., 34, 39
Ginza, see Mandaism
Ginzberg, L., 94, 95
Glasson, T. F., 176
Glory, 18, 34, 36, 37–9, 41, 43, 45, 46,
    58, 59, 67, 71, 78f., 80f., 85, 86, 88,
    90, 92, 101, 118, 119, 121, 135, 146,
    159–63, 167, 193, 194, 199
Glover, T. R., 182
Gollancz, V., 68, 131
Gospel of Philip, 8
Gospel of Thomas, 8, 13
Gospel of Truth, 7, 8, 17, 18, 19, 41,
    42, 54, 64, 117, 137
Grant, R. M., 13, 104
Gregory Nazianzus, 107
Gregory of Nyssa, 107
Griffith, F. Ll., 12
Grobel, K., 8
Guilding, A., 169

Hammurabi, Code of, 111
Harnack, A. von, 47
Harris, J. Rendel, 14, 40f., 82, 107
Hartill, P., 164
Hebrews, Epistle to the, 2, 24, 41, 48,
    59, 64, 77, 78, 81, 88, 90, 92, 105,
    174, 196. See also Biblical Index
Heraclitus, 26, 27, 126
Herford, R. Travers, 34
Herman, E., 140
Hermes Trismegistos, 6, 150. See
    Corpus Hermeticum, in the Index of
    Classical, Hellenistic, and Early
    Christian Writings
Herodotus, 179
Hesychius, 46
Hibil, Hibil-Ziwa, 17, 61, 101, 115–18,
    193
Higgins, A. J. B., 79
Hippolytus, 62, 64, 100f., 104, 111, 116
Hobhouse, S., 60

Hooke, S. H., 55
Hooker, M. D., 79
Hort, F. J. A., 15, 28f., 46, 142f.
Hoskyns, E. C., 14, 35, 132, 166, 178,
    199
Howard, W. F., 35, 48, 59, 62, 64f., 66,
    105, 171, 187, 200
Hügel, F. von, 192
Hunter, A. M., 14, 169, 170
Hypostasis of the Archons, 8

"I am" sayings, 43f., 48, 67, 147, 165,
    205
Ignatius, 100, 107, 133
Image, 18, 19, 32, 33, 36, 55–61, 67,
    73, 77f., 80, 92, 101, 109, 115, 124,
    134, 140, 153, 167, 193, 194, 196, 197
Imitation of Christ, 144ff.
"Innocence" of God, 54, 157ff., 173,
    205
Irenaeus, 24, 41, 61, 100, 102, 107, 116
Isaac, 46, 47, 118
Isaiah, 37, 71, 75, 79, 80, 82, 100, 119,
    164. See also Biblical Index
Isis, 43, 114

Jacob, 36, 47, 59, 60, 69, 76, 79, 80,
    118, 122–4, 129, 135, 140, 193, 204
James, E. O., 26, 27, 114, 126
James, M. R., 95, 126
James, W., 161, 183
Jenssen, H-H., 186
Jeremias, J., 79, 80, 133, 169
John, Apocryphon of, 8, 17, 114, 138
John, Mandean Book of, 7, 62
Jonah, 158, 173
Jones, Rufus M., 66
Jonge, M. de, 51
Josephus, 50, 170
Joüon, P., 47
Judas (not Iscariot), 160
Judgement, 70, 74, 89, 92, 93, 94, 108,
    130, 162, 166, 173, 174, 191, 202,
    205, 206
Julius Caesar, 150
Julius Pollux, 46
Jung Codex, The, ed. F. L. Cross, 17,
    41, 42, 43, 64, 111, 137

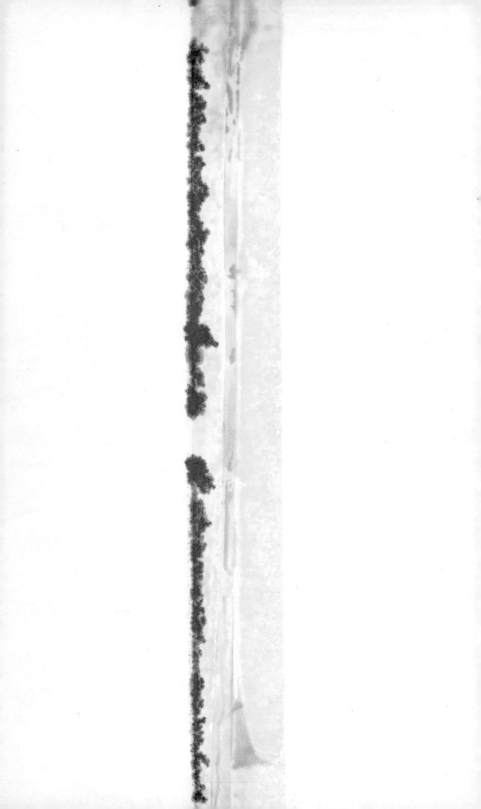

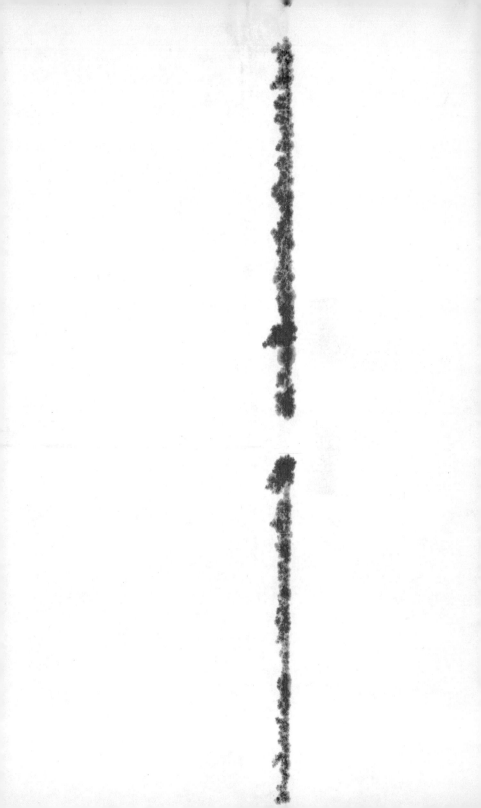